Monstrous Mothers Troubling Tropes

Edited by
Abigail L. Palko and
Andrea O'Reilly

DEMETER

Monstrous Mothers: Troubling Tropes

Edited by Abigail L. Palko and Andrea O'Reilly

Copyright © 2021 Demeter Press

Demeter Press
2546 10th Line
Bradford, Ontario
Canada, L3Z 3L3
Tel: 289-383-0134
Email: info@demeterpress.org
Website: www.demeterpress.org

Demeter Press logo based on the sculpture "Demeter" by Maria-Luise Bodirsky www.keramik-atelier.bodirsky.de

Printed and Bound in Canada

Front cover artwork: Tobiah Mundt
Typesetting: Michelle Pirovich

Library and Archives Canada Cataloguing in Publication
Title: Monstrous mothers : troubling tropes / edited by Abigail L. Palko and Andrea O'Reilly.
Names: Palko, Abigail L., editor. | O'Reilly, Andrea, 1961- editor.
Description: Includes bibliographical references.
Identifiers: Canadiana 2021026070X | ISBN 9781772583335 (softcover)
Subjects: LCSH: Motherhood in popular culture. | LCSH: Women in popular culture.
Classification: LCC HQ759 .M66 2021 | DDC 306.874/3—dc23

Acknowledgments

Abby

It is perhaps wholly unsurprising that a collection about monstrous mothering has had a drawn-out and challenging parturition. We are deeply grateful to the scholars who have contributed to this volume, most particularly for their unwavering belief in its importance and their willingness to grapple with the tropes of maternal monstrosity in respectful ways. This book is now in your hands because of their patience, commitment, and passion for the project.

We would also like to thank the peer reviewers who, through their careful reading and thoughtful feedback, helped us to see the strengths of our draft manuscript and how to improve it to fulfill the vision of the collection. Our deepest thanks also go to Tobiah Mundt, whose stunning photograph graces the cover, making visible some of the paradoxes this collection highlights.

I'm grateful to Linn Baran, who worked on the beginning stages of this book's coming-to-being, including the selection of the contributors, and to Andrea O'Reilly, who coedited the final stages with me, bringing it to birth.

From the moment that Andrea O'Reilly accepted my request to edit this collection, *Monstrous Mothers: Troubling Tropes* has been a labour of love. From the first time I read the abstracts, through every draft of each chapter, the mothers (both fictional and live) whose stories are shared within this book have lived in my head. So, our final thanks are to you, our readers, who will engage with these chapters, and to mothers everywhere, who labour under monstrous conditions.

Andrea

Deepest gratitude and appreciation to Abigail L. Palko for inviting me to become her coeditor for this herstoric volume. And thank you to Demeter's other mothers—copy editor Jesse O'Reilly-Conlin, designer Michelle Pirovich, and proofreader Jena Woodhouse—for delivering this book with such care and expertise.

Contents

Introduction

Abigail L. Palko

Motherhood is one of those roles that assumes an almost-outsized cultural importance in the significance we force it to bear. It becomes both the source of and the repository for all kinds of cultural fears. Its ubiquity, perhaps, is what makes motherhood this perfect foil. After all, while not everyone will become a mother, everyone has a mother. As feminist scholar Jacqueline Rose observes in the opening of her recent book, *Mothers*, "motherhood is, in Western discourse, the place in our culture where we lodge, or rather bury, the reality of our own conflicts, of what it means to be fully human" (1). When we force motherhood to bear the terrors of what it means to be human, we inflict trauma upon those who mother. And traumatized people often—not always but frequently—in turn inflict trauma and abuse on others in their life. Adrienne Rich, whose *Of Woman Born* established a new paradigm through which to understand the impact of cultural and patriarchal violence on motherhood, forces us to confront the harsh reality facing women who cannot bear the burden of motherhood: "Instead of recognizing the institutional violence of patriarchal motherhood, society labels those women who finally erupt in violence as psychopathological" (263).

We can trace a long tradition of bad mothers that shapes contemporary mothering practices (and the way we view them), including the murderous Medea of Greek mythology, the power-hungry Queen Gertrude of *Hamlet*, the emasculating mother of Freud's theories, and the enslaved Sethe of Toni Morrison's *Beloved*. Certainly, there are mothers who cause harm, inflict abuse, and act monstrously. Mothers are human. But mothers are also a favourite—and easy—scapegoat. In this collection, *Monstrous Mothers: Troubling Tropes*, we are interested in representations of mothers that through their very depictions of bad mothering challenge the tropes of monstrous mothering that we lean on while revealing why we turn to them.

The construct of motherhood that Rich and Rose identify (and that we interrogate in this volume) is omnipresent—but not, as philosopher Sara Ruddick reminds us, omnipotent. In this cultural construction, mothers work under surveillance, as "almost invariably the object, either of too much attention or not enough" (Rose 9). We all, collectively, have imbued motherhood with a crucial social role. Motherhood is deployed to do significant cultural work. Politicians and political activists invoke images of mothers to inspire and to police women's behaviours through idealized representations of good mothers. Religious leaders laud the maternal influence that keeps men and children within the institution's control. Media portray women as mothers in humorous and horrific ways to reinforce cultural dictates about women's proper social position. Motherhood, as Rose argues, is the "ultimate scapegoat for our personal and political failings, for everything that is wrong with the world, which it becomes the task— unrealizable, of course—of mothers to repair" (1).

Oddly coexisting with the reverence with which mothers are put on a pedestal are the obsessions with maternal monstrosities. Why do we pay so much attention to monstrous mothers? Mothers and their mothering practices are often easy targets of ridicule and fear in moments of cultural angst or crisis. Widespread obsession with monstrous mothers and their harmful behaviours reflects anxieties about the ways that mothering is an inherently unpredictable endeavour. We cannot guarantee that children will turn out well. And when social structures produce systemic instabilities and inequities, mothers easily become a proxy for other sources of fear and uncertainty.

Thus, it is not coincidental that as instability rises globally—from political tensions to economic disparities to environmental concerns— we see the figure of the monstrous mother operating in a wide variety of literary, media, and artistic texts. The tendency to portray mothers as monstrous hides our fear that we really are powerless in the face of global political and economic forces, environmental degradation and climate change, and even the ordinary moments of daily life with children. Although this desire to find a person or role to serve as the keeper of all our fears may be understandable, the impact of this desire on women's mothering practices is anything but simple.

In this volume, contributors examine a wide variety of monstrous mother figures with the shared objective of offering a more nuanced understanding of what it means to mother under less-than-ideal circumstances in conditions out of your total control. In the process, this volume troubles the trope of the monstrous mother, creating a collective argument that the monstrosity called out in individual instances lies in the society that produces the maternal-child relationship, not in those individual members of the dyad.

This is a radical stance, even as it seems self-evident. As Rose contends, "By making mothers the objects of licensed cruelty, we blind ourselves to the world's iniquities and shut down the portals of the heart" (2). Positioning mothers in such way allows us to ignore any obligations we ourselves bear with respect to the horrors of the modern world. Mothers become the actors, the world, the stage, and us—we are just the audience. Because we need mothers to be this repository (or because we are willing to lay this burden on them), we experience a different kind of horror when a mother breaks the metaphorical fourth wall of mothering. Kelsey E. Henry notes of the mother figure at the centre of the emerging genre of mommy horror films,

> She is *too much,* and thus, *not enough.* She is simply too many things to be a mother. Mothers are one thing: mothers. Or at least this is the dream. Motherhood is mythically imagined as the goal, the promise, and the end game for women. Once a woman is a mother, she is no longer expected to dream herself beyond her scheduled vanishing point, that time and that place where "Mother" emerges and woman recedes.

Films of this canon, she argues, explore "motherhood as a largely unforgiving role with potentially harmful expectations and obligations." Rose, however, insists that mothers are the "original subversives, never—as feminism has long insisted—what they seem, or are meant to be" (18).

In *Of Woman Born,* Adrienne Rich articulates the groundbreaking distinction between the institution and the experience of mothering: "The institution of motherhood cannot be touched or seen.... It must go on being evoked, so that women never again forget that our many fragments of lived experience belong to a whole which is not of our creation" (276). Rich firmly situates motherhood as one of these fragments. Because we do not—cannot—create the whole within which we experience motherhood, some women are driven to "terrible, prevalent acts" (258), in which rage disguises despair and desperation. The geography of maternal practice emphasizes the public-private tensions that shape maternal identities and experiences:

> When we think of the institution of motherhood, no symbolic architecture comes to mind, no visible embodiment of authority, power, or of potential or actual violence. Motherhood calls to mind the home, and we like to believe that the home is a private place.... We do not think of the laws which determine how we got to these places, the penalties imposed on those of us who have tried to live our lives according to a different plan, the art which depicts us in an unnatural serenity or resignation, the medical establishment which has robbed so many women of the act of giving birth, the experts—almost all male—who have told us how, as mothers, we should behave and feel. (Rich 275)

Although mothers have "accepted the stresses of the institutions as if they were a law of nature" (276), Rich contends that the "patriarchal violence and callousness" (277) that women inflict on children serve as a crucial sign of the deleterious and damaging impact of institutional motherhood on everyone—women and men, mothers and children. The monstrous mother, we follow Rich in suggesting, is stitched together from the fragments of lived experiences that have been shattered and scattered by patriarchal motherhood. The results are devastating: "The invisible violence of the institution of motherhood, the guilt, the powerless responsibility for human lives, the judgments and condemnations, the fear of her own power, the guilt, the guilt, the guilt. So much of this heart of darkness is an undramatic, undramatized suffering" (277).

We are living in a moment when the experience of mothering is increasingly shaped by the force of ideals, and a new examination of depictions of monstrous mothers—those who, deliberately or not, definitely fail to live up to this idealization—helps us understand the pressures under which all mothers mother. As Rose points out, the idealization intensifies as cultural realities make it even harder to achieve. In moments of crisis, she argues, mothers are ideally positioned to be the perfect scapegoat; focusing on mothers and their practices diverts attention from urgent social critiques, neutering calls to address the crisis justly (Rose 27). Blame mother, and then we do not need to grapple with the impact of capitalism or neoliberalism, climate change or social backlash.

This is not to suggest that mothers never behave monstrously. Such a claim would traumatically disregard the real experience of the children of monstrous mothers as well as deny such mothers their own individuality (much as efforts to idealize mothers also erase individuality). The horrific stories of the Kerry Babies, Andrea Yates, Melissa Drexler, or Elaine Campione—all of which were further sensationalized by media coverage—remind us that maternal identity is defined by the commitment to the child, not by giving birth (Ruddick 17, 51). These examples highlight the importance of Rich's distinction of the differences between the institution of motherhood and the practice of mothering (or women's lived experience).

Because all mothers occasionally—whether willingly, impulsively, or inadvertently—harm their children, Julia E. Hanigsberg and Sara Ruddick argue that mother blaming affects all mothers. Most mothers, not just monstrous mothers, will, at some point, act in a way that objectively speaking, seems to ignore a child's needs or to humiliate them—or worse. Thus, to challenge social norms of mother blame is to defend yourself. Hanigsberg and Ruddick point out the ways that we culturally use mother blame as self-defence in this environment:

> "Bad" mothers are scapegoats. By turning from them in horror, by devising laws to control and punish them, we can quarantine our own hurtful, neglectful impulses and acts. Scapegoated "bad mothers" are also often poor, unmarried, and targets of racism, burdens that typically make ordinary mothering extraordinarily difficult. But mothers in every class and social group harm their children. The location of "badness" in particular races, classes, or family arrangements—or in female more than male parents— allows the rest of "us" to deny the harms that we have perpetrated as well as those we have suffered. (x)

This is where the chapters in this volume intervene into the conversation; we seek to trouble tropes that have gained cultural power and negatively affected women's mothering. As Hanigsberg and Ruddick note, "Deliberately, helplessly, or inadvertently mothers may use their powers in ways that hurt" (xi). One of the moral dilemmas we face is the fact that when mother blame is pervasive, it becomes challenging to address the harm mothers do. The need to support mothers "under siege" can falsely suggest that any critique of maternal actions is an attack on all mothers (xi). This volume's authors follow Dorothy Roberts in urgently declaring that addressing harm caused by mothers must take as its starting point the circumstances in which women mother (xi). Our chapters urge us to remember, too, the "volatile fragility of motherly love, not as the exception but as the rule" (Henry).

Psychoanalyst Barbara Almond, in her study of the "dark side of motherhood," as she terms the negative side of maternal ambivalence (xiii), points out that it is precisely because contemporary expectations for good mothering are so impossible to achieve—while cultural rhetoric suggests that the stakes have never been higher—that maternal ambivalence has increased. Cruelly, it has simultaneously become more unacceptable to society (xiii). This contradiction can leave mothers vulnerable and isolated in their attempts to achieve a maternal practice that lives up to their personal standards. It can also produce the conditions under which monstrous mothering flourishes (if we can use that verb ironically).

Monstrous Mothers: Troubling Tropes

The chapters that we have collected here present a range of mothering experiences and practices and, consequently, evoke a range of potential social responses to them. Drawing on theoretical engagements with Indigenous knowledge, Josephine L. Savarese asserts in her chapter that "The fact that this tremendous capacity [Indigenous intelligence] is 'always there' underscores the importance of careful listening and theorizing." Both individually and as a collective, the chapters of this collection aim to do this careful listening to mothers' experiences, offering nuanced understandings of maternal practices. We have organized them into three sections: precarious mothering, maternal violence, and the impact of stereotypes and tropes on depictions of maternal practices.

In the first section, Precarious Mothering, contributors explore the impact of modern technology in shaping our conceptions of monstrous mothering. We extend recent scholarly attention with the conditions of precarity to explicitly consider motherhood through this lens. Starting with the deeply understood fact that no one mothers in a vacuum, the chapters in this section question the ways in which technology is deployed in service of the norms that mark the boundary between good and bad mothering—norms that serve to police mothering practices. Even those attempts to subvert our presumptions about what mothering is monstrous end up reinforcing conceptions of a monstrous motherhood. Anitra Goriss-Hunter's chapter offers a close textual reading of the cybernovel *Patchwork Girl* by Shelley Jackson. A "cyberfeminist reworking" of Mary Shelley's *Frankenstein*, as Goriss-Hunter describes it, *Patchwork Girl* explores the intersection of queer desire and maternal love. Jackson's novel moves beyond conventional representations of maternal bodies, Goriss-Hunter argues, to enact a "maternal subjectivity of monstrosity." Her chapter signals from the outset that this collection will use bricolage techniques to trouble the tropes of monstrous mothering we have inherited.

The other chapters in the first section also engage with questions raised by contemporary technology. Josephine L. Savarese uses decolonial love studies to highlight how media accounts of the disappearance of a young Indigenous girl have shaped the child's mother's experience of this loss in her chapter. Whereas media accounts have labelled Laura a deviant mother, Savarese argues that decolonial love studies provide the lens to see how colonial frames of abjection obscured her maternal love. Susan Harper and Jessica Smartt Gullion examine the performance of mothering in a posthuman context through their close reading of the tv series *Orphan Black*. Playing with the consequence of human cloning and human-led evolution, the series questions the use of violence as an extension of mother love and challenges cultural norms of motherhood. My chapter analyses the *Maleficent* franchise and argues that the first film troubles the monstrous mother trope by positing maternal love as true love. The sequel, however, then reinscribes this trope by perverting Maleficent's character and introducing the murderous Ingrith.

The second section of *Monstrous Mothers* more explicitly focuses on maternal violence. Perhaps the strongest emotion driving our tenacious cultural grip on tropes of monstrous mothering is the fear that the same person who gave life can (and at times does) take it away. In a timely critical reading of Anna Burns's novel *No Bones*, Shamara Ransarini focuses on the text's reliance on the ephemeral (in early nationalist imagery of Mother Ireland) and the visceral (its evocations of the Armagh prison strike, including its no-wash protest) to articulate how political and military use of maternal imagery makes mothering monstrous. Set in the height of the Troubles, *No Bones* explores what it means for women—especially women whose identity has been reduced to their maternal status—to adopt "angry and violent" politics (18).

Aidan Moir's analysis of Carrie Mathison, protagonist of *Homeland*, unpacks several monstrous tropes, notably the mother who prioritizes her career over her child and the disabled mother (Carrie is bipolar) who endangers her child. Moir contends that the depiction of Carrie as an "aberrant mother" challenges ideologies of intensive mothering in important ways, particularly in offering an opportunity for her to establish a persona that does not depend completely on her maternal status. Rebecca Jaremko Bromwich explores the deep anxieties triggered by Karla Homolka's postincarceration life as a suburban mom of three. In her chapter, Bromwich performs a critical analysis of mainstream and social media representations of Canada's most notorious female serial killer, paying particular attention to the ways that her maternal status is deployed to heighten anxieties. Finally, Jessica Turcat engages with the maternal persona that recurs in the poet Ai's poetry to consider dichotomous human responses to the capacity of human cruelty and human ability to overcome victimhood. Through the violence inflicted by mothers, Ai can represent the violence patriarchal motherhood inflicts upon mothers themselves.

The chapters in the third section, Mothers Made Monstrous, offer a paradigm-shifting caveat to the cultural impulse that blames mothers and views their failures, weaknesses, or even refusals to conform to maternal idealizations as monstrous. In this section, we explore ways that circumstances can force mothers into adopting monstrous mothering practices. Jennifer Martin poses the question: Can a mother who abandons her children for personal pursuits be anything but monstrous? In close readings of Southern US women's novels from the 1990s, Martin reveals the "erasure of selfhood" that characterizes the protagonists' maternal experiences and urges us to a more sympathetic reading of these works—that these mothers are "victims of a society that makes unrealistic demands on them and denies them any form of individual expression" (20). Through her analysis of maternal omniscience and maternal culpability in Sue Klebold's *A Mother's Reckoning* and Monique Lépine's *Aftermath*, Andrea O'Reilly unpacks the meanings to be gleaned from mothers who have demanded the opportunity to tell their horrific story. Through nuanced readings of the memoirs of two mothers of mass killers, O'Reilly argues that our patriarchal culture's desire and readiness to blame mothers for their children's monstrosities obscure the limits of normative motherhood to prevent trauma.

We conclude this section by looking at stereotypes that control mothering practices and considering the potential insights to be found in speculative fiction. By putting stereotyped images from the nineteenth century in conversation with twenty-first-century depictions, we hope to underscore the ubiquity, the pervasiveness, and the enduring nature of the monstrous mother trope. Melissa Dinsman places an 1897 gothic novel and a 2016 Netflix series in conversation with each other to trace moments that three tropes of bad mothers (the negligent mother, the sexual nonmother, and the working mother) have recurred in literature and television. She outlines the lineage from Lucy, Mina, and Mrs. Harker of Stoker's *Dracula* up through changing cultural hotspots to the women of *Stranger Things* (Karen Wheeler, Nancy Wheeler, and Joyce Byers). Dinsman concludes that even when artistic depictions of mothers may intend to reject monstrous tropes, maternal monstrosity forms a core of contemporary understandings of what it means to be human. She sees a clear concluding message: "The monster is us, and we should embrace it"; this volume as a collective whole seeks to trouble this conclusion. In the final chapter, Andrea O'Reilly undertakes a comparative reading of two recent novels—Helen Phillips's *The Need* and Melanie Golding's *Little Darlings*—and she argues that the genre of speculative fiction opens space for considering the experience of mothering, rather than mothers themselves, to be the monstrosity.

Masks

We are thrilled to have the stunning photograph of Tobiah Mundt's felted needle sculpture for our cover image. On Mother's Day 2020, she posted this photo on Instagram with the caption: "The Mother. a war mask in progress." An artist and mother, she uses various methods of textile arts in her creations. In her artist's statement, she explains her process. It is a method that bears remarkable similarities to the demands of mothering in its reliance on a repetitive action that eventually, finally, draws the final form out of the initial amorphous bundle of wool: "My needle felted sculptures have been poked tens of thousands of times, compacting the wool into its final form. I find that this meticulous repetitious process informs my work, allowing me to enter an almost hypnotic state where I can tap into my own emotions and of those around me."

In all arenas, but particularly for mothers, 2020 elicited and prompted a wide range of emotions and responses. Globally, mothers have disproportionately borne the brunt of caretaking responsibilities during the coronavirus pandemic, and mothers of colour have marched and fought for racial justice in a movement amplified in summer 2020 by new horrors of police brutality (including, but tragically not limited to, the murders of Ahmaud Arbery, Breonna Taylor, and George Floyd), with white mothers marching in solidarity. Mundt's work captures these emotions for us "in frozen moments of change and evolution." Featuring her sculpture on our cover reminds us as readers of the imperative to centre maternal voices in every discussion of mothering practices. It prompts us to question what realities are obscured by the label "monstrous" and to consider what war mask we can offer mothers.

Mothers are expected to be as fearless as lionesses, Jacqueline Rose reminds us, which is often to their own detriment: "A lioness, it is implied, will instinctively protect her cubs because she has no internal life of her own to grapple with. Push a bit further and you might say that having nothing of her own to grapple with—being 'all' for her child at the cost of her own inner life—is the very definition, or at least the unspoken agenda, of being a mother" (193).

The mother who refuses to sacrifice her own inner life—or who protects its sanctity—is often labelled monstrous by Western culture. Such criticism carries with it suggestions that women must surrender their individuality when they become mothers. It also leaves us without appropriate, commensurate ways of discussing those maternal actions that truly are monstrous: genuine abandonment, neglect, and abuse. But Jacqueline Rose challenges us: "Given voice, space and time, motherhood can, and should, be one of the central means through which a historical moment reckons with itself" (17). In this volume, through the contributors' respective chapters, we collectively reckon with the cultural norms that allow us to depict mothers as monstrous.

Works Cited

Almond, Barbara. *The Monster Within: The Hidden Side of Motherhood*. University of California Press, 2010.

Hanigsberg, Julia E., and Sara Ruddick. "Introduction." *Mother Troubles: Rethinking Contemporary Maternal Dilemmas*, edited by Julia E. Hanigsberg and Sara Ruddick, Beacon Press, 1999, pp. ix-xx.

Henry, Kelsey E. "Monstrous Motherhood." *The Point*, 2015, thepoint mag.com/2015/criticism/monstrous-motherhood. Accessed 8 June 2021.

Mundt, Tobiah. "Artist's Statement." *Tobiah Mundt: Textile Artist*, www.tobiahmundt.com/. Accessed 8 June 2021.

Rich, Adrienne. *Of Woman Born: Motherhood as Experience and Institution*. W. W. Norton & Company, 1976.

Rose, Jacqueline. *Mothers*. Farrar, Strauss, Giroux, 2018.

Ruddick, Sara. *Maternal Thinking*. Beacon Press, 1995.

PART I

PRECARIOUS
MOTHERING

Chapter 1

Patchwork Girl–Fractured Maternal Monsters

Anitra Goriss-Hunter

Introduction

Maternity and the monstrous are closely intertwined in cultural, social, scientific, and technological narratives. Monstrous maternal entities are firmly entrenched in the popular imaginary and loom large in countless works of fiction and nonfiction. To problematize the notion of the monstrous maternal as tied to a concept or body, this chapter interrogates how monstrously maternal bodies are constructed as hybridity, fragmented identity, and queer desire in Shelley Jackson's hypertext fiction, *Patchwork Girl* (1995)—a cyberfeminist reworking of Mary Shelley's *Frankenstein*. I argue that *Patchwork Girl* enacts explorations of the monstrous maternal—historically, the site of the Other, embodiment, agency, and pleasure. I consider *Patchwork Girl* in terms of the text's resistance to discourses of conventional maternity (explored in Adrienne Rich's notion of the institution of motherhood). Interconnected with this examination, this chapter also investigates the ways in which the structures and capabilities of the fluid medium of electronic text enable readers/interactors concerned with *Patchwork Girl* to saunter away from normative images and concepts of motherhood.

Patchwork Girl is an early hypertext fiction and is one of the most highly acclaimed texts in this category of electronic literature (Hayles; Landow; Hackman). Like many hyperfictions, *Patchwork Girl* does not possess a linear narrative with a discrete beginning and certain ending. The text is composed of five segments titled "a Graveyard," "a Journal," "a Quilt," "a Story," and "& broken accents." Segments consist of multiple story pathways that connect through text and image. Readers/interactors make their own connections within and between segments as they attempt to patch together story and body parts to resurrect the monstrous Patchwork Girl.

To interrogate the monstrous maternal bodies that run through *Patchwork Girl*, the chapter draws on the work of Judith Halberstam and Rosi Braidotti. The chapter employs Halberstam's notion of the Gothic monster as a fluid porous screen to investigate the different cultural, social, and political interpretations projected upon and resisted by monstrous maternal bodies in the text. Braidotti's concept of the monstrous body as always imbricated in gendered discourses enables the examination of the ways in which maternal bodies in the text represent interconnective flows of gender, flesh, and paradox. To examine the maternal monsters of *Patchwork Girl*, I have combined Halberstam's and Braidotti's concepts of the monster and of the maternal body into a notion I call "monstrous maternity." This combination of monstrous and maternal bodies permits the investigation of how *Patchwork Girl*'s monsters make use of complicated weaves of personal, literary, and political threads to open up spaces for subversive maternal desire and challenges to conventional discourses of motherhood that enable the explication of a queer maternity.

Jackson's *Patchwork Girl* is awash in maternal flows and forces that I interrogate in this chapter. This text is a digital reworking of the Frankenstein story, whereby maternity is monstrous through literary associations with textual monsters, fragmented flesh, and hypertext. Jackson's use of the capabilities of hypertext permits a visual and material birth of the fractured monster Patchwork Girl, mobilizing the metaphor of a monstrous and creative cybermaternity. Jackson returns to Shelley's *Frankenstein* and rewrites the destruction of the female monster. Instead of being destroyed, the female monster is secretly recreated in a rebirthing by the author Shelley, who becomes a character in the hyperfiction. Jackson describes Shelley stitching together the female body parts that Frankenstein had torn asunder. Maternal creator and author, Shelley falls in love with the creature and becomes her lover. The monster then leaves Shelley and embarks upon journeys leading to and through the United States of America (US). After several adventures and an almost literal breakdown(away) of body parts, the monster dies.

(Mary) Shelley Jackson's Patchwork Girl—In the Flesh

The inspiration for *Patchwork Girl* flowed from Jackson's desires to explore the possibilities of hypertext: "My patchworked girl monster emerged ... as a metaphor for a fragmented and dispossessed text that nevertheless had a loud, triumphant voice" (Amerika). In its current form, *Patchwork Girl* is a text that is considerable in size and varied in content. In the work, 323 lexias or sections of text are connected by 462 links, which open many different ways through the text. These lexias vary in length, from passages of over three hundred words to just one sentence. Like other early hypertext fictions, *Patchwork Girl* displays qualities characteristic of mid-1990s hyperfictions such as a strong reliance on intertextuality and a self-reflexive engagement with the medium itself. The narrative is fabricated from Jackson's own prose as well as passages from Shelley's *Frankenstein*, L. Frank Baum's *The Patchwork Girl of Oz*, Donna Haraway's *Cyborg Manifesto*, Barbara Maria Stafford's *Body Criticism*, and Jacques Derrida's *Disseminations*. Excerpts from these texts are often used without obvious referencing. (Bibliographic details of the sources are recorded in separate sections headed "notes.") These sources of theory and story are continually interwoven into a patchworked assemblage of monstrous body parts and narratives.

Patchwork Girl describes herself: "I am tall, and broad-shouldered enough that many take me for a man, others think me a transsexual.... My black hair falls down my back but does not make me girlish. Women and men alike mistake my gender and both are drawn to me.... I was made as strong as my unfortunate and famous brother, but less neurotic" (Jackson). Just as the creature in *Frankenstein* initially looks to his creator for nurturing and support, Patchwork Girl seeks out her mother. While Frankenstein is overcome with horror at the sight of his monstrous creation and abandons the creature, the character Shelley looks favourably on Patchwork Girl and eventually expresses a queer maternal desire for her creation.

Although the term "queer" refuses to be contained in a strict definition, it refers to the interruption of practices of dominant discourse concerning sex, gender, race and embodiment (Ahmed). "Queer" aligns social, political, and personal domains and demands a re-evaluation of some taken-for-granted assumptions. Summing up the drive to dispute that powers the notion of queer, Barbara Creed states the following: "It challenges the view, first, that there is a fixed sexual identity, whether heterosexual or homosexual, bisexual or transsexual; and second, that there is a set of fixed gender characteristics, whether masculine or feminine" (138). Queer readings of bodies, therefore, regard identity as unstable, constantly in formation, and unable to be reduced to one category.

In *Patchwork Girl*, most of the patching together of identities, ideas, and flesh is done by readers/interactors across divisions and segments rather than within chunks of text. Connections are formed by physically clicking on links and through associations of ideas and images. When Patchwork Girl stands before us, she is a hybrid and monstrous creature. Her body parts are sutured together to form a monster whose flesh breaks apart along scar lines, like the links and spaces in hypertext that connect and separate narratives.

Monstrous Bodies

Judith Halberstam examines monstrosity in terms of the Gothic novel and focuses on Frankenstein's monster as an example of how monstrous bodies work: "The monster is able to condense as many fear-provoking traits as possible into one body. Hence the sense that Frankenstein's monster is bursting out of his skin—he is indeed filled to bursting point with flesh and meaning both" (21). For Halberstam, the monster possesses a multiplicity of meanings, disputes notions of unified identity, and is a site of resistance to normative discourse.

Historically, the monstrous is connected to the feminine through discourses of rationality, biology, and gender (Braidotti, "Cyberteratologies"). Culturally, the feminine is often linked to the monster, as narratives of monstrosity position women as always potentially monstrous (Braidotti, "Signs of Wonder"). Braidotti contends that intersections of gender, race and teratology—the construction of "abnormal" or monstrous bodies as objects of ontological examination—connect with discursive forces intent upon the surveillance and control of female bodies ("Signs of Wonder"). Teratological discourses display the connectivities of narratives of gender and race as well as reveal that they are integral to scientific constructions of feminine bodies. Therefore, the monster, in a similar vein to the cyborg, is not an innocent inhabitant of the Garden of Eden. The monstrous is always imbricated in gendered discourses. It is not so much a concept or a body; it is more of a field or plane of interconnective flows of gender, flesh, and paradox. As Braidotti writes, "The monstrous body, more than an object, is *a shifter,* a vehicle that constructs a web of interconnected and yet potentially contradictory discourses about the embodied self" ("Signs of Wonder," 300). Braidotti concludes that "the monster is a process without a stable object. ... It is slippery ... Difference will just not go away" (300). Braidotti's notion of the monster as a "process" connects with feminist notions of female identity as "becoming" (Beauvoir; Braidotti). Monstrous bodies are connected with female bodies due to their inherent disorderly and unstable characteristics, which have the tendency to undermine hegemonic narratives.

The body of the monster is strongly connected to not only femininity but also maternity. Pregnant bodies (mothers-to-be)—in their changing, leaking, noisy, hormonally charged, and multiplying enfleshment—seep and grow beyond the usual limitations and boundaries of the human body. In her investigation of cultural constructions of maternal bodies, Rich identifies narratives of maternity that stand outside what she identifies as the institution of motherhood—mothering defined by the limitations of capitalist patriarchal forces—and explores their connection with the monster and all that is unnatural and not normal. Writing as a mother, Rich explores her own assumptions about maternity and ponders whether she "is a monster—an anti-woman—something driven and without recourse to the normal and appealing consolations of love, motherhood, joy in others" (22). Rich's division of motherhood into institution and personal possibility allows the investigation of subject matter associated with the monstrous in traditional narratives—that is, maternal self-determination as well as maternal sexuality and sensuality. To focus on issues and images of maternity and monstrosity that permeate *Patchwork Girl,* I draw on Rich's division of maternity into institution with its traditional narratives of monstrous maternal bodies and the lived practice of maternal bodies.

Stitch Bitches: How to Sew/Write a Mother of a Monster

Notions of the monster as machine and screen are useful for the investigation of a hyperfiction, and N. Katherine Hayles's concept of the "flickering signifier" adds an important dimension to the examination of this digital text. Hayles argues that the notion of the signifier promoted by de Saussure, Lacan, and others as unitary and flat is particular to print texts, whereas signifiers in cyberspaces are complex and multilayered. Hayles uses the term "flickering" to distinguish the electronic signifier from its print counterpart and to underline its qualities. In contrast to print signification, screenic signifiers are based in computer code, which creates layered and mobile images that are continually being refreshed. Hayles writes "In informatics, the signifier can no longer be understood as a single marker, for example an ink mark on a page. Rather it exists as a flexible chain of markers bound together by the arbitrary relations specified by the relevant codes" ("How We Became Posthuman" 31). These are not trivial differences, as they mark signifiers on the screen and what they represent as crucially more mobile, fluid, and multiplicitous than print or oral signifiers and signifieds.

Hypertexting the notions of flickering signifier and shapeshifting monster, I conceive of maternity in *Patchwork Girl* as a flickering screen that distorts, enfleshes, and subverts the conventional maternal body of motherhood and authorship. I argue that the gerund "flickering" implies moving and shifting, which when applied to monstrosity, in this case, evokes Braidotti's concept of the monster as a "shifter." This constantly moving, flickering screen functions much like the crazy mirrors found in mazes at carnivals, agricultural shows, or sideshows. The crazy mirrors of sideshow alleys distort the body shape of the person looking into the reflective surface. The person looking at the reflection may have a larger or smaller body shown in the mirror than their actual size. The body may be elongated or compacted, or the dimensions could be completely altered from their real-world dimensions. I argue that in *Patchwork Girl*, maternity's flickering screen rewrites conventional notions of motherhood as grounded in heteronormative longing and contained acquiescent flesh to one of queer desire and fleshy monstrosity.

On the text's flickering screen of maternity, collaborative threads of maternal bodies, authorship, readership, queerness, and monstrosity weave together in the birth of the monster, which occurs in the story line and hypertextually on the monitor at the hands of the reader/interactor. The scars and seams of *Patchwork Girl* create a hybrid monstrous maternity of gender indeterminacy and fragmented identity. *Patchwork Girl* draws upon analogies of stitching and piecing disparate parts together to produce an entirely new creation. This techno-needlework echoes Frankenstein's sewing together of corpses in Shelley's novel and enables the reader/interactor to both follow the associations that are directed by the author and forge their own linkages produced by the work's hyperlinks. In this manner of linking and rupture, the text brings together, separates, and then births through the actions of the reader/interactor diverse images, corpo-realities, writings, genres, and ideas. These new monstrous forms lurch along the network of literal and metaphorical scars and sutures that make up the viewer-constructed hypertext. The carefully contrived diversity of *Patchwork Girl* that coagulates on many levels is summed up by George Landow when he states that the text is a "hypertext parable of writing and identity, [which] generates both its themes and its techniques from the kinds of collage writing intrinsic to hypertext" (234). Landow posits the following:

> *Patchwork Girl* makes us all into Frankenstein-readers stitching together narrative, gender and identity…. This digital collage-narrative assembles Shelley Jackson's (and Mary Shelley's and Frankenstein's) female monster, forming a hypertext Every woman who embodies assemblage, concatenation, juxtaposition, and blurred, recreated identities. (237)

Jackson states clearly her intention for viewers of her hyperfiction to go beyond the sedentary role of consumer of text to active participant in the assembling of story, words, and image. She demands that readers/interactors do just that—scan the segments of text and image and then select and assemble the parts into a whole. This project is stated explicitly by the monster in one of the first divisions: "I am buried here. You can resurrect me, but only piecemeal. If you want to see the whole, you will have to sew me together yourself … you will have to put it together any which way, as the scientist Frankenstein was forced to do" (Jackson).

In-text creation of the female monster describes a rewriting of narratives of birth and motherhood. The conventional notion of maternity states that a woman gives birth once at any time. (I am including multiple births as they usually occur in the same way during a relatively short space of time.) In contrast to this finite act, narratives of maternity in the hyperfiction are queered as the birth of the Patchwork Girl is described as the result of many diverse and ongoing acts. According to the narrator, Patchwork Girl's birth takes place more than once: "In the plea of a bygone monster; from a muddy hole by corpse-light; under the needle, and under the pen" (Jackson). This description brings together images of birth in terms of Shelley's male monster asking for a mate; Shelley as an author and as a character; Patchwork Girl's monstrous beginning; Jackson's authorship; and the reader/interactor's creation of meaning by clicking on links. At all times the playful multivocality of *Patchwork Girl* is underlined by Jackson's linking of images and texts that range from academic to popular culture. Patchwork Girl herself is described by Shelley in the text as having skin that was riddled with scars and segments of different types of skin "as distinct as patches in a quilt" (Jackson). Scars show the links and breaks in the narratives—the joins and spaces where the flickering screen of maternity is evident.

Just as the monstrous Patchwork Girl is constructed from disparate body parts, she also seems to be an assemblage of influences and suggestions. For instance, she says: "I am a mixed metaphor. Metaphor, meaning something like 'bearing across,' is itself a fine metaphor for my condition. Every part of me is linked to other territories alien to it but equally mine" (Jackson). Thus, *Patchwork Girl* mobilizes hypertext and hypertextual qualities to interrogate conventional notions of narrative, gender, and maternal identity. The hypertext fiction's multiplicity and nonlinearity enable constructions of female and maternal subjectivities as fractured and complex. Hypertexted connections of fleshy images and multiple narratives create a hyperfiction that rejects traditional representations of motherhood and conventional storytelling in favour of a monstrous queer maternal body of stories.

When Jackson uses Derrida's words to describe her own monster as "An outlaw, a pervert, a bad seed—a monster—a vagrant, an adventurer, a bum" (143), she hijacks his attribution of language to fathers and his evacuation of maternal shapings of language development. Instead, Jackson boldly claims the attributes of language for the unnamed character in this subdivision who could be the monster or Shelley who mothers the creature. The language Jackson cites here—pervert, vagrant, adventurer, bum—stands outside descriptive terms that conventionally adhere to and describe traditional females, especially maternal bodies. In Jackson's text, not only do the mothers (Shelley, Jackson, Patchwork Girl, and the reader) bestow language, but they also play with it and laugh at the hybrid constructions that are birthed from intertwinings of maternity, monstrosity, and queer desire. Jackson's reworking of the Frankenstein myth insists that language belongs to both the maternal creator, Shelley (the author and the character in the hypertext) and her monstrous creation (Patchwork Girl, herself). It is significant that the monster is gendered female and that she and her creator trample upon conventions of femininity. In this text, it is the flickering screen of maternity (Jackson's construction of maternal bodies as queer and abject) that enables the protagonist to poetically use language and offer it to readers/interactors to take, read, and manipulate themselves as bodies who are, in turn, birthing their own textual version of Patchwork Girl.

I argue that the interplay of hypertext, user, and author in *Patchwork Girl* enacts and reflects a maternal dynamic of creation and authorship—collaborative yet fragmented. However, this notion goes only part of the way to recognizing Jackson's reworkings of conventional maternity and the unspoken alliance that readers/interactors enter in their subversion of traditional tropes of maternal bodies. Maternity functions here not as a wan metaphor for authorship or giving birth to a creative venture but as a flickering screen of signification, which calls for the reader/interactor to directly participate in the becoming monstrous of author, character, and viewer/user.

Monstrously Maternal Desire of the Mother

Maternal bodies, in the figures of Shelley and Patchwork Girl (as well as the reader/interactors), are expressed in terms of queer desire and fleshy monstrosity. The flickering screen of maternity set up in *Patchwork Girl* brazenly challenges traditional tropes of motherhood. In this text, maternity is not mired in binary notions of the good and bad mother. For instance, Shelley and the monster she creates move beyond and within texts; Shelley shifts from being the author of *Frankenstein* to a character in *Patchwork Girl*, to birthing and loving a monster, and to becoming monstrous herself. Just as it was impossible for Frankenstein's female monster to survive in the pages of the nineteenth-century novel, Patchwork Girl will not live meekly in cyberspaces. In *Patchwork Girl*, maternal bodies are queered through transformations and renderings of monstrous flesh as well as flows of queer desire.

Maternity in *Patchwork Girl* is dynamic, fragmented, subversive, and queer. Shelley's delight in her creation is often contrasted with Frankenstein's constant spiralling into feelings of abject horror. Frankenstein literally runs away from the monster, thus, avoiding responsibility for his creation. Conversely, Shelley in *Patchwork Girl* joyfully engages in the "responsible creativity" of birthing and caring for her female monster (Hustis 845-58). While Frankenstein is obsessed with "penetrating the secrets of nature" (Shelley 38-39), the character Shelley appears to be an assistant in the harnessing of forces or capabilities she does not fully understand. For instance, Shelley considers whether Patchwork Girl's piecemeal animated self is "more rightfully given, not made; continuous, not interrupted; and subject to divine truth, not the will to expression of its prideful author" (Jackson). This quote suggests a bond between Shelley and Patchwork Girl built on autonomy and respect.

Throughout the text, Jackson implies and states an intimate connection between the characters Shelley and Patchwork Girl. This is depicted in the light of female friendship as well as maternal nurturing and sexual desire. The fractured links between Shelley and Patchwork Girl flesh out Rich's exploration of the complex mother-daughter relationship. The complexity and closeness of Shelley and Patchwork Girl's relationship expresses the cathexis between mother and daughter that Adrienne Rich describes as the greatest unwritten story—essential but often distorted and misused (225). Rich writes the following: "The first knowledge any woman has of warmth, nourishment, tenderness, security, sensuality, mutuality, comes from her mother. That earliest enwrapment of one female body with another can sooner or later be denied or rejected ... but it is, at the beginning, the whole world" (218).

At times, Shelley speaks of her creation in terms of awe and fear. In great contrast to Frankenstein, Shelley does not feel abject regard and horror. Shelley actually expresses her compassion, love, and sexual desire for her creation. Patchwork Girl's huge size is not a cause of alarm for Shelley; rather, she views the creature with a maternal pride that her creature is not bound by traditional tropes of femininity. For Patchwork Girl, gender is a performance that shifts between naturalized gendered roles. Patchwork Girl reveals that the character Shelley's normative female gendered identity is also a performance of "still-polite manners" (Jackson). However, for the character Shelley, a bittersweet maternal pride surfaces when Patchwork Girl asserts her independence and leaves Shelley to set off for the US and a life of adventure.

Maternity in *Patchwork Girl* reworks the traditional notion of maternal bodies as emptied of desire. In this text, hegemonic hetero-sexual longing is remediated via the flickering screen of maternity into queer transgressive desiring that traverses the territory of bisexuality and incest. Maternal bodies do not ghost the narrative but instead are fleshy celebrations of desire, sex, and the written word. These bodies refuse the traditional construction of motherhood that codes as perverse the experiencing of maternity as "erotically pleasurable" (Traina 370). In doing so, they evoke a maternal sexuality that might enable the healthy development and "flourishing" of maternal bodies (Traina 370). Through the flickering screen of maternity in the text, conventional heterosexual motherhood is transformed into the monstrous maternal by the exchange of flesh. The print convention of the author as an omniscient creator of stories is overturned within the economy of the flickering screen of maternity into a collaboration of author, reader/interactor, and character, which births Patchwork Girl. Separations of mother and writer, traditionally occurring through the institution of motherhood, are warped via the textual flickering screen of maternity, whereby Shelley, Jackson and countless readers/ interactors birth Patchwork Girl performing a collective lived experience of mothering (Rich). From the projections of *Frankenstein* cast on the flickering screen of maternity, the authors produce a tale of a maternal body who refuses to abandon her "hideous progeny" (Shelley xii) in an enactment of Rich's division of maternity into conventional institution and specific practice. Instead of parental abandonment, *Patchwork Girl* remediates the *Frankenstein* myth so that love and identification with the monstrous creature are projected on the flickering screen of maternity.

Within the circuits of maternal desire, motherly pride and queer sexuality exist hypertextually. Shelley (the character) expresses an admiring maternal pride in her creation's spirited enjoyment of life and growing independence. This maternal pride is also hypertexted with a strong sexual desire. For instance, Shelley writes of the monster's childlike capacity for pleasure and her own sexual fulfilment and notes that Patchwork Girl's capacious desire "for food and for experience, it surpasses mine, and so I (would-be parent) find my child leading me in pursuit of the pleasures of knowledge and the knowledge of pleasures I had not imagined" (Jackson). In the mention of pleasures previously unimagined by Shelley's maternal imagination, the usual parent-child relationship is overturned and inflected with a queer sexual desire. Shelley writes: "Last night I lay in her arms, my monster, and for the first time laid my hand on her skin ... I touched her skin lightly, and yet she trembled.... It surprised me, then moved me that one so strong should be so susceptible, should tremble and mist at a touch" (Jackson).

Instead of conventional responses of revulsion or horror at the scarred, disparate body, Patchwork Girl's monstrous flesh evokes passion and feelings of identification from Shelley. The character exclaims: "Freed, I pressed myself against her with a ravenous heart.... I clung to her with the full extent of my strength and the length of my body, and she returned the embrace.... We breathed each other's breath" (Jackson). After Shelley expresses her desire for Patchwork Girl, she speaks of her identification with the creature: "Her scars lay like living things between us, inscribing themselves in my skin. I thought I too was rent and sewn, that I was both multiply estranged and gathered together in a dynamic union. What divided her, divided me" (Jackson). It is only after their sexual encounter that Shelley fully understands Patchwork Girl's scars, as she says to the monster: "I see that your scars not only mark a cut, they also commemorate a joining" (Jackson).

To celebrate their union, Shelley and Patchwork Girl exchange patches of skin. Here, monstrosity and "civilized" flesh swap, combine, and transform their bodies. As they consider which patches of skin to exchange, Patchwork Girl states, "The nearest thing to a bit of my own flesh would be this scar, a place where disparate things are joined in a way that was my own" (Jackson). Patchwork Girl's scars are crucial elements of her identity and parts of her body from which she derives pleasure. Shelley takes a patch of skin from her thigh, where she perceives it will not be missed, and her acceptance of Patchwork Girl's monstrous skin affirms and displays the author/character's embracing of her inner monstrosity.

There are obvious connections between the scarred monstrous bodies of author/character, creation/lover, and the reader/interactor of this hyperfiction. Scars, like hypertext links, join and separate, creating something specific to the body/text in the link. Hayles reminds us that "The reader inscribes her subjectivity into this text by choosing what links to activate, what scars to trace. ... the scars/links thus function to join the text with the corporeal body of the reader, which performs the enacted motions that bring text into being" ("Flickering Connectivities"). Scars and links allow Patchwork Girl, Shelley, and the reader/interactor to explore and depart from dominant discourse while feeling the pleasure of this movement.

From would-be parent, to lover, to acting monstrous with another, and to empty-nest mother, the trajectory of desire flickers on the screen of maternity, jumping from Shelley's pleasure in sewing and writing the creature into being to a desire that is both sexual and incestuous. Motherly urges to create transforms into a queer desire, which morphs through the maternal flickering screen in *Patchwork Girl* into an erotically charged enjoyment of monstrous materiality. Jackson, however, hypertexts this sexual maternal to a motherly pride in Shelley's monstrous offspring's leaving home and embarking upon a coming-of-age road trip to the US.

Conclusion

Patchwork Girl is a monstrous cybermaternal text that rejects traditional narratives from the institution of motherhood, preferring the exploration of a lived maternal experience in the sense of Rich's division of maternity. As a hyperfiction, *Patchwork Girl* cunningly and compellingly interweaves threads of *Frankenstein*, technology, maternity, bodies, flesh, hypertext, and authorship. A slippery, brash and charming monster, Patchwork Girl, her equally monstrous textual mother, the character Shelley, and the author Jackson take the already complex Frankenstein myth and hypertext it into a feminist tale of queer maternity.

The character Patchwork Girl is the monstrous offspring of fiction, nonfiction, literary theory, and hypertext technology. Not only is Patchwork Girl birthed by Shelley (the character), but she is also literally pieced together by the efforts of the readers/interactors. The scars of the enfleshed Patchwork Girl and the hypertext links of the hyperfiction demonstrate connectivities between maternal bodies, queer desire, monstrosity, queer maternity, character, text, reader, and author, which exist in fragmentation.

The monstrous bodies of the characters Shelley and Patchwork Girl disrupt traditional notions of how maternal bodies are to be thought of and included in literary works. Their melding of maternal/authorial desires materializes space for collaborative authorship/creation and queers conventional depictions of maternity. The reader/interactor is also drawn into these threads of maternity/authoring, and by direct interaction with the cybertext, they become yet another monstrous maternal creating body. *Patchwork Girl* is, then, a hyperfiction that celebrates and flaunts the collaborative creation of a monstrous queer maternity, which challenges traditional tropes of maternal bodies as well as conventional constructions of readers, authors, and storytelling.

To explore *Patchwork Girl* as an electronic text, a hypertexty fiction, this chapter's investigation of maternity combines concepts of flickering signifiers and screens. In *Patchwork Girl*, the flickering screen of maternity (Jackson's construction of maternal bodies as cheerfully abject and triumphantly queer) reworks traditional notions of motherhood as grounded in heteronormative longing and contained acquiescent flesh. The bodies projected on the screen of maternity in *Patchwork Girl* flaunt monstrous flesh and revel in queer pleasures as they move beyond conventional representations of maternal bodies to create a monstrous queer maternal aesthetic of flickering signification.

Works Cited

Ahmed, Sara. *Queer Phenomenology: Orientations, Objects, Others*. Duke University Press, 2006.

Amerika, Mark. "Stitch Bitch: The Hypertext Author as Cyborg-Femme Narrator." *Amerika On-Line*, www.heise.de/tp/features/Amerika-Online-7-3441257.html. Accessed 9 June 2021.

Beauvoir, Simone de. *The Second Sex.* Vintage Books, 1973.

Braidotti, Rosi. "Cyberteratologies: Female Monsters Negotiate the Other's Participation in Humanity's Far Future." *Envisioning the Future: Science Fiction and the Next Millennium,* edited by Marleen S. Barr, Wesleyan University Press, 2003, pp. 146-172.

Braidotti, Rosi. "Signs of Wonder and Traces of Doubt: on Teratology and Embodied Difference." *Between Monsters, Goddesses and Cyborgs: Feminist Confrontations with Science, Medicine and Cyberspace,* edited by Nina Lykke and Rosi Braidotti, Zed Books, 1996, pp. 135-52.

Creed, Barbara. "Queering the Media: A Gay Gaze." *Media Matrix: Sexing the New Reality,* edited by Barbara Creed, Allen & Unwin, 2003, pp. 136-58.

Derrida, Jacques. *Dissemination.* Translated by Barbara Johnson. Chicago University Press, 1981.

Hackman, Paul. "'I Am a Double Agent': Shelley Jackson's *Patchwork Girl* and the Persistence of Print in the Age of Hypertext." *Contemporary Literature,* vol. 52, no. 1, 2011, pp. 84-107.

Halberstam, Judith. *Skin Shows: Gothic Horror and the Technology of Monsters.* Duke University Press, 1995.

Hayles, N. Katherine. "Flickering Connectivities in the work of Shelley Jackson: The Importance of Media-specific Analysis." *Postmodern Culture,* vol. 10, no. 2, 2000, doi:10.1353/pmc.2000.0011.

Hayles, N. Katherine. *How We Became Posthuman: Virtual Bodies in Cybernetics, Literature, and Informatics.* Chicago: The University of Chicago Press, 1999.

Hustis, Harriet. "Responsible Creativity and the 'Modernity' of Mary Shelley's Prometheus." *Studies in English Literature 1500-1900,* vol. 43, no. 4, 2003, pp. 845-58.

Jackson, Shelley. *Patchwork Girl.* Eastgate Systems, 1995, CD Rom.

Lacan, Jacques. *Ecrits.* Translated by Alan Sheridan, Routledge, 1977.

Landow, George P. *Hypertext 3.0: Critical Theory and New Media in an Era of Globalization.* The Johns Hopkins University Press, 2006.

Rich, Adrienne. *Of Woman Born: Motherhood as Experience and Institution.* Virago, 1979.

Saussaure, Ferdinand de. *Course in General Linguistics.* 1972. Translated by Roy Harris. Open Court Publishing Company, 2000.

Shelley, Mary. *Frankenstein, or, The Modern Prometheus.* Second International Student Edition. Edited by Paul Hunter. W. W. Norton & Co, 1996, 2012.

Traina, Cristina. "Maternal Experience and the Boundaries of Sexual Ethics." *Signs*, vol. 25, 2000, pp. 369-405.

Chapter 2

In Search of Laura's Story: Decolonial Love and Indigenous Mothers of Missing Children

Josephine L. Savarese

To love decolonially is to heal the wound that rejects the other within, to acknowledge the "third meaning" of love that embraces the ambiguity and unknowability of the other, and to unleash the transformative power of that love.
—Carolyn Ureña 99

The hard truth is that we live in a country whose laws and institutions perpetuate violations of fundamental rights, amounting to a genocide against Indigenous women, girls and 2SLGBTQQIA people.
—Marion Buller, Chief Commissioner of the National Inquiry into Missing and Murdered Indigenous Women and Girls

Introduction

This chapter offers the view that the emphasis within love studies on the power of emotion to advance social and political justice can enhance mothering scholarship. A critically and politically inspired decolonial love consciousness might work to challenge discriminatory frames that circumscribe mothering in racialized and gendered ways (Gurusami; Roberts; Lavall-Harvard and Anderson). To demonstrate the value of love studies, I explore how this analytical tool helps to expose how social inequality and systemic oppression influenced the plight of one Indigenous mother referred to by the pseudonym, Laura.

I place together two scholarly streams—decolonial love studies and critical mothering scholarship—to challenge a depiction of an Indigenous mother viewed as monstrous based on her history of involvement in the child welfare system, income inequality, racialization, and other forms of oppression. In her 2017 article, "Mothers Matter: A Feminist Perspective on Child Welfare-Involved Women," Stacey Dunkerley encourages this careful examination of the circumstances that surface in Laura's story she promotes a feminist perspective that contextualizes women's lives by accounting for the "poverty, violence, addictions, and racism" that mothers experience (251). This contextualization is a place "to start the earth moving" or to realize social change (262). Guided by insights like this one based on the feminist-oriented mothering literature, I explore what decolonial love might offer to a rereading of Laura's story to expose the complicated problems that require "complex and dynamic responses," which avoid sternly regulating and even criminalizing mothers who parent from the margins (262).

I am further inspired by the work of Black activist and mothering scholar, Dorothy E. Roberts. In her 1994 text "Deviance, Resistance and Love," Roberts reminds us that responding empathetically to persons who are criminalized and ostracized is a necessary component of radical writing and advocacy. Roberts applies the term "resistance scholarship" to texts that criticized "the dominant construction of outlaws" (191). The knowledge held by outsiders, gained from their lived experience, is essential to building more equitable societies. For Roberts, the most crucial task was "simply to love those whom society has discarded" (191). In the passages that follow, I ponder what insights can be gleaned if Laura's story is viewed from the lens offered by scholars like Roberts and others who see marginalized bodies as worthy of decolonial love rather than abjection. The interviews Laura provided in 2014 and 2016 with reporters from Toronto's *Globe and Mail* and the Canadian news magazine *The Walrus* are the mainstay of this study. The news stories illustrate the ways this mother's knowledge and experiences were suppressed while also suggesting other ways to reread her story by sharing more sympathetic details with readers.

Thoughts on the Embodiment of Alliance

My writing comes from my perspective as a settler scholar, who lives on the traditional unceded territory of the Wolastoqiyik and Wəlastəkewiyik/Maliseet, whose ancestors along with the Mi'Kmaq/Mi'kmaw and Passamaquoddy/Peskotomuhkati Tribes/Nations signed Peace and Friendship Treaties with the British Crown in the 1700s. I am also a former resident of Treaty 6 Territory, known as Saskatchewan. I explored Laura's story in previous research, and, thus, I bring an awareness to the topic (Savarese); however, I can never fully know Laura's experience and may have blind spots, biases, or other limitations, even while aiming for a compassionate reading of her encounters with mainstream systems that disrupts racialized othering. As Lugones argues, one human cannot know another unless one travels to their world. Without this journey, the "other is only dimly present to one". In fact, one is "alone in the other's presence" (Lugones 18).

In her 2019 text "Indigenous Feminist Notes on Embodying Alliance against Settler Colonialism," Maile Arvin queries how we can "embody feminist alliance in relation to resisting settler colonialism" to promote effective engagement between scholars and activists working to end oppression (336). Her assertion that "we have to build worlds" in which Indigenous women are recognized as "activists, artists, and scholars with valuable knowledge and theories about our own lives and our communities' histories and futures" has been inspirational to this text (353). This scholarship is guided by Arvin's vision that meaningful solidarity with Indigenous mothers like Laura may eventually materialize through the collective effort that manifests within the resistance, sometimes small and faltering, which I aim to embody as a newcomer to traditional lands and as an ongoing student of relationships, histories, and knowledges. Arvin's assertion that "Indigenous women should also be seen as essential allies to building just worlds for everyone" is one statement that propels me forward (353).

Part I: Loving the Outlaw

In this chapter, I suggest that placing love studies scholarship—including work by feminist, antiracist, and love studies scholar Carolyn Ureña—alongside mothering scholarship makes it possible to explore the ways in which Laura's mothering, albeit imperfect, was undermined by "hegemonic systems of knowledge and power" (Ureña 88). To oppose the demonized characterizations of Laura found in the news reports and legal decisions highlighted in this text, this chapter foregrounds how a so-called deviant mother can also be a loving mother. Notably, Laura never gave up hope that her daughter, T.K., who went missing in Regina, Saskatchewan, would be found even though over a decade had passed since the pair last saw each other (Carlson). Apart from the attention on Laura and her family, no suspects have been publicly identified.

In "Loving from Below: Of (De)colonial Love and Other Demons," Carolyn Ureña encourages research on persons and communities that experience racialized and gendered oppression due to the "longstanding patterns of power" authorized by colonialism, or "coloniality" (Maldonado-Torres qtd. in Ureña 87). The persistence of the "epistemic rupture enacted by the European encounter in the Americas"—or the "colonial wound"—deserves vigorous challenge through various measures, including through love that is decolonial (88). Ureña applies Chela Sandoval's "methodology of the oppressed" to track the injuries flowing from the imposition of Eurocentric paradigms. Finding new languages of hope, love, and possibility is central to the methodology of the oppressed. Sandoval's approach is best described as "a methodology of love," which is particularly suited to the study of problems that surface in postmodern worlds (Sandoval qtd. in Ureña 90). For Sandoval, the methodology of the oppressed and decolonial love offers a means to "renewal," "social reconstruction," and "emancipation" (Sandoval qtd. in Ureña 90).

Following Sandoval, Ureña explains that decolonial love serves as a counter to more regressive forms of love fuelled by Christian imperialist, Eurocentric ideologies. With her conclusions in mind, it becomes even more possible to question legal summaries and mainstream accounts of Laura's story and to track the institutional rebuke of her life circumstances and parenting. Ureña illustrates her findings through a close reading of Gabriel García Márquez's 1995 *Of Love and Other Demons*. The novel seeks to dismantle "colonial difference" by highlighting "the particular embodied and affective knowledges" of persons who have endured "the violence of coloniality" (91). While examining imagined figures, Ureña, through her method and analysis, offers instruction to decolonial scholarship, like this chapter, by showing how one can read a text to discern "unrecognized subjective and embodied knowledge" (88).

Ureña's support for written narratives that focus on the "lived experiences of female subaltern figures" affirms this chapter's significance given its aims to authenticate alternative modes of existence (87). Laura's story is unique in that her daughter T.K. was a child when she disappeared in 2004, making her one of the youngest entries on Canada's list of missing and murdered Indigenous women. In addition, since her daughter's disappearance, Laura has been treated as a suspect. Disdainful reactions from state agencies, however, are common for many mothers of missing and murdered Indigenous women and girls in Canada.

Only recently, in July 2019, was the crisis acknowledged as one of genocidal proportions with the release of the final report of the National Inquiry into Missing and Murdered Indigenous Women and Girls, *Reclaiming Power and Place*. The Inquiry findings generally align with this decolonial "love story" or this chapter rebuking the treatment of Laura, a mother who experienced the disdain and indifference described by many family members in presentations to the national inquiry.

The Significance of Laura's Story for Mothering Scholarship

Exploring Laura's story is important in a text on monstrous mothering because she has often been depicted as a bad mother (Savarese). Aline Gubrium's 2008 article, "Writing Against the Image of the Monstrous Crack Mother," challenges cultural stereotypes through an African American woman's story of recovery from substance addiction (511–27). Gubrium's deconstruction of such disdainful images of mothers experiencing addiction helps to challenge similarly negative portrayals of Laura and her mothering. Her findings are supported by Charlene Regester's examination of the portrayal of the mother in the acclaimed film *Precious* (30-45). As Regester states, "Any mothers who do not fit the kind of mother associated with the 'traditional nuclear family' constitute 'bad mothers' and are under assault" (Regester 31).

This chapter enhances my earlier study, which tracks the ways in which Laura was deemed monstrous after the disappearance of T.K.

(Savarese 88-111). Although this earlier writing did not reference decolonial love studies, it reframed Laura's experiences to counter the narrow acknowledgement of her humanity, as perpetrated by the presiding gendered, racialized, and colonial worldview. Following a critical read of associated custody cases, my previous study argued that the child welfare system perpetuated and integrated punitive and colonial-inspired scripts to the detriment of Indigenous mothers, like Laura (Savarese 97).

In her 2006 study, "A Case Study of Missing Children in the Canadian Press," Angela Tanner studied news coverage of Laura and her family immediately after T.K.'s disappearance. Notably, Laura and her family were viewed through retributive and denunciatory scripts that highlighted their urban poverty and unconventionality. Tanner found Laura was the least praiseworthy victim among the three mothers studied. While confronting an endangered, missing child, Laura was chastised for failing to live up to the "white, middle class, suburban ideal" (96). Statements from Laura in the more recent interviews scrutinized in this chapter suggest that this negative perception has been only nominally displaced, if at all. Tanner's study lays the groundwork for this chapter's investigation into how love studies may disrupt knee jerk conclusions that mothers are simply monstrous.

Revisiting the Soft Criminalization of Laura

Although I use pseudonyms, Laura's loss is a well-known story (Savarese). Following the 2004 disappearance of her daughter and the apprehension of her children, a distraught Laura provided a telephone interview to the Canadian Press, in which she made statements concerning her family's closeness. Laura stated: "We need each other. We are a family" (qtd. in Cook). They showed affection to one another, helping "each other get through these things" (qtd. in Cook). Laura questioned the police officers' role in the emergency apprehension given the family's cooperation with the investigation. T.K.'s whereabouts still remain unknown, although over a decade has passed. This unresolved crime colours Laura's existence, affording her no closure.

In November 2014, new evidence surfaced on T.K.'s disappearance (Carlson). A hand drawn map with a note advising police to search the wells on an Indigenous territory was brought to law enforcement attention. Although it generated renewed interest in the case, this tip was unreliable and offered no aid regarding the longstanding mystery surrounding T.K.'s abduction (The Canadian Press).

"A Bunch of Nobodies"

The emphasis placed on Laura's neglect in the court rulings alludes to her responsibility, even if indirect, for T'K.'s disappearance. In a 2016 interview with the Canadian news magazine *The Walrus,* Laura voiced frustration with the characterization of her family as the wrongdoers (Pruden). During the interview, Laura was averse to the suggestion she was involved in T.K.'s disappearance. In fact, she bristled when asked if she had anything to do with the abduction. Laura would have harmed her partner, D.M., if evidence had ever surfaced on his involvement in the crime, something he has consistently denied. To Laura, it appeared the police had concluded she and her family were "a bunch of nobodies"—a statement that corresponds with this chapter's worry about monstrous mothers (Pruden). According to Laura, law enforcement subscribed to the view that she "did her own child" (Pruden). In the article, the interviewer makes an ambiguous statement that investigators know that "children are hurt by people closest to them," which subtly hints at nagging doubts about family members' involvement (Pruden). Findings from the 2008 court ruling corroborate Laura's claims to innocence regarding T.K.'s disappearance, yet these statements rest in an obscure, nonpublicized court ruling, a factor that keeps the suspicion of family wrongdoing alive (Savarese).

Part II: Decolonial Love Studies and Definitions of Love

Defining Love

Sandoval's definition of love as "a body of knowledges, arts, practices, and procedures for re-forming the self and the world" (Sandoval 4) provides direction for seeing Laura and her story in a renewed way. Ureña builds on Sandoval's work by understanding love as a "method for determining what kind of political and social actions to take" (89).

Darnell Moore and Monica J. Casper further define love using comparable terms. They describe love as "a radical ethic and apparatus," which is insufficiently theorized as "a tool of social transformation and world-remaking within feminisms and larger left social justice movements invested in the work of transformative justice." Indigenous scholar, poet, and performer, Leanne Betasamosake Simpson, also provides important instruction on centralizing love. In a 2018 conversation, Betasamosake Simpson explained that Elders in traditional societies view love as "a practice of respect, reciprocity, consent and humility" rather than simply an emotion (Dey and Walker). I understand Betasamosake Simpson as encouraging Indigenous peoples to draw from love to reimagine and recreate more viable systems and worlds founded on their innate intelligence and life practices. Her comments, on my reading, are directly relevant to mothering.

Love Studies: What Does Love Do?

As this chapter intends to make clear, interest in love as a research topic is longstanding. In 2000, for example, bell hooks published *All About Love: New Visions*, which highlights caring as a way to counter oppression. In her 2017 examination of the Canadian Truth and Reconciliation Commission, Robyn Green describes love as a "political emotion" (74–94). After an event in Atlantic Canada organized under the theme Zaagi'diwin, an Anishinaabe word for "love," Green writes that she was originally skeptical when Chief Commissioner Murray Sinclair united the sentiments of reconciliation and love (74). To her surprise, though, she felt the "expression of love" within the context of the event united the sentiments of 'reconciliation' and 'love' (76). Ultimately, Green placed value on love as an emotion that could foster visions of "different but equitable futures" beyond preexisting social and political arrangements (90).

Leanne Betasamosake Simpson similarly promotes love as a basis for Indigenous resurgence and collective transformation. Michele Lacombe explores Simpson's "decolonial aesthetics," which calls upon readers to engage in acts of love by attending to the "echoes and repetitions of older creation stories that 'leak' through and reframe the static of neo-colonial violence" (3). Decolonial love is central to this reenvisioning because it "governs relationships between mother and child, between people and land, between physical and spiritual aspects of being, and between ancient and new art forms" (3).

Writing in the Canadian Indigenous context, Rachel Flowers challenges aspects of love studies in her text "Refusal to Forgive: Indigenous Women's Love and Rage" (32-49). For Flowers, anger is justified in light of settler colonial harms and damage, such as the establishment of residential schools and the occupation of Indigenous lands. Outrage disrupts systems of violence and subjugation that bolster settler colonialism. Flowers advocates for self-love and affirmation among Indigenous women. She opposes, however, uncritical approaches to love that silence anger by stressing forgiveness. Flowers illustrates her points through the loving gestures by family and community members of missing and murdered Indigenous women. Their commemorative actions and protests offer opportunities to grieving persons to share sadness, love, and anger. For Flowers, resistance is "written in both rage and love" (40). Indigenous women's expressions of both love and anger are fundamental to "the politics of resistance and approaches to solidarity" (45).

The work of Flowers and others informs this text because they criticize love studies while also affirming love's power to instigate change. Writing in another context, Fiona Wright tracks how Jewish-Israeli politically left activists participate in an affective, dissident politics when they articulate love and mourning for Palestinians who are injured and killed (130–143). Wright is cautious, however, about the outcomes, based on her fieldwork in Israel and Palestine. She has noticed epistemic and practical problems that surface even when activists cite love as the motivation for their resistance work. Loving and mourning the Palestinian Other is meritorious, yet this action objectifies the Other. This objectification is a form of violence that is counter-productive even though the activists want to honour the worthiness of Palestinian life through powerful "expressions of love and grief for the Palestinian Other" (139). Wright provocatively concludes that "relating to and loving Others can also kill them, a little, even as one mourns their loss" (140).

Even while pondering these limitations, I am intrigued by those who argue that love has been undertheorized among contemporary, critical thinkers. Debra Thompson uses the language of hope rather than love, yet she argues that emotions, including anger, play a powerful role in fueling resistance (457-81). Darnell Moore and Monica J. Casper, cofounders of *The Feminist Wire*, a feminist digital publication launched in 2011, speak more directly to love as an important praxis in their text "Love in the Time of Racism." These authors suggest that "lovelessness" is the "epicenter of oppression." Without love, it is reasoned that we see the "various tremors and tsunamis" that destruct our shared world and undermine our wellbeing. Lovelessness, Moore and Casper argue, materializes in "the form of state-sanctioned violence, settler colonialism, bloated prison industries, rape culture, genocide, xenophobia, and so much else" (Moore and Casper). While acknowledging powerful counterforces, Moore and Casper maintain that "love in the time of racism is a radical act that can lead to broader political/social formations and solidarities where 'difference' is not policed or expunged, but acknowledged and celebrated."

For Brazilian, Black, and trans scholar Dora Silva Santana, love is an aid to wellbeing (181-90). Although she experiences multiple transitions across genders, languages, and countries, Santana feels most comfortable when "transitioning along self-collective-familial-intimate-erotic love—love that makes us stand together and shout and echo our voices" (186). For Santana, on my reading, ease comes from "being in movement" and experiencing transitions as a fluid process that emulates water (186). Santana's reflections on the power and possibility of love seem to provide a fitting transition to a reconsideration of some of the aspects of Laura's story that have been made public through the vantage point of love-themed scholarship.

Part III: Decolonial Love and the Brilliance of Laura

With the aid of love studies scholars, particularly decolonial love studies, it is possible to reexamine Laura's circumstances to uncover the ways in which colonial frames of abjection were mobilized to characterize her as irredeemable. When Leanne Betasamosake Simpson asserts that the "brilliance" of Indigenous peoples is "always present," she gives further direction on what scholars should look for in textual reviews (Dey and Walker). This intelligence is sometimes "hidden" or even "coded"; the fact that this tremendous capacity is "always there" underscores the importance of careful listening and theorizing (Dey and Walker).

Through a close reading of the interviews with Laura in 2014 and 2016, it is possible to discern her desire to tell her own story in her own words, even though she risks further stigma. Laura acknowledged her discomfort with talking to reporters in her 2016 interview with *The Walrus* (Pruden). This was the case because Laura disliked reporters' questions and found it hurtful to discuss her losses. Laura's face was described by the reporter as crumpled when she addressed these topics (Pruden). Clearly in distress, Laura explained she needed a "six-pack of Black Ice beer" to open up (Pruden). While uneasy, Laura also valued the opportunity to make her story known. A part of her needed to share what happened.

Even though Laura sees herself as the victim of a serious crime, the new stories demonstrate the persistence of disdain towards her. Blaze Carlson's article, for example, reports that Laura is a self-admitted alcoholic who reports that she became involved in sex work after T.K.'s disappearance. The reader is informed that Laura drank beer during the interview. No information is shared on Laura's nervousness when speaking to the press. Blaze Carlson's depiction of Laura as "a short woman with dark eyes" may convey her sorrow, yet the reference to her worn out appearance may also hint at degeneracy (Carlson). The conversation was described as unpredictable, even erratic, which conveys to the reader that the information may be unreliable and less trustworthy. This uncertainty is emphasized by the conversation vacillating between "past and present, tears and anger" (Carlson). Like the interchange, Blaze Carlson also found the residence to be chaotic. The coffee table in the living room was broken. A door was missing. The frame was covered by a yellow blanket. With a tone of irony, the reader is told that a sign reading "HOPE" was placed on the door frame (Carlson). The description is consistent with the disorderliness dominant societies often apply to Indigenous spaces. The article makes the ambiguous yet potentially value-laden statement that there were "no pictures of T.K. on display in the living room" (Carlson).

The fact that the information on Laura and her living space is only moderately contextualized is problematic from the vantage point of decolonial, mothering love studies. The article briefly references the fact that Laura and her mother both attended residential schools without commenting on the documented horrors that occurred in these institutions (Chrisjohn et al.). Carlson's article notes Laura's upbringing, in what is described as an "abusive, dysfunctional home on White Bear reserve," but does not mention the violent settlement of the prairie regions, as described in James Daschuk's *Clearing the Plains: Disease, Politics of Starvation, and the Loss of Aboriginal Life*. The fact that Laura "ran away to Regina at age 13 and stole food out of the dirt of backyard gardens to survive" is briefly mentioned in a manner that may seem voyeuristic, possibly even sensational, downplaying Laura's precarious existence evidenced by her homelessness and insecurity. Although garden raiding, or gathering produce without permission, is common in farming communities, the article states that Laura's food was drawn directly from the "dirt," the dust and soil, linking her to the earth while also coupling Laura with muck and unclean, soiled spaces.

"Just Gone Now"

The reader is asked to join in the pathologizing of Laura and her community as wild and unruly. Given this narrative stance, it becomes easier to overlook the systemic vulnerability that predisposed Laura and her family to violence. Some of the factors that propelled Laura's earlier status as a missing runaway were replicated in T.K.'s world, seeming to have facilitated her disappearance. *The Walrus* article by Pruden states that T.K. was befriended by an adult man, who was soon discovered to be a pedophile. Pruden mentions other young women who disappeared from the neighbourhood where Laura resided between 1983 and 1993—including Annette Kelly Peigan, age nineteen, Patsy Favel, age eighteen, and Joyce Tillotson—confirming that T.K.'s disappearance was not an isolated phenomenon. In 1995, Pamela George was sexually assaulted and beaten to death by two young, white men. A family friend of Laura's, called Big Aunty, also disappeared from her family's life, a fact that puzzles Laura. Laura woefully described her as "just gone now," a status she shared with Laura's daughter. It is possible this factor is a coincidence, yet it is within the realm of possibility that Big Auntie is also missing, making her one of the many missing, possibly murdered, Indigenous women in Canada.

The fact that Indigenous women disproportionately experience harm is effectively masked by the focus on Laura's shortcomings. This approach normalizes T.K.s disappearance as a natural by-product of

Indigenous criminality and unfitness. For example, Blaze Carlson describes the intense surveillance Laura has experienced by the public and police as a reality that was merely "lamented" by Laura and her partner. This terminology minimizes the psychological harm from the constant scrutiny and diminishes the role it played in the ongoing separation of a mother from her children ("Mother Holds Out Hope").

Monstrous Mothers and Motherwork

In her 2018 work, Susila Gurusami studied Black mothers following prison terms to learn more about the joys and frustrations of parenting outside of closed institutions (128-143). Her study on formerly incarcerated Black women's raced, classed, and gendered parenting labour under the state provides evidence of the strain of state sur- veillance on Black mothers following their release. Gurusami's work may shed light on Laura's predicament, although she has largely been deprived of any meaningful mothering role due to T.K.'s abduction and the apprehension of her other children. The mothers in Gurusami's study used three coping strategies: "collective," "hypervigilant," and "crisis" motherwork (129). Formerly incarcerated Black women adopt these three forms of motherwork on release to enable their negotiation of pervasive surveillance and intervention strategies. These coping methods enable the women to retain a mothering function even while their efforts to assume an authentic parental role were contested. The mother informants in Gurusami's study typically had regained custody or were in regular contact with their children. As a result, they were parenting more actively than Laura, who had lapsed into more passive mothering as her legal struggles progressed (Savarese). The mothers who spoke to Gurusami reported hardship from state scrutiny, especially after incarceration. Their stories offer some insight into the stress Laura may feel from the perpetual punitive gaze engendered by what I have labeled "soft criminalization" through the child welfare system (Savarese).

Perhaps ironically, a sentencing decision from 2005 shows that Laura willingly accepted the criminal justice system's authority to regain her health as a step towards reestablishing custody. In August 2005, she consented to a term of three months of incarceration on several charges, including breach of a probation order (R v. K, [2005]

S.J. No. 545, QuickLaw). At the time, she was thirty-two years old. The sentencing judge was informed that Laura had two boys and four girls in foster care. Laura was then visiting her children twice per week. Her plans included having the children returned to her (R v. K, par. 41). During the sentencing hearing, Laura admitted to addiction problems (R v. K). At various times, she had been presented with treatment options. Though interested in rehabilitation, she had failed to commit to a residential program. As a result, Laura supported a short period of incarceration as "an easier way to help herself out" (R v. K, par. 42).

At the time of the sentencing hearing, it was stated that Laura's physical condition was deteriorating to the point that her "health and safety" was at risk (par. 37). The Crown Counsel argued that Laura needed "some kind of intervention" (par. 37). The defence counsel stated that Laura supported the jail term as a way to stabilize "mentally and emotionally and physically" (par. 42). It was explained that Laura had gone through a "traumatic experience" in the last year, presumably referring to T.K.'s disappearance (par. 42). The judge accepted the joint recommendation on sentencing given her view that Laura required a period of "stability" (par. 45). Two of the charges Laura faced resulted from her failure to observe a curfew imposed under a probation order. The dates given for these breaches were July 4 and July 6, 2005, a year after the date of T.K.'s disappearance. Punishing Laura for lapses on the anniversary date of T.K.'s disappearance may indicate that state agents used their discretion in punitive ways by pursuing charges at times when relapse was more likely. With T.K.'s loss, her breaks from her curfew seem more understandable, even worthy of a different response. While Laura was incarcerated in a provincial women's jail for these charges, the Ministry pursued a further order regarding her children's placement (Savarese).

Deep Colonial Scarring and Decolonial Love

Adding to her difficulties, Laura has been actively targeted by hate-related crimes in response to T.K.'s disappearance and for the mere suspicion of homicide. During the 2014 meeting, Blaze Carlson observed that Laura's body was marked by "deep scars" caused by "being jumped" by three people who claimed she exchanged her daughter for illegal drugs. For decolonial scholars, these injuries have practical and symbolic significance. Though possibly the actions of individuals disposed to violence, Ureña links the persistent victimization of persons, like Laura, to the broader colonial context in which marginalized subjects are routinely harmed. Citing Fanon, Ureña reminds us that "oppressive systems" impose "visible, physical violence" on their subjects, like the beating experienced by Laura. At the same time, the regressive systems also inflict "invisible, affective wounds" or psycho-social harms (88). The fact that Laura was called a "baby killer" by a passerby just prior to the 2016 interview seems to illustrate this tendency (Pruden). The hostility directed towards Laura seemed to be reinforced by the rebuke expressed by dominant institutions. These actions become mutually reinforcing, compounding Laura's susceptibility as a target.

As described in prior scholarship, the most recent (from 2014) family law decision emphasized Laura's parental shortcomings even though the matter was uncontested (Savarese). The judgement overlooks legitimate reasons why an Indigenous mother might distrust mainstream courts (97). It fails to acknowledge ways Laura's struggles were exacerbated by the dominant society's response to T.K.'s disappearance. More theoretically, the judicial approach may coincide with what Maria Lugones calls an "arrogant perception," following Marilyn Frye, which happens when a commentator insists on their own superiority, thereby undermining the humanity of marginalized subjects (4). For Lugones, "arrogant perception" justifies settlers and their institutions when they ignore, ostracize, render invisible, stereotype, or leave women of colour completely alone and interpret them as crazy (7). These characteristics have been attributed to Laura. This insensitivity prohibits a more loving gaze towards a struggling mother, thereby facilitating a view of her as monstrous.

The first court decision offers a more sympathetic evaluation. The Queen's Bench justice who presided over a 2008 custody trial decision refused to focus solely on individualized, mothering shortcomings. The justice chastised the Ministry of Social Services for its failures before and after T.K.'s disappearance. Among other findings, she ruled: "In the midst of a tragedy, instead of helping Laura, the Ministry took her children away" (qtd. in Savarese). Laura was described as a caring mother, even while imperfect, who bonded with her children.

Regardless of this conclusion, the order for the children's return to Laura was later overturned by the Saskatchewan Court of Appeal, who rejected the trial judge's reasoning.

Counter claims of systemic wrongdoing concerning Laura's treatment resurfaced in the summer of 2018. The treatment of Laura and her family was a factor in a class-action lawsuit filed on July 5, 2018, the anniversary of T.K.'s disappearance, by the Regina-based Merchant Law Group. The lawsuit was launched against the federal government for the RCMP's handling of cases involving missing and murdered Indigenous women and girls in Saskatchewan. Counsel for the thirty-six families, Mr. Tony Merchant, is pursuing millions of dollars in compensation for the alleged mishandling of investigations. While the T.K. investigation was not handled by the RCMP, the case was included in the claim (Global News). News reports were not clear on whether T.K.'s family members were directly involved in the lawsuit. Even so, there is evidence that Laura feels shortchanged. In her 2016 interview with Jana Pruden, Laura highlighted her disappointment with law enforcement actions at the time of the 2004 investigation. Laura was concerned that the police failed to shut down the highways leaving Regina and did not issue an Amber Alert. According to Tanner, the frustration Laura voiced to reporters led to portrayals of her as defiant, although sympathetic statements towards Laura's grief were also apparent in these news stories (87-96). It appeared that the lawsuit might provide an opportunity to revisit these characterizations by giving more weight to Laura's concerns.

The Merchant Law Group invited family and community members of a missing or murdered Indigenous woman to complete and submit a form, available through the firm's website. In June 2021, a Federal Court judge dismissed the class action suit to represent family and community members of missing and murdered Indigenous women and girls (MMIWG) (Polischuk). To the dismay of family members, the judge concluded that the application was excessively broad in its scope. Legal counsel for the families, Tony Merchant, indicated that his office would appeal to the Federal Court of Appeal on behalf of the disappointed families (Polischuk).

The failed claim may have permitted a presentation of Laura that has not been prominent in mainstream discourse. T.L.'s Cowan's scholarship is instructive on the more empathetic portrayal that a decolonial lens can provide—it is possible to see Laura in ways that compare to the queer outlaw or the transfeminist killjoy. For Cowan, these figures hold promise because they are the ones who slip "through and into hope, joy, and love and holds them in tension as creative potential" (512).

Through this lens offered by Cowan, Laura may still be a suffering figure, given her losses. On this alternative read, Laura's story can offer teachings on decolonization, liberation, survivorship, and even love. Greater attentiveness to her knowledge might reveal the everyday influence of historic trauma as a lived reality for Indigenous mothers, thereby fostering insight on the inequities that shadow Laura and that seem to have enabled T.K.'s disappearance.

With Cowan, it is possible to rupture the "conceptual and physical" exclusion that seems to characterize Laura's existence given the depth of social, economic, and political disadvantage as well as the stigma that surrounds her (502). Importantly, the tear or gap created by the transfeminist killjoy trickstering manoeuvres is a means to "restructure, claim, and repair feminist happiness" that seems to have eluded Laura and her family due to the discriminatory structures that positioned them for loss (502). Admittedly, these goals seem idealistic after T.K.'s disappearance and Laura's current hardships. Commenting more generally, Ureña stresses that full recovery from colonial trauma may be unachievable for many, which may include Laura and her family. However, she also emphasizes that attempts to advance healing through decolonial love remain laudable as a "worthwhile venture" even if complete success is unattainable (89). While Laura's regenerative potential has been downplayed in the public texts reviewed, a decolonial love lens reminds us of her underlying viability if emancipated from destructive colonial forces.

This scholarship suggests a counter and more radical reading of Laura's story that may afford her more worth as something other than a monstrous mother. Through world traveling, we see that these same persons, or in this context, these same mothers, may be "subjects, lively beings, resistors" and "constructors of visions" even while they "are animated only by the arrogant perceiver and are pliable, foldable, file-awayable, classifiable" in mainstream systems (18)

Comments from Laura seem to vividly illustrate her visionary capacity, albeit through dreams. In a 2016 interview, Laura acknowledged her uncertainty that T.K. would ever be found. Laura described dreams where T.K. emerged. In the first one, T.K. was inside a large house in another city. A grown T.K., with dark, shiny hair was upstairs, sitting on a bathtub edge, putting on stockings. In a second dream, T.K. was still a child who ran into her mother's arms. "There you are!" Laura exclaimed; she picked T.K. up to embrace her. T.K. broke free and disappeared again.

Through combining emancipatory love scholarship with mothering scholarship, we may begin to bring respectful attentiveness to stories like the ones Laura shared, in which T.K.'s presence in her life endures beyond her physical absence. These dream accounts seem important to recognize counter-knowledge about a mother's grief and her ongoing connections to her child, thereby defying the narratives from oppressive systems that seem to convey Laura as hardened to her children's fate. Read in tandem with Ureña, Laura's dreams seem to "complicate" perspectives on "normative categories" by going beyond "hegemonic binaries" of good or bad mothers that reinforce the "colonial wound" of unfitness (99).

A World Traveling Moment: The Justice for Our Stolen Children Camp, Regina, Saskatchewan, 2018

The view that decolonial love is a pathway to justice seems to have found expression with the founders of Justice for Our Stolen Children, a social movement that organized a camp near the Saskatchewan Legislative Building in Regina in February 2018. The fact that the protesters have emphasized the disproportionate number of Indigenous children in care in Saskatchewan as one of their main grievances makes the camp's formation particularly relevant to this scholarship and its call for the recognition of Indigenous mothers as other than monstrous. Their demands for changes to the child welfare system are important to this study, which brings attention to the systemic harms that dramatically affected Laura and her family.

For organizer Prescott Demas, originally from Canupawakpa Dakota First Nation in Manitoba, the purpose of the camp was to resist a system that was "not geared to accept Aboriginal people" (Desai and Gray-Donald). After their July 1 eviction, the protesters immediately reestablished their occupancy. Prescott Demas was one of the persons who kept the camp going. For him, the protest provided Indigenous people with the chance of "joining and rising" (Desai and Gray-Donald).

Notably, some of the protesters identify love as the motivation for their involvement. In a CBC news story, one camp visitor, Chad Pelletier, described his support in ways that coincide with this text. He stated he was drawn by "the teepees," "the fire," and "the medicines" and emphasized that the "respect and honour" shown by the protesters was instructive on "how to be in life" (qtd. in Kendal). Notably, Pelletier hoped the love shown at the camp helped his children. He admired the unity the camp promoted. Pelletier's comments suggest that the camp is a lived example of the decolonial love which may restore what Ureña sees as an urgent priority, namely "intersubjective relation" or close human connection (99). Acknowledging "the experiences of those most marginalized" makes "ethical, loving, and human relation possible" (99).

Part IV: Conclusions: Remembering That "Someone Stole [Her] Child"

In writing this chapter, I aimed to write a feminist, decolonial love story for a struggling mother, Laura, who has a long-term missing child. At the outset, this chapter outlined findings from love studies and decolonial love studies scholarship, which have added further insight into critical mothering scholarship. Along with Dora Silva Santana, this chapter is "interested in what the work of love (hooks) among black women, cis and trans, can do, that is, love embodied in flesh in ancestral energies with potential to heal, to fight death, and to organize, and as praxis of caring for each other against intersecting oppression" (187).

Throughout this text, I explored the effort to grant love a more thoughtful place in critical scholarship. Specifically, I theorized what love studies might offer to a rereading of the account of a mother struggling in the aftermath of her child's disappearance. Although this study is limited to the fragments and pieces from news stories and court cases, it is a step towards envisioning Laura beyond a perpetual wrong-doer, who is read as a monstrous caregiver. This text offers a view of Laura as a grieving parent, who has been structurally rendered precarious. In her 2016 interview, Laura expressed her hope that the broader community would acknowledge that "someone stole [her] child" (Pruden). This chapter has applied the lens of decolonial love with the hope of ensuring that a daughter's disappearance foregrounds the story of Laura by emphasizing her existence as a mother who has been harmed by colonial and criminal victimization, who exists in a nation still reckoning with its traumatic past and the harms to Indigenous bodies.

Postscript

On June 25, 2019, CTV News Regina shared updates on some figures from the Justice for Our Stolen Children camp. At the time of the article, two tipis had been erected in front of homes in Regina's notorious North Central neighbourhood to honour and preserve the camp, which was forcibly disbanded in the fall of 2018. Prescott Demas was one of the main organizers of the Justice for our Stolen Children camp in Wascana Park. In the June 2019 news story, he reported on the birth of his daughter, Tema "Oskana" Demas, with his partner, Shannon Corkery, in April 2019. Demas shared his joy at raising his new daughter as a member of the community that formed during the camp (CTV Regina). In an interview with the *Regina Leader Poster*, Demas said he lost two children to the child welfare system in Manitoba. Demas seemed relieved that the camp had connected him to "an army of advocates" that would ensure that Tema remained in the care of her parents and community (qtd. in White-Crummey). Demas said that his early morning hours were often spent smudging and purifying—a practice he enjoyed sharing with Tema. Demas stated that he was "full of gratitude" regarding the birth of his daughter. In conclusion, Demas said, "I mean I love her, every minute," a statement that seems to offer an appropriate ending to this chapter by reinforcing the value of love (qtd. in CTV Regina).

Acknowledgments

Tema's parents granted their permission for the inclusion of these details. The author also thanks Joshua Sallos for his editorial assistance in finalizing this manuscript.

Works Cited

Arvin, Maile. "Indigenous Feminist Notes on Embodying Alliance against Settler Colonialism." *Meridians*, vol. 18, no. 2, 1 Oct. 2019, pp. 335-57.

Buller, Marion, et al. *Reclaiming Power and Place: The Final Report of the National Inquiry into Missing and Murdered Indigenous Women and Girls*. National Inquiry into Missing and Murdered Indigenous Women and Girls, 2019.

Carlson, Kathryn Blaze. "Mother holds out hope in missing girl search: 'I want her to come home.'" *The Globe and Mail*, 7 Nov. 2014, theglobeandmail.com/news/national/tamra-keepness-a-haunting-reminder-of-an-unsolved-mystery/article21490589. Accessed 11 June 2021.

Chrisjohn, Roland David, et al. *The Circle Game: Shadows and Substance in the Indian Residential School Experience in Canada*. Theytus Books, 2006.

Cook, Tim. "Tamra's siblings removed from home", Canadian Press. 22 July 2004, *Tribe Magazine*, https://www.tribemagazine.com/board/threads/stupid-hypocritical-police-media-and-soceity-re-tamara-keepness.72621/. Accessed 11 June 2021.

Cowan, T. L. "Transfeminist Kill/Joys: Rage, Love, and Reparative Performance." *TSQ: Transgender Studies Quarterly*, vol. 1, no. 4, 1 Nov. 2014, pp. 501-16.

CTV Regina. "Members of 'Justice for Our Stolen Children's Camp" Share Special Connections One Year Later." *CTV News*, 25 June 2019, regina.ctvnews.ca/members-of-justice-for-our-stolen-children-camp-share-special-connections-one-year-later-1.4480953. Accessed 11 June 2021.

Daschuk, James. *Clearing the Plains: Disease, Politics of Starvation and the Loss of Aboriginal Life*. University of Regina Press, 2013.

Desai, Saima, and David Gray-Donald. "Camped out for Justice." *Briarpatch Magazine*, 9 Mar. 2019, briarpatchmagazine.com/articles/view/camped-out-for-justice. Accessed 11 June 2021.

Dey, Sayan, and Jonnelle Walker. "Reviving Indigenous Spaces: Echoes of a Native Spirit – An Interview with Leanne Betasamosake Simpson." *Writers in Conversation*, vol. 5, no. 1, 28 Jan. 2018, pp. 1-3.

Dunkerley, Stacy. "Mothers Matter: A Feminist Perspective on Child Welfare-Involved Women." *Journal of Family Social Work*, vol. 20, no. 3, 16 May 2017, pp. 251-65.

Flowers, Rachel. "Refusal to Forgive: Indigenous Women's Love and Rage." *Decolonization: Indigeneity, Education & Society*, vol. 4, no. 2, 2015, pp. 32-49.

Galloway, Gloria. "Proposed Class Action Suit Accuses RCMP of Inadequately Investigating Murdered, Missing Indigenous Women." *The Globe and Mail*. 5 July 2018, theglobeandmail.com/canada/article-proposed-class-action-suit-accuses-rcmp-of-inadequately-investigating.

Global News. "T.K. One of Many Missing Indigenous Girls Listed in Class Action Lawsuit against RCMP." *Global News*, 5 July 2018, globalnews.ca/video/4315745/tamra-keepness-one-of-many-missing-indigenous-girls-listed-in-class-action-lawsuit-against-rcmp. Accessed 11 June 2021.

Green, Robyn. "Loving to Reconcile: Love as a Political Emotion at the Truth and Reconciliation Commission." *Power Through Testimony: Reframing Residential Schools in the Age of Reconciliation*, edited by Brieg Capitaine and Karine Vanthuyne, UBC Press, 2017, pp. 74-94.

Gubrium, Aline. "Writing Against the Image of the Monstrous Crack Mother." *Journal of Contemporary Ethnography*, vol. 37, no. 5, 1 Oct. 2008, pp. 511-27.

Gurusami, Susila. "Motherwork Under the State: The Maternal Labor of Formerly Incarcerated Black Women." *Social Problems*, vol. 66, no. 1, 13 Feb. 2018, pp. 128-43.

Latimer, Kendall. "Who Is There? Meet the People of the Indigenous Protest Camp: People have flocked to Justice for Our Stolen Children Camp for a Variety of Reasons." *CBC News*, 29 June 2018, cbc.ca/news/canada/saskatchewan/faces-of-the-justice-camp-1.4728833. Accessed 11 June 2021.

Lavell-Harvard, D. Memee, and Kim Anderson, editors. *Mothers of the Nations: Indigenous Mothering as Global Resistance, Reclaiming and Recovery*. Demeter Press, 2014.

Lacombe, Michele. "Leanne Betasamosake Simpson's Decolonial

Aesthetics: 'Leaks'/Leaks, Storytelling, Community, and Collaboration." *Canadian Literature*, vol. 1, no. 230, 2016, pp. 45-63.

Lugones, María. "Playfulness, 'World'-Travelling, and Loving Perception." *Hypatia*, vol. 2, no. 2, 1987, pp. 3-19.

Moore, Darnell, and Monica J. Casper. "Love in the Time of Racism." *Ada: A Journal of Gender, New Media, & Technology*, no. 5, July 2014, adanewmedia.org/2014/07/issue5-moorecasper.

Polischuk, Heather. "Federal Court Tosses Out Attempted MMIWG Class Action Led by Regina Mother. The Federal Court Has Ended a Class-Action Attempt by MMIWG-Impacted Families, Finding the Claim 'Overly Broad'." *Regina Leader Post*, 17 June 2021, leaderpost.com/news/saskatchewan/federal-court-tosses-out-attempted-mmiwg-class-action-led-by-regina-mother. Accessed 22 June 2021.

Pruden, Jana G. "What Happened the Night Tamra Keepness Disappeared from Her Regina Home?" *The Walrus*, 24 June 2016, thewalrus.ca/little-girl-lost/. Accessed 11 June 2021.

Regester, Charlene. "Monstrous Mother, Incestuous Father, and Terrorized Teen: Reading Precious as a Horror Film." *Journal of Film and Video*, vol. 67, no.1, 2015, pp. 30-45.

Roberts, Dorothy E. "Deviance, Resistance, and Love." *Penn Law: Legal Scholarship Repository*, 1994, scholarship.law.upenn.edu/faculty scholarship/1386/. Accessed 11 June 2021.

Sandoval, Chela. *Methodology of the Oppressed*. University of Minnesota Press, 2000.

Santana, Dora Silva. "Transitionings and Returnings: Experiments with the Poetics of Transatlantic Water." *TSQ: Transgender Studies Quarterly*, vol. 4, no. 2, 1 May 2017, pp. 181-90.

Saskatchewan Court of Appeal. *Re S.F. SKCA 121*. 2009, canlii.ca/t/26jd3.

Saskatchewan Court of Queen's Bench. *Re S.F. Regina. F.S.M. No. 80 of 2001*. 9 July 2008.

Saskatchewan Court of Queen's Bench. *Re S.F. SKQB 179*. 2014, canlii.ca/t/g82q0.

Savarese, Josephine. "Theorizing Soft Criminalization in the Child Welfare System, An Analysis of Re S.F." *Criminalized Mothers*,

Criminalizing Mothering, edited by Bryan Hogeveen and Joanne Minaker, Demeter Press, 2015, pp. 88-111.

Tanner, Angela. "A Case Study of Missing Children in the Canadian Press." *Carleton University Research Virtual Environment*, *Carleton University*, 2006, curve.carleton.ca/system/files/etd/c6c44906-e87c-4a26-8928-868798ab421f/etd_pdf/39f48d09cc7d2affa58fc0d52a04b963/tanner-acasestudyofmissingchildreninthecanadianpress.pdf. Accessed 11 June 2021.

The Canadian Press. "Regina Police Say Map, Search Yield No Evidence of Tamra Keepness." *CTV News*, 7 Nov. 2014, regina.ctvnews.ca/regina-police-say-map-search-yield-no-evidence-of-tamra-keepness-1.2092462. Accessed 11 June 2021.

Thompson, Debra. "An Exoneration of Black Rage." *South Atlantic Quarterly*, vol. 116, no. 3, 1 July 2017, pp. 457-481.

Ureña, Carolyn. "Loving from Below: Of (De)Colonial Love and Other Demons." *Hypatia*, vol. 32, no. 1, 8 Oct. 2017, pp. 86-102.

Wright, Fiona. "Palestine, My Love: The Ethico-Politics of Love and Mourning in Jewish Israeli Solidarity Activism." *American Ethnologist*, vol. 43, no. 1, 14 Feb. 2016, pp. 130-43.

White-Crummey, Arthur. "Regina Protest Camp Lives on in Family Ties, Resurrected Teepee, and Google Street View." *Regina Leader-Post*, 20 June 2019, leaderpost.com/news/saskatchewan/regina-protest-camp-lives-on-in-family-ties-and-resurrected-teepee. Accessed 11 June 2021.

Chapter 3

"Science Put Babies in My Belly": Cyborg Mothering and Posthumanism in *Orphan Black*

Susan Harper and Jessica Smartt Gullion

In 2013, the BBC premiered the science fiction dystopia *Orphan Black*.[1] The series raises questions about what it means to be human after significant technological interference with the body and explores the role of mothers in technologically mediated biology. As the series unfolds, we learn how newly created human forms can be both monstrous and hopeful.

Science fiction, and in particular dystopian science fiction, has long served as a venue for exploring society's fears about technology and social change. Speculative stories that take place in worlds not far removed from our own, such as *Orphan Black*, are rich sites of exploring the possibilities and pitfalls of scientific and technical progress. Firmly located within—and often drawing on the themes and motifs of— classic science fiction and dystopian fantasy such as Aldous Huxley's *A Brave New World*, Phillip K. Dick's *Do Androids Dream of Electric Sheep?* (and its film adaptation, *Bladerunner*), Margaret Atwood's *A Handmaid's Tale*, and George Orwell's *1984*, *Orphan Black* delves into fears of unte- thered technology. Set in a world much like our own, in a time that is roughly contemporaneous or only slightly in the future, *Orphan Black* locates its characters in a social world that confronts issues the audience is familiar with, as those characters also must navigate an ever-unfolding mystery and the dangers it uncovers.

The Series

The premise of *Orphan Black* is that a secret organization (known as Dyad) successfully cloned humans in the early 1980s as part of an experiment in human-led evolution. When the show begins, these humans are now young adults. The audience is unaware of Dyad's existence as the show opens. They enter the world of *Orphan Black* through the eyes and experiences of Sarah Manning. Sarah is one of the Dyad clones, but neither she nor the audience know this in the opening episode. Sarah's chance encounter with a woman who looks exactly like her—in fact, one of the other clones—sets in motion the chain of events that will reveal to Sarah and the audience the extent of the Dyad experiment and all its far-reaching repercussions.

Using a chimera as their initial DNA, Dyad created both a male and female line of clones. The members of the female line, called Leda, were allowed to mature naturally, living out in society but kept unaware of their status as clones while researchers covertly monitored them. The notable exception is the Leda clone Rachel Duncan, who is raised self-aware from birth and is parented in a highly scientific manner by Dyan founders Ethan and Susan Duncan and then by Aldous Leekie. They groom her to take over both the Leda project and the Dyad Corporation upon adulthood. Meanwhile, the members of the male line, known as Castor, were raised together by the military as super soldiers. The audience—and most of the Leda clones—remain unaware of the Castor clones' existence until close to the end of season two.

The show starts as some of the female clones discover each other's existence. By the end of the series, we learn there are 247 Leda clones dispersed throughout the globe. Cloning humans was part of Dyad's larger agenda in eugenics. The Leda clones were engineered to be sterile. The Castor clones carry a pathogen that they pass on to women through sex; this pathogen renders those women infertile. This was intended to be a weapon in the Castor project's aim to "end war within a generation." Eventually, the world would be run by the Dyad corporation. The clones would serve as a controllable workforce, and the rest of humanity would die out.

Biology is notoriously difficult to control, however. In an unexpected twist, a set of Leda clones twinned. The twins had an anomaly that allowed them to become pregnant. These twins—Sarah Manning and her twin Helena—were raised in separate environments and were lost to the experiment and Dyad monitoring. Sarah and Helena are unaware of their relationship until later in the series.

We soon learn that the clones are dying. The antifertility gene in both clone lines mutated and caused an autoimmune disease that ravages their organs. The Leda clones develop uterine tumours, which not only render them sterile as planned but also lead to a respiratory disease that ultimately kills them. The Castor clones experience neurological anomalies—known as "glitching"—which eventually lead to neurological failure and death.

Both lines have a synthetic DNA sequence, which has been patented by the Dyad corporation, marked with the words "This organism and derivative genetic material is restricted intellectual property." This raises the question of the clones' fundamental humanity.[2] The series explores the consequences of human cloning, human-led evolution, eugenics, corporate ownership of humans, and ultimately how we define what is human.

Cyborg Mothering in the Posthuman Era

Notions about the posthuman are rampant in science fiction, and cloning itself is far from fantasy (Griffin and Nesseth). In 1957, researchers cloned HeLa cells (which would later become the heart of a controversy about who owns biological data) (Skloot). This was the first time that human cells would be cloned. Stillman and Hall cloned the first human embryo in 1993. In 1996, the first cloned mammal, Dolly the Sheep, was born, followed the next year by Cumulina the cloned mouse. Cumulina was part of the OncoMouse project and was the first patented transgenic mammal. Late in 2002, a company called Clonaid claimed that the first human clone, Eve, was born.[3] While the company claims to have created additional living clones, none of the company's claims have been independently verified, nor have any of their results been published in the scientific literature, leading many skeptics to refer to Eve's status as a clone as a hoax. In 2003 the Human

Genome Project was completed, providing a complete map of all human genes. In 2013, the US Supreme Court ruled that naturally occurring genes cannot be patented, but that synthetic sequences (such as those in the clones of *Orphan Black*) could be. Thus, as in the television show, it is conceivable that human beings could become corporate intellectual property. In 2017, the first human-pig chimera embryos were created; human genes were injected into a pig embryo to create the creature. Theoretically, such a creature could be used to grow human replacement organs. While this was not the first mixed-species chimera, it was the first involving human genes.

Beginning with Donna Haraway's manifesto for cyborgs, feminist theorists have taken the lead in theorizing the cybernetic human and the emancipatory potentialities of the posthuman. Jessica Dickson writes that such a creature is "a fictional being where gendered subjection through epistemologies of science and taxonomy is challenged by the blurring of the socially constructed (rather than natural) boundaries between human, animal, and machine" (79).

Whereas Haraway has envisioned the cyborg as a body outside of gendered and racialized categories, Dickson writes that the agency of cybernetic beings in science fiction is determined by their subjugation to established gendered and racialized roles. For example, *Star Trek's* Data, an android, is regularly used in the show as a proxy challenge for "a Western ideal concept of personhood as an individual with consciousness" (Dickson 79). Tests of his personhood include his ability to form friendships and intimate relationships with humans, his career success, and even his caretaking of a pet cat. Emphasizing that relationality becomes the signifier of subjectivity, Dickson writes, "Humanness in the biomedical Western sense is not an empirical given of natural kinds in the world, but of socioculturally constructed boundaries that purport a particular, but not necessarily homogeneous or static model of personhood" (81). Questions of biology and consciousness arise in other recent science fiction works, including the series *Westworld* and *Battlestar Galactica*, and such films as *Her* and *Ex Machina*. In all of these depictions, we find that the dream of the cyborg is not of electric sheep but of becoming human.

Mothering and Monstrosity in *Orphan Black*

If the defining feature of humanity is relationality and agential cyborgs are subjected to gendered roles, it is no wonder that motherhood plays such a prominent role in *Orphan Black*. Mothering (the act of caring for children) and motherhood (the social construction of how children are to be borne, cared for, and raised) are central themes throughout the series (Rich). Andrea O'Reilly makes this distinction: "The term motherhood refers to the patriarchal institution of motherhood which is male-defined and controlled, and is deeply oppressive to women, while the word mothering refers to women's experiences of mothering which are female-defined and centred, and potentially empowering to women." We see the tension and sometimes contradictions between these two concepts—which are so often conflated in Western culture— as the Ledas and their families grapple with raising and caring for their children (and adult children), making reproductive choices, and even looking after each other. Motherhood and mothering are portrayed in ways that are complex, often morally ambiguous, and that challenge cultural norms of what it means to be a mother. The trope of the monstrous mother and the monster as mother in *Orphan Black* raises larger questions of what a mother is, the role of nature versus nurture, violence as an extension of mother love, and the various ways in which a being can become a mother and perform acts of mothering in a posthuman context.

The characters in *Orphan Black* are situated as monstrous mothers, but as the series unfolds, we find that their mothering reflects the monstrous context in which they were created. The characters must perform their acts of mothering in ways that seem monstrous from the viewer's standpoint but that are in fact rooted in deep love and determination to survive.

In this chapter, we focus on three main characters in the series: Sarah Manning, her twin sister, Helena (who is never given a surname), and their sister clone, Alison Hendrix. These three characters are the only Ledas who are raising children. Sarah and Helena both give birth to children; Sarah is already mother to seven-year-old Kira when the series opens, and Helena goes on to give birth to twins in the final episodes of the series. Alison, in contrast, is infertile, like the other Leda clones, but has adopted two children. The sharply different ways in which these characters embody and enact motherhood provide an excellent lens through which to examine motherhood and mothering writ large in *Orphan Black*. However, we would like to note that the series is ripe for analysis and that most of the female characters could be situated within the context of monstrous mothers; indeed, larger issues of reproductive autonomy, eugenics, surrogacy-for-hire, and the exploitation of Brown and Black childbearing bodies permeate the series as well.

Sarah Manning

Sarah and Helena are anomalies among the Leda clones. They are mirror twins, monozygotic, with some features as reflections. (For example, Helena's heart is on the right side of her chest while Sarah's is on the left.) They were lost to the Dyad experiment when their surrogate mother, an Afrian immigrant named Amelia, learned of the project, escaped, and hid the twins.[4]

Sarah was sent to live with a Siobhan Sadler ("Mrs. S") in London, who was part of a network that knew about the cloning project and wanted to protect the babies from Dyad. They later fled to Toronto, along with Sarah's foster brother, Felix, and this is where most of the series takes place.

We are introduced to Sarah in the midst of a conflict with Mrs. S surrounding Sarah's daughter. During a phone call, we learn that Sarah has returned to Toronto and wants to see her daughter, Kira, whom Mrs. S has been caring for. Mrs. S refuses, to which Sarah replies, "Well, I'm her mother." Later in the episode, Sarah's foster brother Felix reminds her that she "left Kira with Mrs. S overnight and [was] gone for *ten months*."[5]

This episode sets up Sarah in the role of bad mother. She abandoned her daughter. She is a criminal and a grifter. She is involved with an abusive drug dealer. She is willing to be violent herself, as she indicates when she tells Felix she "hit [her boyfriend] first *this time*."[6] She plans to steal a dead woman's identity (the first indication of another clone) and to use money from the sale of stolen cocaine to finance an escape for herself, her daughter, and her foster brother.

We see the trope of the bad mother, the monstrous mother, played out throughout the series regarding Sarah, even as viewers get to know her mothering as much more complex than the initial scenes of the series might indicate. These opening scenes establish motherhood and mothering as a central conflict of the series—though in ways far different than viewers might expect.

Sarah's pregnancy with Kira was unplanned; we learn in the final episode of the series that she had considered having an abortion.[7] Kira is not Sarah's first pregnancy; she had an abortion previously.[8] Kira's paternity is also uncertain. While viewers eventually learn the father is a man Sarah ran a con on,[9] the long-standing uncertainty about who fathered Kira also plays into the monstrosity of Sarah's motherhood: it is unintended; she seriously considered terminating the pregnancy; she is young and unmarried; she is promiscuous, leading to uncertainty about her child's paternity; she is a criminal; and Mrs. S urges her to reconsider carrying the pregnancy to term and keeping the child because Sarah "can barely take care of [her]self."[10]

Helena

As an infant, Helena was placed in a convent in the Ukraine, where she was brutally abused. At twelve years old, a religious extremist group called the Proletheans took her. The Proletheans are a proscience religious cult who know about the Dyad experiment and believe that cloning and human engineering are God's will. They convinced Helena that she was the only real human in the experiment, that she was the original from which all the others were cloned, and that the clones were abominations in the eyes of God. The Proletheans trained her and sent her out to murder the other clones.

Helena believes the clones are "dirty, dirty copies" of her.[11] When viewers meet her, she's on a killing spree. She kills with extreme brutality and without remorse; she is on a mission from God. She leaves dismembered Barbies behind as her calling card. Even after her true nature as one clone of many is revealed, she is willing to take life without much self-reflection, as when she still plans to assassinate a fellow clone.[12]

Helena has a feral aura, with uncontrolled and uncontrollable hair, wild red-ringed eyes, a lack of table manners, and unquenchable hunger for all things sugary. She lives in abandoned places, outdoor lairs, and hidden and dirty spaces, which are more like dens than domiciles. The stick figures with which she decorates the walls of her homes recall cave paintings as well as "primitive" or childlike art. The fact that she is on a murder spree only underscores this monstrosity.

The antagonist of the first season, Helena is a clear and present danger to the clones. Even when that relationship shifts in season two, Helena remains wild, distinct from her "Seestras," as she refers to the other clones. She marks her body with razor cuts that scar into angel wings, which shows that Helena herself is perhaps not sure whether she is human, divine, or evil. She is, as one character calls her, "an angry angel,"[13] or in the words of the hosts of the podcast *Tatiana Is Everyone*, a "precious murder angel."[14]

Even as Helena becomes integrated into the sisterhood of the clones, monstrosity remains a key aspect of her character. This monstrosity only becomes more apparent when she becomes pregnant with twins. Helena's pregnancy is the result of a forcible insemination by the leader of the Protheans. In a violent scene, Helena is raped in a barn with cattle insemination tools. It is an experiment to see if she, like Sarah, will be fertile. The key moments of her motherhood journey take place in wild places—she is fertilized in a barn, spends a significant portion of her pregnancy living in a national park in a fur-covered hut and hunting food (often with her bare hands), gives birth in an abandoned building, and lives with her babies in a converted garage. Is she human or some type of animal? The question put forth in our first encounters with her remains unanswered even after five seasons.

Despite the violent circumstances under which she becomes pregnant, Helena embraces motherhood. She never considers terminating the pregnancy—in contrast to what we learn about Sarah's reaction to pregnancy. Instead, Helena becomes fiercely protective of her babies. Helena discovers that the Protheans created many embryos during her "procedure," some of which were also implanted into the leader's biological daughter, Gracie, and others of which were frozen and kept in cold storage. The Protheans planned to impregnate other women with the remaining embryos. Despite their origins, Helena considers all of the embryos to be her "babies." She assures Gracie that Gracie does not have to "carry [her] babies" if she doesn't want to,[15] but she also ensures that she retrieves the remaining frozen embryos when she kills the leader of the Protheans and burns the compound down.

Helena is especially willing to kill for her babies, whether they be the twins she carries or the fertilized embryos in the cryotank. In a later episode, her cryotank of embryos is stolen by a gang of drug dealers. In response, Helena slaughters the drug dealers, exiting the building with tank in hand and blood dripping from her clothing.[16] When she is taken to the hospital because one of her babies has been injured by her fall on a sharp stick during an altercation with the Neolutionists, agents of the organization behind the Leda Project and other attempts to control human evolution, in her forest lair, Helena is immediately suspicious of the medical personnel and the tests they want to do. She knows that people are interested in her babies' genetics the same way they are interested in Kira's genetics. When a doctor encourages her to undergo an amniocentesis for a genetic test, Helena is wary and protective; rather than undergo the test and put her babies' genetic material at risk, Helena stabs the doctor with the amniocentesis needle.[17] Helena seems to have an intense, mother-bear instinct for protecting her young, aligning to the theme of her character.

Interestingly, Helena seems to know that she is a monstrous mother. She discusses having Sarah raise her twins because she does not want them to turn out like her. Later, when she is in labour at Dyad, Helena is taunted by Virginia Coady, the "mother" of the Castor line, whom Helena has called a "shit mother" for her treatment of the Castor clones.[18] Coady goads Helena that her babies will be better off being raised by Dyad because "what kind of mother could [she] possibly be?"[19] Helena takes Coady's words to heart; she has already expressed fear that her babies will turn out like her, an outcome she is desperate to avoid. When she is left unattended in the ersatz labour suite Coady has constructed, Helena slits her own wrists so that she will die and save her twins from being mothered and raised by her. Helena's birth experience is grisly, savage, and monstrous—she gives birth on a piece of cardboard on the dirty floor of a disused room at Dyad, with no professional medical help and only Art and Sarah to assist.

Following the birth of her sons, Helena makes a home in Alison's converted garage. She sleeps in a hammock and decorates the space with homemade toys. In defiance of convention, she does not give children names until several months after they are born, instead using socks and wristbands in different colours—Orange and Purple, which become the boys' nicknames—so she can tell them apart.

Alison Hendrix

If Sarah and (especially) Helena represent the archetypical monstrous mother, then Alison Hendrix embodies the role of the good mother—or at least on the surface. Alison is the mother of two adopted children. When we meet Alison, she is preparing to serve orange slices at their soccer game. Sarah surprises her in the act, and Alison's immediate concern is that her children do not see Sarah and discover the secret of the clones.[20]

Alison has discovered the existence of the clone experiment (though not the details of it), and she has been working with fellow clones Beth and Cosima to find others and to get to the bottom of their situation. She has carefully protected her children and her husband from the knowledge of the other clones and her involvement in the mystery. Alison is stereotypical in her motherhood. She is a white, middle-class, and suburb-dwelling soccer mom. She drives a minivan, does not pursue a career outside the house, is involved in church and in community theater, and provides the snacks for soccer games. The neighbours regularly come to her home for potluck dinners. Her well-appointed craft room ensures that she is prepared for any occasion.

The one "flaw" in Alison's motherhood is that she has been unable to bear children herself; her two children, Oscar and Gemma, are adopted. (Although it is never remarked upon in the series, her children are also not white.) Her inability to have biological children is a source of pain for Alison, as we see several times throughout the series. When Sarah arrives at Alison's house for the meeting with Cosima, Alison is clearly surprised to hear that Sarah has a daughter. Alison asks if Sarah's daughter is "adopted, like [her children]" and visibly reacts when Sarah, puzzled, replies that Kira is not adopted.[21]

However, as with so much in *Orphan Black*, all is not as it seems. While Alison's interactions with her children, and with Kira, are kind, firm, and maternal, she is harbouring secrets. Alison clearly questions whether the life she has chosen—full-time mothering, suburban life, marriage—is all there is. In a series of flashbacks, we see Alison have an existential crisis about her role as a full-time mother.[22] This revelation that Alison has questioned whether the life she has—the so-called perfect life of a full-time, middle-class wife and mother—gives new context to her behaviour throughout the series. Because even though Alison seems to be the ideal good mother, she engages in a variety of behaviours that people associate with bad mothers. Under the patina of suburban bliss, Alison performs monstrosity in her own way.

Our first indication that something is amiss occurs when we learn about Alison's addiction to pills and alcohol. At first, she seems to be keeping her use of these substances from everyone, even her husband. However, she soon finds herself the object of an intervention[23] led by her best friend Aynsley, who Alison suspects is an undercover monitor working for Dyad. Alison's addictions come to a head when she drinks too much and falls off the stage during a community theatre performance, leading her to end up in rehab and have her children withheld from her.[24] When her husband loses his job, he and Alison begin selling drugs throughout the neighbourhood, using her mother's soap shop as a cover. She ends up in serious debt to a drug gang (who, as mentioned in the previous section, Helena dispatches). These episodes make Alison the subject of gossip in her affluent suburb; she loses leadership positions in the church and community and finds herself shunned by people she once considered friends. When her husband falls on stage during a Highland dance because he has unknowingly consumed a bottle of iced tea that Alison spiked with pills, Alison lashes out. She reminds her neighbours that most of them bought pills from her—that they are in fact not as squeaky clean as they like to pretend they are. She clearly knows that her past addictive behaviour causes others to label her as a bad mother, and she is unwilling to let others off the hook.[25]

Although the public incidents stemming from her addictions are the most obvious ways in which Alison performs monstrosity, they are not the most severe. Alison has sex with Aynsley's husband to get back at Aynsley for (supposedly) being her Dyad monitor. Later, she stands by while Aynsley is choked to death by her scarf in the garbage disposal. She helps her husband dispose of Leekie's body in the floor of their garage after her husband murdered him—an experience that unexpectedly rekindles the passion in their marriage.

Alison is by all accounts a good mother, and we see her acts of mothering as confirming this. However, despite her ability to perform mothering and motherhood according to cultural standards—even to exceed those cultural standards—it is hard to ignore that Alison engages in monstrous behaviour. Like Sarah and Helena, Alison engages in some of this behaviour to protect her children. She wants

Aynsley dead so that she herself is no longer monitored (even though Aynsley is not, in fact, her monitor). She signs Leekie's documents submitting to some regular checkups but discharging the monitors, believing this will keep her children safe from the web of violence that surrounds the Ledas. But she also selfishly—that most lethal of all charges—pursues her own pleasures through substances and extra-marital sex. She cannot admit that her "ideal" life is somehow unfulfilling—no mother is as monstrous as the one who admits she is not happy being a mother—so she seeks other ways to either numb the pain or to bring in some excitement. As she remarks to Aynsley, Alison wonders how many of the women in her suburb are also questioning whether mothering, soccer practices, and minivans are all there is to life, if there might not be something more.

Alison's doubts and fears about the value of her life as a good mother are put into stark relief in her confrontation with Frontenac, who says to her, "Sarah and Helena are valuable because they are fertile. Cosima is a real scientist. And then there's *you*." Called upon to defend her own value, Alison replies that she is a wife, a mother, and a homemaker—all roles for which she is rewarded by society. Frontenac responds that she can go back to her "vapid" life, indicating that she has no value to the clones, to Neolution, to anyone. Even embodying the good mother is not, in the end, enough. Her fertile sisters, previously considered failures for their fertility, have become a valued commodity; once again, Alison's infertility makes her less valuable, less of a mother, less of a woman.[26] It is this confrontation that causes Alison to take off on her own for a while—to explore herself and discover who she is apart from the roles of good mother and good wife.

Embracing the Monstrous

Fertility

Dominant cultural narratives hold that being fertile is a key part of what it is to be a woman. Birthing and rearing children are normative in most human societies, even as options for reproductive choice have expanded in many industrialized societies and the use of reproductive technologies has expanded (Greil, McQuillan, and Slausen-Blevins; Ulrich and Weatherall). Infertility is seen as a disruption of the natural life course and can cause significant personal and relationship stress as women grapple with having failed to live up to societal expectations around motherhood (Becker). Infertile women are seen, and may see themselves, as somehow less-than, not exactly entitled to full womanhood; they are to be pitied, but are also seen as defective (Ulrich and Weatherall; Gonzalez). Because infertility is considered a "stigmatizing condition," women in the US have successfully used the Americans with Disabilities Act to gain access to reproductive technology (Sternke and Abrahamson). We see some of this discourse reflected in Alison's and Beth's experiences in *Orphan Black*. We find out that Alison and Donny have two adopted children when Alison asks whether Kira is "adopted like" her children and is visibly shaken to realize that Sarah birthed Kira. Alison draws on this narrative (as a ruse) later in the series, when she spots a friend at the Brightborn Agency and explains how she really wants to carry a baby of her own, as much as she loves her adopted children. In another instance, Paul tells Sarah that he was with Beth when Beth found out she couldn't have children; the audience is clearly meant to infer that this news was upsetting to Beth, although since she dies in the first minutes of the first episode of *Orphan Black*, the audience never gets her perspective. Among the clones themselves, the underlying assumption about Sarah's fertility—Helena's would not be revealed until *Orphan Black*'s second season—is that she is the most successful clone. Indeed, the audience is complicit in this assumption; we are, after all, encouraged to root for Sarah generally, and our dominant cultural narratives tell us that a fertile woman is a successful woman. Rachel Duncan, the clone reared by Dyad, says as much during a confrontation with her father, Ethan Duncan. She is surprised and enraged to find out that Dyad considered Sarah (and Helena) failures due to their fertility. The Ledas were always intended to be infertile, Ethan Duncan goes on to explain. Rachel's frantic destruction of her office in the aftermath of this news is a rare show of emotion on her part.[27]

In their attempt to control human evolution (which they refer to as "Neolution"), Dyad could not afford the risk of clones who could breed and possibly spread mutated genes—or move their patented synthetic sequences out into the general population. In contrast to the dominant cultural narratives that portray infertile women as somehow monstrous, in *Orphan Black*, fertility makes Sarah, and ultimately Helena, an outlier and representative of scientific failure.

Good Mothering through Bad Motherhood

Sarah, Helena, and Alison all perform monstrosity in their motherhood in different ways. Arguably, they all fail to one degree or another at the cultural institution of motherhood—even Alison, who has all the trappings but still manages to fall rather spectacularly from grace. Even as they miss the motherhood mark, however, it cannot be denied that all three of them enact mother*ing* in ways that are incredibly tender, loving, protective, and (to put it simply) good. Each one of them ends up having to do horrible things, violent things, in the course of the series, in protection of their families. Objectively, these acts of violence and criminality are monstrous. But put into the context of what the Ledas are up against, the monstrous context in which they and the Castors were created, and the violent, confusing, and dangerous context in which they live—about which they can confide to no one but each other—these acts of violent mother-love, of deception, of criminality become the ultimate acts of love. In the end, Sarah, Helena, and Alison are neither good mothers nor bad mothers—they are mothers doing what they must to ensure the survival of their children.

If Sarah is set up to be a bad mother by moral and cultural standards, Helena is set up to be a bad mother because her humanity is somehow suspect. Both Sarah and Helena embody the monstrous mother in their own ways—Sarah because she is selfish (arguably the worst thing a mother can be accused of being); Helena because she is volatile and dangerous. Sarah is a monstrous mother because she is supposed to understand how motherhood is performed yet chooses to flout those conventions and norms. Helena is a monstrous mother because she has absolutely no grounding in cultural expectations of motherhood.

While both Sarah and Helena embody the monstrous mother trope in their own distinct ways through their mother*hood*, it is noteworthy that in the actual mother*ing* of their children, this trope is somewhat turned on its head. It is true that Sarah's motherhood of Kira is first introduced to viewers through its absence, her ten months' leave from Kira's life, along with what seems to be a rather long track record of moving in and out of Kira's life and putting her own needs and desires before Kira's. At the same time, however, we see a tender relationship between Sarah and Kira when they are together. Sarah has regard for Kira and talks to her like she can understand, reason, and make decisions, which she demonstrates that she can. There is a playful rapport between them, but Sarah is also not afraid to draw boundaries with Kira. Despite Sarah's disappearances, there is genuine affection between the two of them. Although she can certainly be characterized as having acted selfishly in choosing Vic, the abusive drug dealer and conman she has just left when the audience meets her in the first episode of the series, and life on the road over living a settled life with Kira, Sarah has also ensured that Kira would have a stable home with Mrs. S. She appears to at least attempt to give Kira stability, although Kira does admit to clone Rachel that she often moved around and has not been able to keep friends as a result.[28]

Despite Sarah's assertion in the final episode that she feels like a "shit mum," throughout the series, we see her step up to protect Kira at all costs, including putting herself in danger by surrendering to Dyad[29] and going to the island to prevent the further cloning planned that will use Kira's eggs.[30] Like Helena, Sarah does not hesitate to enact violence to protect Kira. Violence as an extension of mother love and an act of mothering is perhaps one of the pervading themes of *Orphan Black*, as we see women willing to perform "monstrous" acts of violence in the course of protecting their children.

Helena, who outwardly portrays monstrosity at nearly every step of the way in the series, presents an even more surprising subversion of the monstrous mother trope. Like Sarah, she is fiercely protective of her babies—even the frozen embryos—and is willing to enact violence to protect them. But she is also amazingly tender in her mothering. When Helena discovers that the embryos in her cryotank are dead, she buries them in the Hendrix's garden. She apologizes that she "did not know [she] needed to feed [them] liquid nitrogens." She clearly considers these embryos to be her children and as lives for which she is responsible.[31] Like Sarah, Helena is not a good mother. She in no way meets the cultural imperative of motherhood—from a socially prescribed standard, Helena is clearly a monstrous mother. Yet Helena's acts of mothering are beautiful. In the final episode we see her care for her twins in a way that seems to be a perfect depiction of how to mother. In her interactions with Orange and Purple (later known as Arthur and Donnie), Helena is clearly completely besotted with her babies. She is gentle, loving, patient—the last qualities one might expect from her, given what we know of her and the degree to which she has been constructed as monstrous.

Conclusion

Stacey Abbott writes about the "scientific hubris and masculine desire to co-opt the power of woman and God to create life" (157). This hubris is on vivid display in *Orphan Black*. But ultimately it is not male scientific hubris and desire that triumph. Instead, it is the Ledas themselves. Although they were created to be intellectual property, they have stepped into something beyond that. As Sarah tells Westmorland, she and her sisters have evolved beyond him—"THIS is evolution!"[32] They have secured a safe future for their children, for each other, and through the cure for the Ledas' disease, for all the Ledas around the world. They have become in some ways mothers to themselves, to each other, and to all their sister clones.

Orphan Black leaves unanswered the question of how the Ledas will mother their children now that the clear and present danger of Dyad, the Neolutionists, and the Protheans is gone. Without the monstrosity of their circumstances, can they also mother without monstrosity? Or is it even possible for any mother—any human, fallible, imperfect mother—to escape the trap and the trope of the monstrous mother? Given Kira's super healing powers and psychic connection—abilities that might also be present in Helena's twin boys—will the Ledas be faced with mothering children who are not quite human but not quite something else?

It is fitting that *Orphan Black* ends as it began with a scene that foregrounds motherhood. As the clones and their friends and allies celebrate Helena's baby shower at the Hendrix house, they begin to reflect on what it has meant to them to be a mother. Sarah, who has just failed to take her GED test, confesses that even after all that's happened to the Ledas, she still feels like a "shit mum." This opens a heartfelt discussion in the backyard in which it is revealed that Helena and Alison, too, feel as though they fall short in mothering. Alison, the very image of the good mother, confesses that she got so frustrated with her daughter that she threatened to hang her up by her thumbs. Helena tells the group that every time she turns around, the babies are eating sand and that she lets them do it, although she does not know "where does this sand come from?"[33] Cosima confesses that she does not know if she will ever be ready to be a parent. There is both humor and pathos in this scene, as the mothers confess to one another that they also fear they are failing at motherhood and that they share a sense of never really being good enough, of never really fulfilling the role the way the culture says they should. And it opens up the question of what it means to be a good mother, especially when one must mother in the face of violence and monstrosity.

Endnotes

1. For ease of reading, we have placed all episode references in the endnotes.
2. "Endless Forms Most Beautiful"
3. www.clonaid.com
4. "Unconscious Selection"
5. "Natural Selection"
6. "Natural Selection"
7. "To Right the Wrongs of Many"
8. "By Means Which Have Never Been Told"
9. "Mingling its Own Nature With It"
10. "To Right the Wrongs of Many"
11. "Variation Under Nature; Effects of External Conditions; One Fettered Slave"
12. "Ipsa Scientia Potestas Est"
13. "Variation Under Nature"
14. *Tatiana Is Everyone*, "Episode 54: Helena and Sarah" https://tatianaiseveryone.com/post/108061651173/helena-and-sarah-orphan-black-podcast
15. "Things Which Have Never Yet Been Done"
16. "Insolvent Phantom of Tomorrow"
17. "Clutch of Greed"
18. "Newer Elements of Our Defence"
19. "To Right the Wrongs of Many"
20. "Instinct"
21. "Variation Under Nature"
22. "Beneath Her Heart"
23. "Unconscious Selection"

24. "Governed As It Were by Chance"
25. "Beneath Her Heart"
26. "Beneath Her Heart"
27. "Variable and Full of Perturbation"
28. "Let the Children and the Childbearers Toil"
29. "By Means Which Have Never Been Tried"
30. "From Dancing Mice to Psychopaths, The Few Who Dare"
31. "The Collapse of Nature"
32. "To Right the Wrongs of Many"
33. "To Right the Wrongs of Many"

Works Cited

Abbott, Stacey. "Clone Club–*Frankenstein's* Daughters." *Science Fiction Film and Television*, vol. 11, no. 2., 2018, pp. 157-76.

Becker, Gay. "Metaphors in Disrupted Lives: Infertility and Cultural Constructions of Continuity." *Medical Anthropology Quarterly*, vol. 8, no. 4, 1994, pp. 383-410.

"Beneath Her Heart." *Orphan Black: Season Five*, written by Alex Levine, directed by David Wellington, BBC America, 2017.

"By Means Which Have Never Yet Been Tried." *Orphan Black: Season Two*, written by Graeme Manson, directed by John Fawcett, BBC America, 2014.

"Certain Agony of the Battlefield." *Orphan Black: Season Three*, written by Aubrey Nealon, directed by Helen Shaver, BBC America, 2015.

"Clutch of Greed." *Orphan Black: Season Five*, written by Jeremy Boxon, directed by John Fawcett, BBC America, 2017.

Dickson, Jessica. "Do Cyborgs Desire Their Own Subjection? Thinking Anthropology with Cinematic Science Fiction." *Bulletin of Science, Technology & Society*, vol. 36, no. 1, 2016, pp. 78-84.

"Effects of External Conditions." *Orphan Black: Season One*, written by Karen Walton, directed by Grant Harvey, BBC America, 2013.

"Endless Forms Most Beautiful." *Orphan Black: Season One,* written by Graeme Manson, directed by John Fawcett, BBC America, 2013.

"From Dancing Mice to Psychopaths." *Orphan Black: Season Four*, written by Graeme Manson, directed by John Fawcett, BBC America, 2016.

Gonzalez, Lois O. "Infertility as Transformational Process: A Framework for Psychotherapeutic Support of Infertile Women." *Mental Health Nursing*, vol. 21, no. 6, 2009, pp. 619-33.

"Governed As It Were By Chance." *Orphan Black: Season Two*, written Russ Cochrane, directed by David Frazee, BBC America, 2014.

Greil, Arthur, Julia McQuillen, and Kathleen Slauson-Blevins. "The Social Construction of Infertility." *Sociology Compass*, vol. 5, no. 8, 2011, pp. 736-46.

Griffin, Casey, and Nina Nesseth. *The Science of Orphan Black: The Official Companion*. ECW Press, 2017.

Haraway, Donna J. "A Manifesto for Cyborgs: Science, Technology, and Socialist Feminism in the 1980s." *Socialist Review*, vol. 80, 1985, pp. 65-108.

Haraway, Donna J. *Manifestly Haraway*. University of Minnesota Press, 2016.

"Insolvent Phantom of Tomorrow." *Orphan Black: Season Three*, written by Russ Cochrane, directed by Vincenzo Natali, BBC America, 2015.

"Instinct." *Orphan Black: Season One*, written by Graeme Manson, directed by John Fawcett, BBC America, 2013.

"Ipsa Scientia Potestas Est." *Orphan Black: Season Two*, written by Tony Elliot, directed by Helen Shaver, BBC America, 2014.

"Knowledge of Causes, and Secret Motions of Things." *Orphan Black: Season Two*, written by Aubrey Nealon, directed by Ken Girotti, BBC America, 2014.

"Let the Children and the Childbearers Toil." *Orphan Black: Season Five*, written by Greg Nelson, directed by David Wellington, BBC America, 2017.

"Mingling Its Own Nature With It." *Orphan Black: Season Two*, written by Alex Levine, directed by T.J. Scott, BBC America, 2014.

"Natural Selection." *Orphan Black: Season One*, written by Graeme Manson, directed by John Fawcett, BBC America, 2013.

"Newer Elements of Our Defense." *Orphan Black: Season Three*, written by Russ Cochrane, directed by Chris Grismer, BBC America, 2015.

O'Reilly, Andrea. 2014. "Ain't I A Feminist? Matristic Feminism, Feminist Mamas, And Why Mothers Need a Feminist Movement/ Theory of Their Own." Keynote speech, induction into the Motherhood Hall of Fame and Museum of Motherhood, Procreate Project, www.procreateproject.com/andrea-oreilly/. Accessed 11 June 2021.

"One Fettered Slave." *Orphan Black: Season Five*, written by Alex Levine, directed by David Frazee, BBC America, 2017.

Rich, Adrienne. *Of Woman Born: Motherhood as Experience and Institution*. Norton, 1976.

Skloot, Rebecca. *The Immortal Life of Henrietta Lacks*. Broadway Paperbacks, 2010.

Sternke, Elizabeth A, and Kathleen Abrahamson. "Perceptions of Women with Infertility on Stigma and Disability." *Sexuality and Disability*, 33, 2015, pp. 3-17

Tatiana Is Everyone. "Episode 54: Helena and Sarah." *Tatiana Is Everyone*, tatianaiseveryone.com/post/108061651173/helena-and-sarah-orphan-black-podcast. Accessed 11 June 2021.

"The Collapse of Nature." *Orphan Black: Season Four*, written by Graeme Manson, directed by John Fawcett, BBC America, 2016.

"The Few Who Dare." *Orphan Black: Season Five*, written by Graeme Manson, directed by John Fawcett, BBC America, 2017.

"The Scandal of Altruism." *Orphan Black: Season Four*, written by Chris Roberts, directed by Grant Harvey, BBC America, 2016.

"The Stigmata of Progress." *Orphan Black: Season Four*, written by Aubrey Nealon, directed by Ken Girotti, BBC America, 2016.

"Things Which Have Never Yet Been Done." *Orphan Black: Season Two*, written by Alex Levine, directed by T.J. Scott, BBC America, 2014.

"To Hound Nature in Her Wanderings." *Orphan Black: Season Two*, written by Chris Roberts, directed by Tom Sullivan, BBC America, 2014.

"To Right the Wrongs of Many." *Orphan Black: Season Five*, written by Renee St. Cyr & Graeme Manson, directed by John Fawcett, BBC America, 2017.

Ulrich, Miriam, and Ann Weatherall. 2000. "Motherhood and

Infertility: Viewing Motherhood Through the Lens of Infertility." *Feminism and Psychology*, vol. 10, no. 3, 2000, doi.org/10.1177/0959 353500010003003. Accessed 11 June 2021.

"Unconscious Selection." *Orphan Black: Season One*, written by Alex Levine, directed by T.J. Scott, BBC America, 2013. DVD.

"Variable and Full of Perturbation." *Orphan Black: Season Two*, written by Karen Walton, directed by John Fawcett, BBC America, 2014.

"Variation Under Nature." *Orphan Black: Season One*, written by David Frazee, directed by John Fawcett, BBC America, 2013.

Chapter 4

The Maternal Maleficent

Abigail L. Palko

Anyone who has watched the Disney Princess movies might very well ask themselves, why does Disney hate—or fear?—mothers so much? Peggy Orenstein's analysis of Disney's marketing strategy in *Cinderella Ate My Daughter* identifies the ostensibly individual, stand-alone animated movies as a coherent, critical cohort, which she terms the "Princess films." Critically understood to uphold heteronormative patriarchal norms, the Princess films depict a world in which an absent (typically, dead) mother has been replaced by a surrogate maternal figure marked by a seemingly irredeemable malevolence: They are the monstrous mothers of the Disney Princess universe. In the process, these characters—and the films they appear in—also indirectly reinforce ideologies of good mothering and simultaneously imply the impotence of good mothers to protect their children. The 1959 animated *Sleeping Beauty* is one such film in this Princess oeuvre,[1] pitting Aurora's nameless birth mother against the villain Maleficent who threatens Aurora's life and whose emotional investment in Aurora is framed as malevolent. Maleficent embodies the vampiric not-mother who seeks the suffering and death of an innocent child, incapable of maternal love. Two recent live-action updates to *Sleeping Beauty*—*Maleficent* and its sequel *Maleficent II: Mistress of Evil*—shift the narrative focus to tell the story from Maleficent's perspective. The *Maleficent* films both repudiate and depend upon notions of monstrous mothering. This chapter will unpack the ways in which the live-action films first trouble this trope by reimagining the villainess in *Maleficent* but then reinscribe the trope in the sequel by leaning on matrophobia to pervert Maleficent's character and introduce another stereotypical monstrous mother, Ingrith, as an additional obstacle and foil. With the enormous influence that Disney films exert on the ways that children understand gendered roles, the franchise's retrenchment of the monstrous mother trope offers children a harmful, outdated role model.

Reimagining the Villainess: *Maleficent* (2014)

Maleficent retells the classic fairy tale "Sleeping Beauty" from the perspective of the villainess Maleficent, using Disney's 1959 animated film *Sleeping Beauty* as the primary source. Screenwriter Linda Woolverton uses this shift in narrative focus to explore Maleficent's backstory. Depictions of the trauma she endures as a teenager explain and justify the hatred she feels towards Stefan and then inflicts on his infant daughter. Maleficent, a Dark Fey, is guardian of the Moors; Stefan is an ambitious but poor orphan in the adjoining (unnamed) human kingdom. In scenes set temporally before the opening of the animated film, Woolverton creates a romantic history between Maleficent and Stefan. Power-hungry, Stefan betrays Maleficent in a (successful) bid to be named King Henry's heir. Ordered to kill Maleficent, Stefan falters, only able to cut off her wings, which he presents to King Henry. Stefan is named Henry's heir and marries his daughter (still unnamed!), becoming king upon Henry's death. When Stefan and his queen's daughter, Aurora, is born years later, Maleficent appears uninvited at the christening to curse the infant and exact revenge. As in the animated version, the three pixies spirit Aurora away to the forest, where they raise her in hiding to protect her from Maleficent's curse. In this version, Maleficent knows where they are hiding in the Moors, and she displays a vested interest in keeping Aurora alive until her sixteenth birthday. Here, the film diverges from the source material: Aurora is aware that Maleficent watches over her from the shadows and a relationship develops between Aurora and Maleficent, whom Aurora calls "Fairy Godmother" in a nod to the older woman's liminal presence in her life.

On the cusp of Aurora's sixteenth birthday, Maleficent tries first to undo the curse and then to warn Aurora. She tells her: "There is an evil in this world, and I cannot keep you from it." When the pixies tell Aurora she has been cursed, she realizes that Maleficent is the source of this evil. She flees to her father's castle, expecting to find comfort and refuge there. In these final scenes of *Maleficent*, Woolverton offers her most salient revisions to the source material. Driven by revenge, fear, power lust, and guilt, Stefan has descended into madness and is laying traps for Maleficent. Maleficent goes to the castle, desperate that Phillip save Aurora from the curse. Once Aurora has awoken from the curse (I'll turn to that scene below), Maleficent tries to get her, Phillip, and Diaval (Maleficent's man/crow familiar) out of the castle. Stefan discovers her presence in the castle and orders his army to capture and kill her; she only fights Stefan in self-defence. In Stefan's assault on her, it becomes clear that he is the "evil in the world" who must be purged. After he plunges to his death, Maleficent and Aurora return to the Moors to live happily ever after.

Accepting Maternal Responsibility

Maleficent rehabilitates the character of Maleficent through a series of scenes that depict her growing maternal identity. When Maleficent appears at the infant Aurora's christening, she comes as both envoy of the Moors and as Stefan's scorned love. Knowledge of her traumatic loss of her wings suggests hints of a wounded bird. Her actions reinforce this reading. When she curses Aurora, she is both the wild, wounded creature lashing out and the maternal figure preemptively harming her child to preclude a potential future greater harm. Psychologist Barbara Almond explains infanticide as follows: "Child murder is almost invariably the result of maternal despair about conditions in which it is impossible to raise children, at least, *for that particular mother, at that particular time*" (186). In a perverted way, by cursing Aurora to die at age sixteen, Maleficent ensures that this infant—who as Stefan's daughter might so easily have been her own daughter and whom she might very well have dreamed of being mother to—will never reach the age that Maleficent was when Stefan assaulted her. Thus, Maleficent's curse, which bears elements of both revenge against Stefan and protection of Aurora, is at its core a maternal act.

The scene depicting the first sustained interaction between Maleficent and Aurora reveals the ways in which mothering in *Maleficent* is inextricably linked to shielding daughters from sexual assault. The narrator highlights Aurora's curiosity about the world:

"She wondered at the world about her, and at what lay beyond the fearsome wall of thorns." Stefan's soldiers trespass in the Moors and threaten to assault Aurora. Maleficent, who until now has not directly intervened herself to assist Aurora, steps in to protect her, in the process claiming a Ruddickian maternal identity. Philosopher Sara Ruddick asserts in *Maternal Thinking* that the hallmark of a maternal status or identity is the acceptance of maternal responsibility. Maleficent knows herself to be a monstrous mother. She articulates her fear that she will frighten Aurora. The younger woman reassures her however, accepting the claim Maleficent has just given her. Aurora affirms Maleficent's identity: "I know who you are ... You're my fairy Godmother.... You've been watching over me my whole life.... Wherever I went, your shadow was always with me." Aurora embraces her "Fairy Godmother" as the truest maternal figure in her life.

With a relationship established, Aurora and Maleficent explore its cathexis. In her groundbreaking analysis of patriarchal motherhood, Adrienne Rich observes that "This cathexis between mother and daughter—essential, distorted, misused—is the great unwritten story... The materials are here for the deepest mutuality and the most painful estrangement" (225, 226). Yet she continues: "This relationship has been minimized and trivialized in the annals of patriarchy" (226). As *Maleficent* depicts them, Maleficent and Aurora embody the figures Rich theorizes. Forces stronger than Maleficent's magic shape the unfolding of the story. Maleficent tries to revoke the curse, but her love and regret cannot yet overcome her earlier hate and revenge. Aurora's desire to live in the Moors with her so that they could look after each other disarms Maleficent's resolve to tell her about the curse. Having grown up comforted by Maleficent's shadowy presence, Aurora is strong enough to confront her when the fairies reveal the truth about the curse. Throughout their confrontation, the film insists on Maleficent's simultaneous maternity and monstrosity, suggesting the former may ultimately subdue the latter.

Rewriting the Script

I vividly recall my experience seeing *Maleficent* for the first time: I was teaching a summer course on gender studies in a university program for high schoolers. One morning, I screened *Sleeping Beauty* and they analysed it; they bravely took a critical look at a beloved childhood film while unflinchingly deconstructing its encoded patriarchal messages. That afternoon, we took a field trip to the local cinema to see *Maleficent* on its opening day. I'd watched the trailers with interest, and I was excited to see it with this group of highly engaged, intelligent students. For most of the movie, a small part of my attention was split from the screen to track their reactions. After that morning's discussion, I thought that witnessing them watching the film would be the best part of the movie experience.

Then came the scene that made the movie—and the experience—for me: Aurora is angelically arrayed on her bed; the bumbling pixies drag Philip into her room and order him to kiss her. My students hissed at their demand and cheered Philip's concern for consent. I remember my joy at their response but then I forgot their presence with Maleficent's entry on the screen.

Knowing the source tale—something must wake up Aurora, even if it's not Philip's kiss—I felt my anticipation rise, the tension increase, with each expressive twitch of Angelina Jolie's face as Maleficent expresses her scorn of a belief in true love. Maleficent is so certain that she has created an unexploitable loophole to her curse. And then, the mother-daughter cathexis: "The flow of energy that moves between mothers and daughters as they navigate the meaning, significance and context of their connection" (Grassau ii): Maleficent plants a gentle kiss on Aurora's brow, and Aurora asks in a wondering voice, "Fairy God*mother*?" (my emphasis). At some point, I realized tears were streaming down my face, prompted by this Hollywood depiction of maternal love as true love.

With *Maleficent*, Woolverton sets out to tell a new story that humanizes a cartoon villain. The film does more than just provide a backstory that fleshes out the villain's character. It first depicts the ways that society would deem Maleficent a monstrous mother: the curse that Maleficent casts on Aurora, which results in the infant being removed from her birth mother; Maleficent's use of the innocent Aurora to exact revenge on Stefan; and her cold, nonmaternal distaste of the child. In the process of developing Maleficent's character, the film also develops the relationship between the two women. Through her interactions with Aurora, Maleficent learns how to allow herself to be vulnerable and feel love for someone again. This growth is the core of *Maleficent*, and it culminates in the scene when the spell is broken. When Phillip's kiss fails to wake Aurora, Maleficent fully opens up to the sleeping girl: "I will not ask your forgiveness because what I have done to you is unforgivable. I was so lost in hatred and revenge. Sweet Aurora, you stole what was left of my heart. And now I have lost you forever. I swear, no harm will come to you as long as I live. And not a day shall pass that I don't miss your smile." She seals this promise with the kiss. Rather than merely reforming Maleficent, the film completely upends the monstrous mother trope. When only true love's kiss can end the spell, it is Maleficent's maternal kiss that does—a kiss that offers her apology and affirms her commitment to protecting Aurora that succeeds.

According to Larissa Schlögl and Nelson Zagalo, the animated Maleficent functions as the antimaternal:

> Her presence is solely as an embodiment of malevolence. She brings power and depth to the story and presents the necessary opposition for the construction of the narrative's conflict. Her character has no trace of goodness and has no understanding of love or kindness. She behaves with imposing self-possession, has a frenetic laugh, her blocked out but angular vestments represent power ... she is also willowy with fine, long fingers, acting pettily and meanly in her nefarious choices. (162)

They claim that the significance of the character chosen to awaken Aurora lies in its challenge to "old story models and established cultural myths of masculine power and heterosexuality" (167-68). Such a reading, however, returns attention to the presumptive future patriarch by linking it to hegemonic masculinity. The much greater challenge to old models and cultural myths is the film's rewriting of maternal love. Woolverton sees Maleficent as a "woman of all different colors who struggles with the evil that's inside her and how it overtook her and being able to learn to love after she has been so incredibly wronged" (qtd. in Silverstein). Woolverton's ending to her revision of *Sleeping Beauty* upends conventional understandings of maternal love as oppressive, not liberatory.

A Maternal Love Story

In the concluding segment, the narrator revels herself to be an older Aurora. With the story told by Aurora, the film becomes a love story and homage to her mother. The revisions to the source tale create the opportunity of developing a maternal-filial relationship between Maleficent and Aurora. Aurora's ability to see Maleficent clearly challenges the monstrous mother trope: "In the end, my kingdom was united, not by a hero or a villain as legend had predicted, but by one who was both hero and villain. And her name was Maleficent." This embrace of the maternal and the monstrous offers a radical ending to the film because of the cultural weight that motherhood bears. As Almond argues, "If you hate your children, you are considered monstrous—immoral, unnatural, and evil" (2). The villainous half of Maleficent that Aurora not only embraces but also praises at the end of the film is the aggressive half who was willing to harm the infant Aurora. Again, Almond's insights are instructive:

> Aggression in women—the *behavioral* manifestation of their hating feelings—is generally considered problematic, that is, not feminine. But when women's aggression is aimed at their children, it becomes even more unacceptable. It is one of those societal problems that fill us with outrage and horror, even as some part of us secretly understands its normality. (4)

Perhaps the film's greatest contribution to contemporary conversations about mothering practices is the way it speaks the truth aloud about maternal aggression. The film invites recognition from those who "secretly understand [the] normality" of women's aggression. *Maleficent* redeems the titular character, the surrogate mother figure, even though she has harmed her adopted daughter, and her daughter in turn embraces her mother in her full complexity.

Leaning on Matrophobia: *Maleficent II: Mistress of Evil* (2019)

Benjamin Justice asks us to consider "what *Maleficent* tells its viewers about how girls and women are supposed to act and, further, what Disney's assumptions are about who would view this message and how they would receive it" (195). Woolverton's moves to develop the nuances of Maleficent's character succeed, in part, because the film is "frank in its repudiation of the cult of domesticity" (Justice 196). Repudiating the cult of domesticity, *Maleficent* suggests, frees women to claim a "powerful station in the public realm" (Priyanka 39), as both Maleficent and Aurora do. As a sequel to *Maleficent*, *Mistress of Evil* is a film concept that had great potential. How could the maternal Maleficent of the first film support Aurora as queen of the Moors? As fiancée of Prince Philip? How would Aurora's gradual reengagement with the human world impact her relationship with Maleficent? In an interview, director Joachim Rønning[2] explains how he positions the sequel firmly as a continuation of the maternal story begun in *Maleficent*. He highlights his interest in discovering what he terms a "more mature Maleficent":

> Because her little girl is not a little girl anymore. Aurora is becoming a woman. Any parent fears when that day comes and you're not the most important person in that person's life anymore. I was interested in seeing how Maleficent can go to that level. Also as a parent you sacrifice yourself, you try to change as a person in order to make your child happy. Or do the best for your child. In this movie, I was interested in how far Maleficent would change for Aurora. And she really tries. She goes to meet the parents [of Aurora's future husband Prince Phillip, the King and Queen Ingrith]. The in-laws! And then that backfires. But that journey was very interesting for me to explore. (qtd. in Schaefer)

Here, Rønning hints at the maternal experience of sending a grown child into the world, affirming Maleficent's maternal status. He thus lays out a vision of maternal practice that subjects Maleficent to institutionalized patriarchal ideologies of motherhood. Mothering within these strictures will always be limited by the impact of matrophobia, which Rich defines as "a womanly splitting of the self, in the desire to become purged once and for all of our mothers' bondage, to become individuated and free" (236). Whereas Rønning is curious about how much Maleficent can change for Aurora, the true emotional power of the film lies in its exploration of how Maleficent and Aurora can eschew matrophobia.

The Vampiric Mother

The film does not merely suggest that Maleficent is no longer the most important person in Aurora's life, as Rønning asserts. It thrusts her into a dangerous surrogate home, where a vampiric mother, Aurora's future mother-in-law Ingrith, will threaten her life. Almond describes what she terms an "ominous form of maternal vampirism" as the "forcing of 'food' *into* the child—food in the form of ideas, behaviors, allegiances, and beliefs, in particular, beliefs about the nature of human relationships—to a degree that may totally co-opt the child's autonomy, defeat creative effort, and lead to a paranoid view of the world" (165-66). This is how Ingrith's manipulations of Aurora, Maleficent, and the community function, but their (near) success depends upon a regression of the growth that Aurora and, to an even greater extent, Maleficent experienced in the first film and a disintegration of the trust built between them. By forcing Aurora back into the human world and replacing the central maternal figure in her life with a vampiric one, *Mistress of Evil* implies that a key conflict women face is with a (literal) evil mother, reinforcing an old archetype that *Maleficent* had helped to repudiate. The character thus goes from the campy villain of *Sleeping Beauty* to the maternal heroine of *Maleficent* to the cartoonish victim of *Mistress of Evil*.

Mistress of Evil perverts the character of Maleficent as we knew her at the end of *Maleficent*. Where the original leaves us with an understanding of a woman who has embraced both her power (her magic) and her vulnerability (her love)—as well as her anger and her fear—and forged a maternal strength that depends on both aspects of her identity, the sequel introduces us to a different woman. The sequel opens with humans despoiling the forest and kidnapping fairies. The narrator speaks over their carnage to frame the tale:

Once upon a time... or perhaps twice upon a time, for you may remember this story ... there was a powerful Fey named Maleficent. For some reason, the mistress of evil and protector of the Moors ... was still hated after all this time. True, she had cursed the princess, Aurora ... but that was before she found light in the heart of a human child ... and raised the girl as her own. After all, it was Maleficent's love which broke that very same curse. But that detail was somehow mysteriously forgotten.

For as the tale was told over and again throughout the kingdom
... Maleficent became the villain once more.

With this declaration that Maleficent was the "villain once more,"
the film pulls off a bait and switch that simultaneously undercuts what
we come to know about Maleficent's maternal identity at the end of
Maleficent and depends upon the machinations of a different monstrous
mother—Queen Ingrith.

While the title (*Maleficent: Mistress of Evil*) and the opening narration
prime us to see Maleficent as the monstrous mother of the film, Ingrith
is in reality the monstrous one. Her monstrosity lies principally in her
efforts to malign Maleficent, and her success on this front in turn
drives a wedge between Maleficent and Aurora. Ingrith manipulates
matrophobia to her own advantage, exacerbating the disharmony she
has sown. At the dinner she hosts to celebrate Aurora and Phillip's
engagement, she slyly promises: "Now Aurora will finally get the love
of a real family, a real mother. Tonight, I consider Aurora my own." In
an extended exchange that is painful to watch for the ways that Ingrith
is so easily able to manipulate everyone's perceptions, she others
Maleficent in a clear analogy to the settler colonialism and racism that
poisons contemporary life. Insidiously, she uses the poison Maleficent
originally created with her spell in *Maleficent* against her: Ingrith
poisons her husband, John, and accuses Maleficent of casting another
spell, amplifying cultural fears of the threat that angry mothers pose to
their children. When Maleficent, wounded by Aurora's inability to see
what really happened and believe in her instead of Ingrith, explodes in
a green fury at the end of the dinner, she seemingly confirms Ingrith's
insinuations of her unfit mothering

Through the regression of Maleficent's maternal identity that it
depends upon, *Mistress of Evil* explores "the narrow and shifting border
between maternal love and protection and maternal possessiveness and
unconscious aggression" (Almond 198). Rønning seems to be suggesting that maternal growth is only ever provisional and that each
subsequent developmental stage reached by the child will trigger a new
regression on the part of the mother.

Mistress of Evil also mirrors *Maleficent* in providing glimpses into
Maleficent's history. Whereas the first film depicts the arc of her
relationship with King Stefan, Aurora's father, the sequel reconnects
her with her Dark Fey brethren. After the assassination attempt that

Ingrith orders fails, Maleficent is saved by another Dark Fey; taken to their nest to recuperate, she must grapple with the psychological wounds of the past five years, during which her integrity and her maternal love for Aurora have been perverted in the tales that Ingrith has spread. In Rich's extended description of matrophobia, we can see elements of the internal attunement process that Maleficent is engaging in. Rich writes: "The mother stands for the victim in ourselves, the unfree woman, the martyr. Our personalities seem dangerously to blur and overlap with our mothers'; and, in a desperate attempt to know where mother ends and daughter begins, we perform radical surgery" (236). Maleficent must grapple with deep psychic wounds, unmothered herself and feeling rejected by Aurora.

In the nest, we see Maleficent for the first time in the company of those like her, including Conall, the dark fey who saves Maleficent from drowning and takes her to the nest, and Borra, their leader who seeks war and revenge against the humans. We also see that her magic and fury are hers alone, as the last descendant of the Phoenix; it is fed through her connection to the Moors. They save her life, give her purpose. Conall truly sees Maleficent and restores her to her maternal line:

> You are the last of her descendants. Her blood is your own. You are her. In your hands, you hold the power of life and death... destruction and rebirth. But nature's greatest power is the power of true transformation. You transformed when you raised Aurora. When you found love... in the middle of your pain. I'm asking you to take all of your fury... all of your pain... and not use it. Help us broker peace with the humans. Because peace... could be the Dark Fey's final transformation.

Maleficent initially resists, telling Conall: "I have no daughter. She has chosen her side." She, too, chooses a side, agreeing to Borra's demand that she lead the Dark Fey in an attack on Ulstead to vanquish the humans who threaten the Moors, their "last true nature on earth." It is only after Aurora claims Maleficent in the height of the resulting battle that the wounding spell Ingrith's machinations have cast over Maleficent is broken and that she can see the wisdom of Conall's vision.

The Disney Influence

Some of the film's complexity lies in the ways it simultaneously revises and reinforces stereotypes. Although the film depends on the dead mother trope, for example, it also expands understandings of who can mother. This rewriting of who can mother follows the example of *Finding Nemo*, which "paves the way for new images of mothering" when "Marlin chooses to embody mothering in the film" (Brydon 137, 138). This redemption of the maternal figure also builds on the ending of *Brave* (2012), in which Merida rides off into the sunset with her mother, Elinor, rather than one of the three suitors invited to win her hand. This image offers a liminal moment in which girls can have freedom; it envisions a mother-daughter bond that does not depend upon the mother's indoctrination of the daughter into institutional, patriarchal motherhood. As Justice notes, "It's Merida's betrayal of her mother, and subsequent rapprochement, that provides the emotional arc of the story" (196)—not the scripted quest for her hand that the heirs of the other clans enact.

Disney films are powerful cultural artefacts, as Orenstein demonstrates in *Cinderella Ate My Daughter*, which extend the role of traditional fairy tales. They bear and reinforce cultural fears about monstrous mothers. Suzan Brydon summarizes the stereotypical Disney portrayal of mothering (focusing on the studio's feature-length animated films):

Disney mothers who remain as part of the story have historically been expected to focus on the nurture, protection and education of children. With minor exceptions, their bodies have been images of health and unobtrusiveness, with mixed messages about sexual potency and age. Disney characters engaged in mothering need not have given birth biologically to the children (they could be grandmothers or adoptive mothers), but they have been required to be women and to desire an existence in/around the home. These somatexts appear as strong and confident while performing the mothering function, but not actively pursuing roles or activities outside of mothering. More than anything, mothering in Disney discourse, as in the larger cultural discourse described above, has focused on performing the everyday caring for children—the grooming, the feeding and the protecting. (136-37)

Applying this rubric to Maleficent produces a mix of insights, as she conforms to some of these maternal expectations and eschews others.

Yet there are progressive elements to the script: *Mistress of Evil* offers Maleficent the transformative opportunity of rebirth as a phoenix, facilitated by Aurora, the daughter who truly sees her mother for who she is. In both films, Maleficent's identity depends on Aurora recognizing her and calling her "Godmother." These scenes illustrate how fragile Maleficent's maternal subjectivity is, in that it depends on Aurora's articulation of her as mother. Digging deeper, Aurora can only recognize Maleficent as a being herself outside of her maternal role because of Philip's reminder. Philip is one of the most authentic feminists in the films. Building on his advocacy of informed and affirmative consent in the first film, in *Mistress of Evil*, he assures Aurora that she does not have to change herself to fit into his world. His championing of her autonomy prompts her realization that she has held Maleficent to a different standard, as we see in a scene where she expresses her discomfort with palace life:

Phillip: Tell me what's troubling you.

Aurora: It's nothing.

Phillip: Aurora, I know you better than that.

Aurora: This jewelry... my hair... all these rules. I can't breathe. I feel like I'm not Queen of the Moors anymore. I feel like a different person.

Phillip: Listen... I fell in love with a girl in the forest and only her. You don't have to change. I don't want you to change.

Aurora: I should have never asked her to wear that scarf.

Secure in his reassurance, Aurora can see how she told Maleficent she had to change by asking her to cover her horns when they went to dinner with Phillip's family, revealing Aurora's discomfort with Maleficent as she is. She brings this new insight to the climactic battle scene where she releases Maleficent from her fury in an inversion of Maleficent's freeing of her from the spell in the first film:

Aurora: Stop! I'm sorry I doubted you, but this isn't you. There's another way. I know who you are. I know you.

Maleficent: You do not.

Aurora: [tearfully] Yes, I do. You're my mother.

It is at this moment that Ingrith hits Maleficent with an iron arrow, disintegrating her into ashes. But she has been called by name, and Aurora's tears combine with her magic to power her regeneration as a phoenix.

The sequel changes Maleficent's personality, doing violence to the maternal persona celebrated at the end of the first film. Schlögl and Zagalo conclude their analysis of *Maleficent* with this reminder: "Each new narrative requires different approaches not only to justify fresh filmic productions, but also to serve as a mirror of and contributor to processes of social change" (169). This matters deeply for the audience consuming the films. As Suzan Brydon notes of Disney films: "Although the characters are fictional, the part they play in the overall, and very real, cultural discourse is not" (131). Woolverton discusses her deep sense of responsibility with respect to the first film:

> I feel enormous responsibility, especially when you are working for the Disney company, because I know that these movies are going to be seen in China and all parts of the world, so I take it really seriously. I look at what the message is going to be for young, evolving minds. I'm more interested in what the story is going to make young minds believe and think because these Disney movies become a part of your soul when you are a kid. They are in you forever. For me, that is an enormous responsibility. (qtd. in Silverstein)

Why does it matter that the sequel deforms Maleficent's personality? For a brief moment at the beginning of the 2010s, Disney movies seemed to have evolved in their depiction of mothers and maternal figures from the stereotypes that characterized decades of their movies. They had so heavily leaned upon tropes of missing and dead mothers and evil stepmothers, but with *Brave*, they began to offer a vision of loving, emotionally healthy maternal relationships. For the young children watching—daughters and sons of mothers (as Nancy Chodorow reminds us, maternal lessons and examples powerfully shape children's understanding of gendered family roles)—the value in seeing the maternal figure embrace her daughter's passion and make space and time to play with her, whereas previously only the father had encouraged her interests, is incalculable. *Maleficent*, for a brief moment, seemed to solidify this new, multifaceted, and more nuanced vision of who and what a mother could be.

But with *Mistress of Evil*, this expansive vision was repudiated. Although the opening scene offers ample justification for Maleficent's fear and distrust—and Ingrith's machinations throughout prove her right—the film works hard to present her as simultaneously irrational and evil. It never, for example, offers a believable explanation for Maleficent's sense of being betrayed by Aurora. Is it because she wants to marry? Or because she might return to the human world? Does she feel abandoned? Aurora has already claimed Maleficent as her mother by the time they meet Ingrith. When Maleficent asks, "Why on earth would I go to Ulstead?" Aurora's response is immediate: "Because they want to meet my mother." The discord between them is present from the opening of the film is never satisfactorily explained, which reinforces tropes of monstrous mothering.

In Maleficent's first appearance on screen, Diaval has come to break the news to her that Phillip has proposed to Aurora. He clearly anticipates her anger, and her displeasure is immediately evident:

D: Mistress.... I have a little bit of news.... It's nothing of any real consequence ... and it's certainly no reason to overreact. It's just that... Prince Philip has, um...

M: Disappeared?

D: No. No. Philip has...

M: Yellow fever? No, wait! Leprosy!

D: No, Mistress. Prince Philip has asked Aurora if she'll become his...

Maleficent's refusal to let him finish the sentence—punctuated by her dramatic cut-off "Don't. Ruin. My morning" and a freefall off the cliff's edge—confirms that something has changed drastically, and for the worse, since the end of the previous film. Whereas *Maleficent* offers an expansive vision of maternal love as true love, *Mistress of Evil* gives a more regressive message of maternal jealousy and distrust, wrapped in progressive filmography. The movies target both young girls (setting up the next generation to submit to the patriarchal institution of motherhood) and their mothers (reinforcing patriarchally-induced doubts such as the fear of producing monstrous offspring through "faulty—even monstrous—mothering" Almond 10).

Conclusion

Maleficent carries over a salient detail from *Sleeping Beauty*. In both versions, Aurora's biological mother is nameless, and although the script for *Maleficent* assigns her a name, it is never spoken aloud. As a child, my daughter was obsessed by *Sleeping Beauty*, vociferously demanding to watch "Aurora" on a frequent basis. As evidenced by her renaming of the film, she knew at age three the power of names. The feminist in my core could not allow her to watch it unedited, so we named Aurora's mother Queen Eleanor (in homage to Eleanor of Aquitaine). Another commonality carries over: The birth mother's presence must be erased. *Maleficent* goes one step further, and Aurora can only find and embrace a maternal relationship after her mother's death. Significantly, Maleficent is also portrayed as motherless, even in the film crafted to explore her backstory. This literal elimination of birth mothers from the picture demonstrates just how challenging it is to overcome proscriptive stereotypes and expectations of mothering.

Repeat viewings tell me that I should not have been so surprised by *Maleficent*'s twist in ascribing the true love to the maternal figure rather than the teenaged crush from *Sleeping Beauty* nor by *Mistress of Evil*'s ultimate affirmation of it. The films carefully set down multiple markers of her maternal "instincts," or what critics Schlögl and Zagalo term "a surreptitious kindness" (163) in their reading. The film depicts Maleficent in a range of roles, including military leader, assaulted and scorned lover, social worker, and diplomat. As "matriarch and guardian of the Moors" (Priyanka 39), Maleficent displays a maternal ferocity in her defense of the Moors and her people when King Henry tries to conquer the Moors, evoking the trope of the mama bear protecting her cubs. As Stefan's scorned and victimized lover, she sees her opportunity to exact revenge through threatening the infant Aurora, but she is also impelled to shield the child from the assault she herself endured. Throughout the years that the pixies raise Aurora in the woods, Maleficent's maternal watchfulness prompts her to intervene each time their incompetence threatens to kill the child, offering the valuable protections social workers provide to vulnerable children. And when Aurora and Phillip decide to marry, Maleficent travels to Ulstead in a diplomatic role, overcoming her discomfort with entering the human world that threatens her life in order to fulfill the role her daughter needs of her.

In *Mistress of Evil*, Queen Ingrith assumes the role of villainess, portraying a monstrous mother driven by her political ambitions to destroy the woman she views as both competition for power and for her son's maternal affections, manipulating the subjects of Ulstead (and the vaguely defined neighboring lands) into fearing Maleficent. Rønning ties this plot element to this current moment; he implies that he is referring to politics in the message of kindness he sees the film offering. He explains: "Our villain in the shape of Queen Ingrith is very much controlling the narrative, using that as part of her power and dividing people. Yes, there's definitely some parallels to today in society" (qtd. in Schaefer). The ultimate message of the film, he suggests, is as follows: "At the end of the day you have your family, you come together, you show an openness. You come to an acceptance of others and show kindness" (qtd. in Schaefer). *Mistress of Evil* offers a powerful message about the power of discourse to shape perception—the power in controlling the narrative. But it also reflects how public discourse shapes our perceptions of mothers. For evidence, consider how easily Ingrith is able to cast doubt on Maleficent as a mother:

> Do you know what makes a great leader, Aurora? The ability to instill fear in your subjects, and then use that fear ... against your enemies. [Breathes deeply] So... I spread the story of the evil witch and the princess she cursed. It doesn't matter who woke Sleeping Beauty, they were all terrified. And the story became legend.... I know you think I'm a monster, with what I did to the king, to Maleficent, to... my son... I did for Ulstead. You are a traitor to your kind, and you will pay for it! [to her kingdom] Maleficent is dead! We will never again live in fear!

When Ingrith says, "It doesn't matter who woke Sleeping Beauty, they were all terrified," she reveals the harsh reality that mothers are so easily judged and that recovering from an error is so nearly impossible. Maleficent's fury at the rumours, looking back to the opening of the film, becomes more understandable after learning of Ingrith's fearmongering. Her fury seems to represent women's power-lessness as individuals to undo the impact of oppressive norms of institutionalized understandings of good mothering. *Mistress of Evil* reinscribes tired—yet still dangerous—tropes of monstrous mother-hood.

Endnotes

1. *Snow White and the Seven Dwarves* (1937), *Cinderella* (1950), *The Little Mermaid* (1989), and *Tangled* (2010) are other notable examples of this model, and as their distribution dates indicate, the trend is enduring.

2. Whereas Woolverton holds sole writing credit for *Maleficent*, *Mistress of Evil* was co-written by Woolverton, Noah Harpster, and Micah Fitzerman-Blue; additionally, Rønning describes working on the script with Angelina Jolie during production (Schaefer), and final responsibility for the vision of *Mistress of Evil* seems to lie with Rønning.

Works Cited

Brydon, Suzan G. "Men at the Heart of Mothering: Finding Mother in *Finding Nemo.*" *Journal of Gender Studies*, vol. 18, no. 2, 2009, pp. 131-46.

Grassau, Pamela Anne. *Navigating the Cathexis: Mothers and Daughters and End of Life.* 2015. Factor-Inwentash Faculty of Social Work, University of Toronto. PhD dissertation.

Justice, Benjamin. "Maleficent Reborn: Disney's Fairytale View of Gender Reaches Puberty." *Social Education*, vol. 78, no. 4, 2014, pp. 194-98.

Orenstein, Peggy. *Cinderella Ate My Daughter.* HarperCollins, 2011.

Priyanka, M. C. "Malevolence Subverted:(Re) Defining Gender Roles in the Film *Maleficent.*" *Singularities: A transdisciplinary Biannual Research Journal*, vol. 3, no. 2, 2016, pp. 38-42.

Rønning, Joachim, director. *Maleficent: Mistress of Evil.* Walt Disney Studios Motion Pictures, 2019.

Schaefer, Stephen. "From Norway to Mighty 'Maleficent.'" *Boston Herald* reprinted on *Fussy Eye Blogspot*, Oct. 2019, fussyeye. blogspot.com/2019/10/blog-post_14.html. Accessed 13 June 2021.

Schlögl, Larissa, and Nelson Zagalo. "From Animation to Live-Action: Reconstructing Maleficent." *Body and Text: Cultural Transformations in New Media Environments*, edited by Kenneth Callahan and Anthony, Barker, Springer, Cham, 2019, pp. 157-71.

Silverstein, M. "Interview. Women in Hollywood; *Maleficent* Screen-writer Linda Woolverton on What's Changed and What Hasn't." *Fussy Eye Blogspot*, Oct. 2014, fussyeye.blogspot.com/2014/10/makers-presents-in-hollywood.html. Accessed 13 June 2021.

Stromberg, Robert, director. *Maleficent*. Walt Disney Studios Motion Pictures, 2014.

Üner, Ayşe Melda. "Intertextual Transformation Of A Fairy Tale From Sleeping Beauty To Maleficent." *Balikesir University Journal of Social Sciences Institute*, vol. 20, no. 38, 2017, pp. 371-82.

PART II
MATERNAL
VIOLENCE

Chapter 5

"She Laughed at Anything": The Portrayal of the Monstrous Maternal in Anna Burns's *No Bones*

Shamara Ransirini

This chapter rethinks the monstrous maternal as a possible troubling of the masculinist anxieties surrounding nationalist women in Northern Ireland. I argue that in her debut novel, *No Bones*, Anna Burns explores the trope of the monstrous mother as a means to protest the uneasiness generated by Republican women's feminine embodiment in nationalist iconography. I engage the historical event of the Northern Irish Republican women's no-wash prison strike in 1980 to argue that the fear and uneasiness evoked by the menstruating Republican women prisoners is caricatured in the darkly satirical and carnivalesque portrayal of Bronagh McCabe, the IRA woman and monstrous mother in Burns's novel. I read Bronagh's portrayal as a possible questioning of the allegorization of women as placid, restrained, and asexual mothers in Irish nationalist imagery and suggest that by collapsing the constructions of the maternal and the monstrous, Burns seems to unravel the somatization of feminine anger as political agency.

My argument expands the feminist position that the monsterization of the maternal reveals the sociopolitical anxieties of the times. As Margrit Shildrick argues, the complex intersections between the monstrous and the maternal have historically depicted the particular uneasiness towards female embodiment (30). I suggest that Burns's portrayal of the monstrous maternal highlights and protests the fears of female corporeality in violent politics. Bronagh McCabe's portrayal in the novel as an angry, hysterical, and hypersexual IRA mother, I argue, is a metafictional rendering of the monstrous maternal that queers the gaze on the nonnormative female body.

The monster embodies a liminality and ambivalence, which is not predicated on absolute difference but on its very absence. As Shildrick argues: "It is not that the monster represents the threats *of* difference, but that it threatens to interrupt difference—at least in its binary form —such that the comfortable otherness that secures the selfsame is lost" (45). It is the monster's uncanny resemblance to the self that is threatening. In a patriarchal economy of representation, the links between the monstrous and the maternal body are forged on the grounds of these uneasy slippages between binary categorizations. The intimate relationship between the maternal body, the fetus, and child is ironically idolized as well as seen as threatening. The mother's capacity to give life also evokes the possibility that she holds the capacity to take away that life, which invests in her the double bind of being the source of both life and death. The material maternal body is also regarded as an unpredictable site of excess—her body that changes shape, that lactates, that oozes body fluids, and that defies containment and knowledge of paternal lineage fuels both anxiety and fascination. Accordingly, the coupling of the monstrous and the maternal becomes a convenient but also complex means to invite the overseeing gaze on the feminine that denies her subjectivity. *No Bones* presents a textual troubling of that gaze—the gaze of the reader but also the other characters—on the IRA woman/mother in the novel and the absence of a vocabulary of representation for women's anger outside hysteria and hypersexuality.

By evoking the fear, repulsion, and intrigue generated by the angry IRA women during and after the Troubles, Bronagh's portrayal in the novel also protests the disembodied allegorization of women as the ideal, suffering maternal in nationalist iconography. As Bronagh's portrayal remains restricted to a trope of the monstrous maternal, which bars the reader from gaining insight into her subjectivity, it raises a series of pertinent questions. What does it mean for a woman, a mother, to adopt angry and violent politics? How can feminine anger in politics be reimagined beyond a framework that does not normalize the generation of repulsion and fear? While I do not propose to provide definitive answers to these questions, my attempt is to throw some light upon them.

Published in 2001 and shortlisted for the Orange Prize the following year, *No Bones* centres on young Amelia Lovett and her dysfunctional family. It spans Amelia's childhood and youth in a working-class Catholic community in West Belfast. Opening at the beginning of the street riots in 1969 when Amelia is six years old and ending in 1994 when she is thirty and the peace process is underway, *No Bones* portrays the most turbulent years of the modern Northern Irish Troubles. It depicts, with dark humour, the occupation of Northern Ireland by British troops, the criminalization of the IRA by the British government, and the anticipation of the signing of the peace accord in 1998.

As the title implies, the narrative makes "no bones" about the range and scale of the violence and its effects as they are replayed in the fragmented memories of Amelia, her family, and her friends, a point underscored by the opening lines: "The Troubles started on a Thursday. At six o'clock at night. At least that's how Amelia remembered it" (Burns 1). Amelia's world—where, as she notes towards the ending of the novel, "in order to relax, they needed to fight first" (318)—is one where violence defamiliarizes and displaces the temporal and spatial certainties of the everyday. As family members, relatives, and friends are killed, disappeared, or become abusive, the roles of perpetrators, victims, and witnesses are blurred, as are the distinctions between political and interpersonal violence. For instance, whereas homes were safe houses for Republican activists during the Troubles, the domestic in the text is also a site of horrendous violence: Amelia is raped in the kitchen by her brother and his female partner (128-33), and young Mary Dolan, who walks the streets pushing a pram with her dead baby wrapped in a plastic bag, is repeatedly sexually assaulted by her own father (65-70).

Bronagh McCabe is Amelia's schoolmate who later becomes an IRA agent, and although she is not a main character, she appears in several crucial chapters. Even though Bronagh and Amelia both embody the nonnormative, working-class feminine corporealities trapped within a militarized society, on the surface, they appear to be polar opposites. Subdued Amelia is submissive and is presented as a victim to sexual and domestic violence. Her anger is suppressed and turned inwards. Even though hardly anyone in the novel seems to take notice, she suffers from anorexia and addiction, and despite claiming to have no capacity for aggression, she is "warring with her body" (74). In contrast, Bronagh, "bigger than most big beefs of girls" (74), with her "big voice" (106) embodies unrestrained anger and violence. While Amelia is the overt victim, Bronagh is a perpetrator both of political and interpersonal violence. A crucial difference between them, however, is that while Amelia is portrayed as protesting her abjection and (dis)embodiment and struggling to reclaim ownership of her fragmented and fractured subjectivity, Bronagh is devoid of such aspirations. Unlike Amelia, Bronagh is always the object of narration and never the narrator. She is also constantly driven by anger and is never presented as a rational subject, which is corroborated by the not so subtle theatrical carnivalesque aspects of Bronagh's comportment across the novel. Consistently a spectacle, Bronagh seems to push the dominant image of the monstrous maternal to its unruly if not horrifying (il)logical limit, which queers the violent disembodiment of the gendered material body in nationalist imaginary. To foreground my engagement with the monstrous maternal in *No Bones*, I will first briefly map the allegorization of nationalist gendered political activism and the imposed absence of the material, feminine body in the iconography of the modern Northern Irish Troubles.

The Maternal in Irish Nationalism

Feminists have protested the symbolic feminine images in Irish nationalist imaginary—that is, a woman or mother passively sacrificing and inertly suffering for the nation—and have called for reimaginings of women as autonomous subjects who make their own decisions and act upon them (Mac Crossan 126; Pelan 129). Although in the late 1960s, with the emergence of widespread violence in Northern Ireland, women's direct participation in the Irish Republican Army as volunteers increased (Alison 140), women have always played a pivotal role in the nationalist struggle. Irish women's political roles, however, have been historically linked to their maternal roles. Polly Radosh points out that as early as the mid-nineteenth century, the operation of patriarchy in Irish society was different to other Western societies: Mothers were in charge of the management of domestic finances and were responsible for important family decisions (306). During the famine in the mid-nineteenth century, mothers played an important role in the struggle for the children's survival. After the famine, the British state, which had earlier suppressed the Catholic church, now actively exploited the close link between the church and family, using the mother as the conduit to reinforce heightened religiosity that advocated strict sexual codes and frugal forms of living (Radosh 308). Radosh argues that the characterization of Irish motherhood as strict and devout is linked to the social and cultural transformations that originated in the mid-nineteenth century and permeated well into the twentieth century and that reinforced "humility, physical deprivations, denial of physical and sexual needs" (312) as virtues of motherhood. In other words, the ideal of Irish motherhood was historically premised on the notion of shunning excess of any form.

As Irish nationalism increasingly idealized the rural life and the hard-working farming classes associated with it, a predominant image of motherhood was Mother Ireland. Imaged as a grieving or suffering mother who bemoans the loss and the pain suffered by her sons, the subdued, nurturing, suffering image of motherhood became symbolically the most idealized (Aretxaga, *Shattering* 62). Despite this cultural script of the maternal, however, women's actual maternal agency in nurturing their children in a militarized society—protecting their families and struggling against all odds on a daily basis to keep their children alive and safe—was often effectively made invisible by displacing their suffering into their nationalist sons' wounded or killed bodies (Aretxaga, *Shattering* 50). The traditional allegorization of women's bodies as Mother Ireland thus obscures the lived experiences and material bodies of women (Weekes 100; del Pozo 21; Steele 96) and primarily feminizes the land, signalling both the female body and the land it signified as "rapable" (Lyons 141).

IRA Women Prisoners

As part of the "forgotten episodes and hidden discourses" of Northern Irish history (Aretxaga, "Dirty Protest" 125), the Armagh prison strike featured in the Irish nationalist imaginary only as "auxiliary" to the main protest (McAuliffe and Hale 181). Whereas the male no-wash protest and the male hunger strikers in Long Kesh prison, led by Bobby

Sands, acquired celebrity status as martyrs in the nationalist imaginary, the IRA women's experiences in prison, their hunger strike, the no-wash protest, and the routine strip searches to which they were subjected rarely featured in nationalist narratives. The women's no-wash protest, in which approximately thirty female IRA inmates participated, commenced in the Armagh prison on February 7, 1980, and lasted until December 1 1980 (McAuliffe and Hale 178-79). The women's protest was motivated not only by the denial of political status but also by specific events of gendered violence in Armagh. When the female inmates ignored the banning of Republican uniforms and meetings inside the prison, and subsequently refused to appear for their disciplinary hearings, male prison guards forcibly rounded them up and abused them. In Mairéad Farrell's words, "It was obvious they were after our black uniforms[1] and by the look of things our blood as well" (qtd. in Neti 79). Following this event, the women were subjected to further violence when they were denied the right to basic sanitation (Neti 79). As with the male prisoners in Long Kesh, the women resisted the prohibition by smearing their body fluids on the prison walls and continued to do so even after they were permitted to use the washrooms.

Although the menstrual blood on the walls evoked the very notions of dirtiness and primitiveness within which the Irish were framed by colonial British ideology, it also confounded the notions of purity that the Irish Catholic Church and Irish nationalist patriarchy typically associated with women (Neti 80; Corcoran 243). For instance, when Nell McCafferty's report on the women's no-wash strike was first published in the *Irish Times* in 1980—exclaiming, "There is menstrual blood on the walls of Armagh prison in Northern Ireland" (qtd. in McAuliffe and Hale 181)—it was met with silence. Menstruating bodies—leaky, fluid, and abject—amplified the anxiety associated with feminine corporeality and threatened the fiction of a clean and proper body. Begona Aretxaga cites a woman prisoner whose brother, an IRA member, was so repulsed by her striking that he tried to discourage her yet was unable to name menstruation: "They didn't say that; they said that we were women, that we were different. But we knew it was because of our periods. These were men who had killed, and had been imprisoned and they couldn't say the word 'period'" (qtd. in McAuliffe and Hale 182). Whereas the male no-wash protest and hunger strike were seen as political resistance, women's anger and protest were channelled as hysteria and unruly sexuality, which normalized women's reclamation of agency on grounds of sexual and gender difference (Corcoran 244). Paula Burns suggests that the women IRA inmates' "weaponization" of menstrual blood challenged the phallo-centric economy of representation as well as the dominant feminist notion of shared oppression among women (29). In other words, the dirty protest reveals the feminist need for specific and heterogeneous women's narratives that trouble the dominant tropes of female embodiment (P. Burns 30).

No Bones

As mentioned above, Bronagh McCabe in Burns's novel *No Bones* is not presented as a subject beyond her angry, hysterical self. I read the novel's silencing of Bronagh's voice, her thoughts and desires, as deliberate. It reflects back to the readers their own willingness to oversee and not see Bronagh as a subject. In her performativity of the monstrous maternal as excessively irrational, hysterical, and hyper-sexual, Bronagh amplifies and contests dominant forms of representing Northern Irish Republican women. However, she is not the only angry woman or mother in the novel. Although there are other women who are presented as irrationally violent as the men, it is only women who are portrayed as hysterical and spectacular in their violence. This violence is exemplified by the description of Amelia's mother when she fights with her sister—"Mariah Lovett was mad.... Sister or no sister, she was a savage and something should be done to restrain her" (53)—and in the description of Amelia's sister Lizzie, who is so "addicted to fighting" that even the IRA does not want her (127): "Most people took time off, at least sort of, to have, say, sex, but not her. Lizzie's mindset was such that she forewent lovemaking at every opportunity for anything properly confrontational that might lead to a brawl" (126).

Meanwhile Bronagh's and Amelia's narratives can be read as counterpoints to each other. Amelia's struggle with mental illness, including anorexia and addiction, which makes her gradually more and more subdued, is intensely embodied: "She was counting calories, swallowing laxatives, shoving up suppositories, turning round mirrors, being friends with food, not being friends with food, nightmaring about clothes, being at war with her body" (128). The more Amelia collapses into her body, becoming almost invisible through anorexia, however, the more Bronagh grows out of her body and into her anger. Even though there are sporadic references to the violence of the other women in the text, Bronagh's violence does not strike the reader as exceptional; it is interesting that hers is the only portrayal in the novel of a Republican woman activist. Even as a young woman, before she becomes a mother, Bronagh is driven by unrestrained anger that evokes a combination of ridicule, disgust, and fascination in Amelia, who narrates the first two episodes featuring her. In these two episodes, Bronagh's links to the IRA are speculated but unconfirmed. In the first episode that features her, which is set in the school both girls attend, Amelia notes her fear of big, "beefy" Bronagh, who takes up "too much" space: "I was left standing in shock for Bronagh is one big beef of a girl, bigger than most big beefs of girls I knew" (74). Amelia also speculates whether any boy "would be mad enough to take up with" Bronagh (73). Amelia's gaze, which constructs Bronagh as the big, sexually undesirable young girl, is implicitly underlined by the associations that are often drawn between body fat, overconsumption, and gendered working-class subjectivity (Ellmann 7-9). This stereotype is reiterated by another classmate who provokes Bronagh: "Ye're fat, ye're ugly, yer boy doesn't want ye, ye're a big waste of space and ye're out" (75). Amelia narrates how Bronagh responds to the insult by producing a gun hidden beneath the flowery cover of her school basket and shooting the girl, who survives from the "minor gunshot wound" (75). In narrating how Bronagh's carnivalesque performance of anger in the school ground draws attention, as it becomes the subject of much sensationalized speculation among the school and the wider community—bringing "the RUC, the Brits, a helicopter and an ambulance ... and the other, invisible, sometimes not invisible people" (75)—Amelia also admits how it overwhelms her: "I can't stand it. It was doin' my head in" (75).

Although the two women seemingly inhabit opposing ends of a spectrum of femininized embodiment, they are both denied subjectivity. It is, however, only Amelia who seems to struggle against it, however fraught that struggle might be. She does try to reclaim herself: "Why can't I have what I want? She wondered and that, had she but known it, was the big question of Amelia Lovett's life" (247). Towards the end of the novel, as Amelia begins a complex, at times circular journey of healing and recovery, she also seems to develop a critical perspective of her mother. Amelia's mother is presented as a fierce, violent woman, who was either oblivious or indifferent to her daughter's plight: "Now she could see her mother's way of doing things was one way of doing things, and that she, Amelia Lovett didn't have to do things that way. She didn't have to have the last word. She didn't have to annihilate in order not to be annihilated" (291). As Amelia seems to distance herself from her mother's strategies of survival, she also begins to adopt her own tools that interestingly reflect the maternal principles of self-care and care for others. Her self-recovery, though a complex journey, does entail a degree of self-awareness, as she observes in one instance: "I might be having a mental breakdown, but I am not sure. I am not feeling connected" (253). Megan Rogers identifies maternal principles of care and self-care as not exclusive to biological mothers or even only to mothers but as important elements to reimagine female insanity outside a "madness-as-rebellion emplotment" (167). Amelia's continued suffering and struggle with depression, anorexia, and addiction does indeed problematize the reading of mental illness as gendered resistance. Mental illness obscures Amelia's sense of reality and often hurls her into states of vulnerability and fear. Rogers argues that the feminist emplotment of insanity as subversion in women's texts mutes the maternal subjectivity of female protagonists (166) and women's agency for transformation (167). In stark contrast to Amelia's slow and difficult work towards reclaiming herself, however, is Bronagh's performativity of the hysterical maternal in the third and fourth episodes in which she is featured, which caricatures the feminized somatization of anger and the channelling of her agency through hysteria.

It is in the third episode featuring Bronagh, after an implied lapse of time, that she is presented in the novel as an adult and an IRA woman for the first time. In this episode, Bronagh is also a mother of six young boys. Her maternal role amplifies her subversion of the Irish maternal in several significant ways, particularly in her role as mother to six young boys—a set of triplets, twins, and a toddler—all under the age of six. If multiple births are already excessive and abnormal (Russo 110), Bronagh's multiple births within the limited timespan seem to correspond to her uncanny monstrosity. It also signals to her darker side. In contrast to the previous two episodes, where teenage Bronagh was presented as irrationally angry and spontaneous, these two episodes reveal that adult Bronagh is manipulative: "For everybody knows a Bronagh. They are a laugh and a geg, the life and soul of every party but they tend to have a whole other side to them you just don't want to know" (221).

The shift in the narrative gaze from Amelia (in the two earlier episodes) to a third-person narrator is also striking. Whereas Amelia's gaze registered teenage Bronagh mostly with uneasiness and dread, the third-person narrator here is both repulsed and fascinated by Bronagh. The narrative voice in this episode also appears to correlate with the perspective of Marseillaise, another colleague from Bronagh's school days who features in the episode. The accidental encounter between the two women occurs in a tense suspension of linear time, where one bomb has just exploded, and the Royal Ulster Constabulary (RUC)[2] is unsuccessfully struggling to locate a second, which eventually explodes (206). Abused by her husband, a RUC official, Marseillaise is depressed and drunk: "Oh, her heart was broken. Everything was cruel and how much she suffered in this world. Nobody ever saw her point of view or cared what happened to her" (208). Irony and tension underlie this episode. Whereas abused Marseillaise drowns her rage and pain in alcohol to make her emotions invisible so that nobody ever saw or cared what happened to her, unbeknownst to the others, the smiling and laughing mother of six, Bronagh, is at that very moment planning an explosion to kill Marseillaise's husband and colleagues from RUC intelligence (211).[3]

The shift in the gaze in this episode is registered through Marseillaise's surprise by Bronagh's "unexpected" transformation: "Although convinced that Bronagh McCabe must have turned into the dirty ankled, Provo hussy everybody thought she would, there was something in that love bitten throat, the long legs, the way she took up all that room, that was just a bit too much to have to put up with. And she didn't have dirty ankles either"(203).

Similarly to the earlier episode, Bronagh is seen as occupying too much space, yet she now does so with elegance and poise. While drawn in by her "sensuous" body movements (211), Marseillaise is at the same time intimidated by the spectacle Bronagh creates. It is Bronagh's transformation into a seemingly elegant mother who at the same time owns an excessive and unrestrained laughter that is confounding as well as incongruous: "Bronagh threw back her head and laughed. Marseillaise remembered that laugh—how teachers used to scream when they heard it. And Bronagh McCabe laughed at anything—burnt cakes in cookery, plants falling out windows, cockroaches, bruises, bodies. Marseillaise never laughed like that. Her life would not have allowed it" (203).

Bronagh's performance in this episode (and the next), with its heightened theatricality, exponentially intensifies the element of performativity in her comportment. Her excessive laughter that enacts the female hysteric—the predominant trope through which women IRA prisoners were depicted during and after the no-wash protest (Corcoran 55)—demonstrates in both the episodes the anxieties evoked by the hysterical maternal body. It also raises questions about how the portrayal of the angry IRA woman as violent and excessive feminizes and illegitimates women's anger in politics. As Marseillaise notes, Bronagh seems to claim ownership to her laughter. It is this seemingly confident reclaiming of laughter that unsettles and frightens both Marseillaise and the RUC officer: the confident, laughing woman's maternal body both heightens and complicates the incongruity of the female hysteric. Bronagh's laughter clearly unsettles Marseillaise and the RUC officer in different ways. Whereas Marseillaise is both confused and seduced by her friend's laughter, the RUC officer responds with hostility and aggression. He threatens to take Bronagh into custody (210) and not so subtly reminds her that, as a mother, she has much to lose, malevolently wishing that the bomb would kill her children: "It would save me the trouble of having to shoot them later on" (210). Bronagh responds to him in equally sinister style: "You could be going around your business when—bang! What d'ye know? You'll be dead." And she then laughs because "to her, indeed, everything was funny" (210). Similar to the hidden bomb, which the police fail to find or defuse, Bronagh's laughter not only infuses the scene with menace but also helps her escape military surveillance.

If in the previous two episodes Bronagh was constantly subjected to laughter, a spectacle that was "seen but not heard" (Russo 68), in this episode, through owning her laughter, she becomes the subject who laughs. But what does it mean for a woman, a mother in particular, to claim subjectivity through hysteria? In *Rabelais and His World*, Mikhail Bakhtin perceives the figurines of the laughing and pregnant "old terracotta hags" as modelling "a principle of growth" that he maintains was a part of his notion of gothic realism: "Life is shown in its two-fold contradictory process; it is the epitome of incompleteness.... Moreover, these old hags are laughing" (26). In Mary Russo's feminist rereading, she complicates the laughter of Bakhtin's maternal (pregnant) terracotta hags and raises the question that clearly escaped Bakhtin: "But why are they laughing?" (Russo 63). I suggest, however, that Bronagh's subversive laughter opens up the possibility for another question: But what does that laughter do?

At one level, Bronagh's inexplicable laughter subverts the silent laughter, the covert disgust and ridicule she engenders in others, including, perhaps, the reader. At the same time, however, Bronagh's laughter also masks her anger. Bronagh's performativity of the maternal hysteric—which stems from anger—conceals the violence she plans. Her grotesque, excessive laughter mocks the sovereignty of a threatened state/military apparatus and its fear and anxiety of militant insurgency, particularly militant female insurgents. But her laughter allows her to be in control and to mask her planned counterviolence against the state. In rendering laughter and anger indistinguishable, Bronagh also renders it intensely ambivalent. Similarly to anger, laughter interrupts (Massumi 9). Her laughter strategically interrupts the gaze that misreads her as an irrational, hysterical mother. It conceals her manipulation of Marseillaise's anxiety and drunkenness in order to plan her husband's murder.

Occurring in the suspended time and space of an interregnum, Bronagh's laughter is also dialogical. It both enacts and disturbs the very suppression of female anger by militarized patriarchy. "Dialogical laughter," Russo argues, is the "laughter of intertext and multiple identifications. It is the conflictual laughter of social subjects in a classist, racist, ageist, sexist society" (73). Bronagh's manipulative, cold-hearted approach to her political activism, heightened by her suppressed rage masked as laughter is at one level juxtaposed, at another confirmed, by her maternal role. Bronagh in this episode exemplifies the enactment of the female hysteric as a monstrous, angry mother. Her hysterical anger that evokes anxiety and fear also gestures to how the anger of IRA women prisoners as political protest was muted and accordingly made invisible in dominant narratives of the Troubles.

The fourth episode featuring Bronagh focuses on her in a domestic space for the first time. Though set in Bronagh's home (in her kitchen and the children's bedroom), the location, ironically, highlights the unrealness of the entire episode. When Amelia visits her, seeking information about her brother who has disappeared, Bronagh appears to be carrying out the typically maternal role of nurturing her children but is in fact preparing to carry out an act of terror. "Housewifely, innocently" peeling potatoes for the children's dinner, Bronagh is planning an explosion that very afternoon (221).[4] Recalling that the figure of Mother Ireland is one that is frozen in time—stagnating and unable to move forwards and suspended at the particular historical moment of the past—Bronagh's children are "doomed by a legacy, by Ireland, by England, by prehistory, by everything that had gone before them, always and forever to be one, four and six years old" (226). Meanwhile Amelia, who is "not endearingly childlike, but frighteningly childlike" (224), is acting and feeling "peculiar" (221). Suffering from intense stomach pains caused by alcohol withdrawal, she can no longer recall her reason for visiting Bronagh (221). Feeling emotionally drained as if in a "blank mode" at a funeral (224), Amelia struggles to distinguish between the real and the imagined. Amelia's childlikeness also intensifies Bronagh's abuse of her maternal role, for it is indeed a monstrous mother who would violently exploit the vulnerability of a child. While Amelia's precarious emotional state in this episode serves as a precursor to the series of nervous breakdowns she will later suffer, it also contributes to the sense of incongruity underscoring this episode, as do Bronagh's excessive sexual desires, the explosives on the kitchen table, and the children's constant interruptions about playing with them (225):

> The build up to committing murder, as anyone will tell you takes its toll and Bronagh was no exception to that. Luckily for her though, her unconscious had created an antidote. It was absolutely fool proof and had worked every time so far. All she had to do before killing people, was to get some obsessive-compulsive human contact, and the obsessive-compulsive drug of choice for Bronagh was dominating and very fast sex. (222)

In enacting an "obsessive-compulsive" desire for human contact, Bronagh reevokes the irrational and excessive female hysteric. This desire also uncannily reproduces and mirrors wartime masculine sexual aggression. Her need for "dominating" and "fast sex" echoes the ubiquitous rationalization underlying the sexual abuse of women by male soldiers during war.[5]

The episode portrays Bronagh's predatory desires targeting Amelia first in the kitchen. As Amelia gradually gives into to Bronagh's sexual aggression, the narrator ironically notes that both women seem to believe "that sex with a woman didn't matter at all" (225). From the kitchen, the women move to the triplets' room: a windowless box room strewn with children's toys in various stages of deconstruction. With the intensified sense that time has been suspended, the minuscule, cavelike room evokes the "grotto-esque," or the orifice of the female womb (Russo 116) and recalls the blood-smeared prison cells of the Irish women inmates. Here, the loudly intrusive children are replaced by a silent toy action man in military fatigues; with "his plastic rifle at the ready," he is "peeping over at the two women from a single shelf that ran the length of the wall" (227). Although the action man might signify the militarized masculinist gaze and surveillance that objectify women's bodies, its power is undermined by its presence in the grotto-esque space of the womblike room. As Fiona McCann has noted, the inert toy solider with a plastic rifle is more of a miniature version of "an impotent Peeping Tom" (76), which undermines the power of the militarized gaze.

But the miniaturized version of the male gaze continues as the narrative gaze shifts to a child's. When one of the triplets is coerced by his siblings to sneak into the room, his child's gaze registers with horror:

His mammy was sitting up, on top, back to front, her eyes yellow, and she lifted her gaze and yelled and the sound was a fathomless, wordless roar. Her face looked not like his mammy's but like a contorted face from one of his kicking, kicking-awake nightmares, and not inches from himself were monster adult thighs and a giant hairy under bum. Those legs, his mammy's were twisting, twining, spiderling the head of that drunk person. That drunk person, apart from her head, was nowhere else to be seen at all. Her body was missing, maybe under the blankets or maybe not under the blankets, maybe under his mammy, doing invisible things. (228)

In the six-year-old's gaze, the mother is registered as disembodied and monstrous. The maternal body is monsterized mainly through dismemberment into body parts: "yellow eyes," "contorted face," "monster adult thighs," and "giant hairy under bum." This amplifies not only the monstrosity of the maternal body but also its strategic disembodiment in the male gaze. The child's gaze also disembodies Amelia: Her head is seen, but her body is missing. It is through the mutilation and the disembodiment of the monstrous maternal and the other "drunk person," her victim, that the child's gaze maps the horror she evokes in him. The gaze that simultaneously disembodies and depersonifies the woman perpetrator and the woman victim also corresponds with the dominant gaze. The monstrosity of the mother and her capacity to horrify are further magnified in the narrative gaze through Bronagh's metaphorical devouring of the flesh of children: When she later awakens from a short nap with the "tiny wee war worries taken care of" (228), her body now "contented, all buttery and honey and slippy slidy lovely" (228), she swallows the heads of the jelly babies her son has refused to eat. Brongah's swift transformations, between "slippy, slidy lovely" and "yellow eyes" and "monster adult thighs" also reinforces the masculinist anxieties underlying the slippages between the ideal and the monstrous maternal.

Bringing together the deformed, disfigured, and dismembered bodies of the monstrous mother and her woman victim—the children's toys, the jelly heads, the plastic military figure, and finally, the piece of flesh Amelia encounters—the scene continues to evoke the disgust and repulsion associated with menstruating female bodies in prison. Unable to distinguish sleeping from waking, only recalling that she has been having "dreams of alcohol" (229), Amelia struggles to distinguish between the real and the imagined and hallucinates a bloody piece of meat from which she recoils in horror. The animated chunk of meat, which Amelia sees and feels, moves around her legs and slides up her ankles (again, it is not clear whether by this stage Amelia is awake or still sleeping):

Raw, bright, red, glistening and crawling over the teddy bears ... coming closer and closer to her thigh. When it touched her thigh, she kicked and kicked and kicked herself awake again ... she was afraid to turn around, but she turned around and the piece of meat was gone again. The ripped up teddy bears and the jelly heads were lying in bits, unbloodied, as before. (229-30)

The bloody piece of meat further signifies the fears evoked by the excessive maternal body. Similarly to its dismemberment into fleshy parts—thigh, face, breasts—the monstrous maternal can only be represented and contained in fragments. If in this episode, Amelia was on autopilot up to this point of "going through the motions" as the narrator notes (225)—and before she runs away from Bronagh's house and all the "unholy things it stood for" (230)—the bloodied piece of flesh forces her to relive the horror of encountering the maternal body and its monstrousness. Taken together with the image of the room as a gothic cave, the bleeding that uncannily resonates with women's bleeding during menstruation and childbirth evokes those often silenced but pertinent affects underlying maternal embodiment as well as the IRA women's protest. Similarly to the bloody piece of flesh that appears and disappears before Amelia, women's rage against oppression materializes as the abjected excess—or the "blood on the walls." This gestures to what cannot be materialized in the dominant imaginary and what subjects the noncompliant maternal body to "grotesque distortions of the gaze" (Araujo 103)—that is, the monsterizing gaze that silences female anger and protest.

Conclusion

I read the textual imperative of No Bones in the form of a question: How can women, and mothers in particular, own their rage at social and political injustice and how can this anger be heard, acknowledged, rescripted, and channelled positively for social and political transformation, without been dismissed or ridiculed? As a trope for the violent feminine, Bronagh's portrayal of the monstrous mother troubles the heteronormative, masculinist anxieties surrounding women's political activism and gestures towards the gaps and omissions in representational economies through which the embodied narratives of women struggle to materialize. The feelings and sensations Amelia experiences in the fourth episode also resonate with the tensions underlying her later struggles in the text to reclaim herself through practicing the maternal principles of care and self-care. Later in the text, when Bronagh makes a final and brief appearance in the form of a possible hallucination, Amelia challenges the gaze that controls and dispossesses her anorexic body. In this episode, Amelia is seen to be recovering from addiction, but she is in the throes of a nervous breakdown while walking the London streets when a passerby accidentally knocks her down and helps her back up. As she observes him wiping his hands on his trousers, she shouts defensively, "My clothes may be dirty ... but ... Inside's my body, and my body's *my* body. My body is very clean" (250). Amelia's desire to reclaim herself accordingly articulates the tensions underlying the feminist project of reowning the gendered self without reducing her to a trope or icon that serves a functional role in the masculinist, nationalist imagery.

Endnotes

1. Once the IRA prisoners lost their special category status, they were required to wear the standard uniform worn by other inmates. The female IRA prisoners challenged this by wearing a black uniform.

2. The RUC, the Northern Ireland police force, had paramilitary characteristics until 2001.

3. Instead of being a coldblooded killer, however, Bronagh does display some concern for her friend's safety (211).

4. It is striking how kitchens become dark, sinister spaces of gendered brutality in the novel. As mentioned earlier, Amelia is raped by her brother and his partner in her family's kitchen.

5. McCann contends that Bronagh's inversion of the male militant is, ironically, the only embodiment of a "good terrorist" in the novel, particularly given the dearth of "effective" IRA men in the text (76).

Works Cited

Alison, Miranda. *Women and Political Violence: Female Combatants in Ethno-National Conflicts.* Routledge, 2009.

Araujo, Susana. "The Gothic-Grotesque of Haunted: Joyce Carol Oates's Tales of Abjection." *The Abject of Desire: The Aestheticization of the Unaesthetic in Contemporary Literature and Culture,* edited by Konstanze Kutzbach and Monika Mueller, Rodopi, 2007 pp. 89-106.

Aretxaga, Begona. "Dirty Protest: Symbolic Overdetermination and Gender in Northern Ireland Ethnic Violence." *Ethos*, vol. 23, no. 2, 1995, pp. 123-48.

Aretxaga, Begona. *Shattering Silence: Women, Nationalism and Political Subjectivity in Northern Ireland.* Princeton University Press, 1997.

Bakhtin, Mikhail. *Rabelais and his World.* Translated by Hélène Iswolsky. Indiana UP, 1984.

Burns, Anna. *No Bones.* Flamingo, 2002.

Burns, Paula. "Rethinking the Armagh Women's Dirty Protest." *Theory on the Edge: Irish Studies and the Politics of Sexual Difference*, edited by Noreen Giffney and Margrit Shildrick, Palgrave Macmillan, 2013, pp. 29-37,

Corcoran, Mary. "'Doing Your Time Right': The Punishment and Resistance of Women Political Prisoners in Northern Ireland." 2003, Dissertation, Liverpool John Moores University, PhD dissertation, researchonline.ljmu.ac.uk/5637/1/406844.pdf. Accessed 14 June 2021.

Del Pozo, Mercedes del Campo. "'Mother Ireland, get off our backs': Gender, Republicanism and State Politics in Prison Short Stories by Northern Irish Women Writers." *Estudios Irlandeses*, vol. 9, 2014, pp. 13-23.

Ellmann, Maud. *The Hunger Artists: Starving, Writing and Imprisonment.* Harvard University Press, 1993.

Lyons, Laura. "Feminist Articulations of the Nation: The 'Dirty' Women of Armagh and the Discourse of Armagh Women." *On Your Left: The New Historical Materialism*, edited by Anne Kibbey et al., New York University Press, 1996, pp. 110-49.

Mac Crossan, Elizabeth. "Bin Lids, Bombs and Babies in Free Derry: Reading the Troubles as a Woman's War." *Irish Women at War: The Twentieth Century*, edited by Gillian McIntosh and Diane Urquhart, Irish Academic Press, 2010.

Massumi, Brian. *The Politics of Affect.* Polity, 2015.

McAuliffe, Mary, and Laura Hale. "Blood on the Walls: Gender, History and Writing the Armagh Women." *Irish Women at War: The Twentieth Century*, edited by Gillian McIntosh and Dianne Urquhart, Irish Academic Press, 2010.

McCann, Fiona. "The Good Terrorist(s)? Interrogating Gender and Violence in Anne Devlin's 'Naming the Names' and Anna Burns' No Bones." *Estudios Irlandeses*, vol. 7, 2012, pp. 69-78.

Neti, Leila. "Blood and Dirt: Politics of Women's Protest in Armagh Prison, Northern Ireland." *Violence and the Body: Race, Gender, and the State,* edited by Arturo Aldama, Indiana University Press, 2003, pp. 77-93.

Pelan, Rebecca. *Two Irelands: Literary Feminisms North and South.* Syracuse University Press, 2005.

Radosh, Polly. "Can Ruddick's Maternal Thinking be Applied to Traditional Mothering?" *Journal of Family History*, vol. 33, no. 3, 2008, pp. 304-15.

Rogers, Megan. *Finding the Plot: A Maternal Approach to Madness in Literature.* Demeter Press, 2017.

Rolston, Bill. "Mothers, Whores and Villains: Images of Women in Novels of the Northern Ireland Conflict." *Race and Class*, vol. 31, no. 1, 1989, pp. 41-57.

Russo, Mary. *The Female Grotesque: Risk, Excess and Modernity.* Routledge, 1994.

Shildrick, Margrit. *Embodying the Monster: Encounters with the Vulnerable Self.* Sage, 2002.

Steele, Jayne. "And Behind Him a Wicked Hag Did Stalk: From Maiden to Mother, Ireland as Woman through the Male Psyche." *Irish Women and Nationalism: Soldiers, New Women and Wicked Hags,* edited by Louise Ryan and Margaret Ward, Irish Academic Press, 2004, pp. 96-113.

Weekes, Ann Owens. "Figuring the Mother in Contemporary Irish Fiction." *Contemporary Irish Fiction: Themes, Trope and Theories,* edited by Liam Harte and Michael Parker, Macmillian, 2000, pp. 100-24.

Chapter 6

Central Intelligence and Maternal Mental Health: The Apparently Aberrant Bad Mother in *Homeland*

Aidan Moir

The archetype of the monstrous mother remains a prominent representation in contemporary media and is most particularly evident with Showtime's popular television series *Homeland* (2011–2020). This chapter explores the depiction of *Homeland*'s lead character Carrie Mathison (portrayed by actor Claire Danes) as an aberrantly monstrous mother, particularly regarding how this woman prioritizes her career over what her family believes should be her more natural maternal obligations towards her daughter, Franny. The analysis provides insights into the contradictions pertaining to the social construction of motherhood, as Carrie's personal maternal identity crisis is situated within the larger ideological context of maternity that circulates throughout public discourse. Representations of motherhood in popular culture work to negotiate social desires and values regarding acceptability and maternity, and the discursive authority of such imagery is reflected in the rhetoric, motifs, and language used by both television critics and viewers to harshly portray Carrie as a bad mother (Walters and Harrison).

Carrie is a single, bipolar Central Intelligence Agency (CIA) officer, who is depicted as a woman prioritizing her job and public obligation to matters of national security over her health and personal life. Viewers become immediately engaged with this storyline, as Carrie struggles to gain control and balance over her mental health and professional and personal commitments. The first three seasons of *Homeland* focus on Carrie's suspicions regarding Nicholas Brody, a former United States (US) marine, congressman, and spy for the fictional Al-Qaeda terrorist, Abu Nazir. Brody, once viewed by the public as a celebrated war hero after spending twelve years as a prisoner of war held captive in Afghanistan by Nazir, attempted to murder the vice-president of the United States by detonating a suicide vest and is eventually executed for treason in Iran. Carrie's own personal association with Brody is clearly defined as incredibly tumultuous from the first episode, in which she commences a sexual relationship with Brody to maintain surveillance operations on his activities.

Following their affair, Carrie becomes pregnant with Brody's child and gives birth to their daughter, Franny, during a period in which she is mourning his death. Carrie struggles to accept, let alone acknowledge, any type of innate maternal desire following Franny's birth. In one particularly unnerving scene, she contemplates infanticide while giving her daughter a bath. Carrie ultimately abandons a more natural and closely attentive role in Franny's life by requesting overseas fieldwork positions in Kabul and Islamabad. Remarking upon the episode containing *Homeland*'s infamous bathtub scene, Hayley Krischer notes:

> Despite all of the ambient awareness about maternal mental illness and post-partum, and the horrific headlines that come along with it—the culture of motherhood can be all-consuming. Carrie is supposed to love her daughter after not seeing her for months. Period. She's supposed to be thrilled about dropping her dangerous, adventurous, beloved job in the CIA to stroll her baby around a park.

Krischer's commentary is one of the few cultural critiques of Carrie's internal battle to accept her maternal identity that recognizes the larger social discourses informing how audiences will potentially interpret the character's actions and choices regarding her own daughter's care. Although Carrie's decisions concerning the safety and wellbeing of her daughter are certainly problematic, *Homeland* offers an intriguing representation of motherhood that directly challenges ideologies of intensive mothering that continue to govern hierarchies of maternal acceptability in public discourse. Cultural intermediaries perform a critical role in maintaining the hegemonic power of intensive mothering that dictates practices of respectable motherhood. The reproduction of intensive mothering as a dominant discursive formation is best illustrated through the intense reactions by many critics and viewers following the introduction of pregnancy and motherhood into the narrative of *Homeland*, as they fervently denounced Carrie's troubles in acknowledging her new maternal identity. Few commentaries have addressed the influence of Carrie's marginalized identity as a bipolar mother conceivably suffering from postpartum depression (PPD). *Homeland*'s depiction of Carrie as a monstrous and aberrant mother struggling under difficult circumstances ultimately offers a cultural representation that can potentially create new possibilities for visualizing different maternal subjectivities.

Scholarly Approaches to the Social Construction of Motherhood

Popular culture exhibits a persistent fascination with motherhood, which is well illustrated by television representations categorizing mothers into varying hierarchies of maternal acceptability. Suzanna Danuta Walters and Laura Harrison argue that the concept of motherhood as an ideological construction is "so overdetermined that a singular hegemonic trope rarely emerges, although there have certainly been historical moments when the power of the dominant produces a more singular frame" (39). Contemporary society has privileged the notion of intensive mothering, which Sharon Hays argues is a "gendered model" that demands maternal figures devote extensive attention and financial resources to support their children. Mothers who fail to achieve such unattainable standards are stigmatized as selfish and unfit to any type of maternal responsibility (Hays x). The ideology of intensive mothering has emerged as a dominant representation of motherhood in part due to the power of celebrity and popular culture, with Elizabeth Podnieks arguing that the "mass media praises and vilifies mothers, keeping them under constant surveillance and judging them according to the extent to which they adhere to ideologies of good motherhood" (14). Susan J. Douglas and

Meredith W. Michaels address the intersections between motherhood, the intensification of neoliberal consumer capitalism, and socio-economic changes to journalism, leading to the promotion lifestyle and tabloid content contributing to what they refer to as the "new momism"—a trend influenced by dynamics of class and race that requires mothers to constantly scrutinize themselves and others through new forms of cultural surveillance practices (19-20). Such arguments theorize how cultural trends and practices have produced a dominant construction of contemporary motherhood that is employed by various social institutions to judge and discipline mothers, including fictional characters on television like Carrie Mathison.

As a social construct, motherhood is open to numerous contradictions and competing representations, enabling the emergence of the aberrant mother within popular culture. In their analysis on representations of motherhood in television, Walters and Harrison critique E. Ann Kaplan's argument that controlling and overindulgent mothers are the dominant tropes depicting cruel motherhood in cultural texts (48). They argue that such tropes do not account for contemporary culture's fascination with the aberrant mother: "Neither monster nor angel, the aberrant mother is not quite a twenty-first-century feminist heroine but she does upend more traditional depictions of maternal identity. Unabashedly sexual, idiosyncratic to a fault, and seriously delirious in her caretaking skills" (40). They situate their analysis of television's aberrant mothers within the context of intensive mothering and Douglas and Michaels's argument of the "mommy myth," which suggests that "in a culture that chastises middle-class mothers for one missed soccer practice, this brazen disregard for maternal mandates of (over) protection is both shocking and strangely exhilarating" (43). Walters and Harrison contend that although the aberrant mother can be characterized and criticized as monstrous for some of the maternal choices she makes, this mother figure is still a progressive representation because for her, motherhood is a secondary identity—one that is behind other professional and personal roles and obligations (48). In contrast to other depictions that can be characterized as constituting the trend of intensive mothering, the aberrant mother on television provides opportunities for women to establish a persona that is not entirely dependent upon a maternal identity. Representations of aberrant mothers, including *Homeland*'s Carrie, offer further openings to interrogate how motherhood is a complex ideological construction that continues to challenge preexisting singular hegemonic beliefs. Walters and Harrison's arguments are well suited to analyze the maternal narrative in *Homeland*, since the notion of the aberrant mother allows for a more nuanced exploration as to how Carrie's shocking actions are reflective of the larger complexities that shape her identity.

Conveying Sexuality, Mental Illness, and Carrie Mathison's Pregnant Body on *Homeland*

Adapted from an Israeli series and produced by the creators of *24*, *Homeland* touches upon numerous issues central to contemporary geopolitics. Diane Negra and Jorie Lagerwey describe the program as a "dense, polysemic text that provides rich grist for readings in relation to class, gender, and genre" (126). Previous scholarship on *Homeland* analyzes how the program negotiates central themes of post-9/11 culture regarding domestic security, surveillance, intelligence, and terrorism within the larger context of the Obama administration's foreign policy (Castonguay; Steenberg and Tasker). Other work addresses the ways in which Carrie's mental illness is framed as a unique ability abetting her professional endeavours (Bevan; Wessels). Further supporting Walters and Harrison's notion of the aberrant mother, Negra and Lagerwey discuss Carrie's decision to leave her daughter in the US to take up postings in Kabul and Islamabad, and they note that such career-orientated decisions reflect how she prioritizes patriotism and public duty over her maternal identity and familial obligations (126).

The celebration of premium television by critics and other cultural commentators often downplays female contributions by heralding male characters, yet programs that have received attention for featuring complex female characters often contain storylines that showcase matters of politics and security (Castonguay 140). Characters like *Homeland*'s Carrie perform a metaphorical role that cannot be achieved in masculine-centred programming, in which Alex Bevan argues that Carrie's body and sexuality, in addition to her mental health, function narratively as a "battleground" for negotiating changing notions of citizenship and investigative labour (145). For Negra and Lagerwey, the struggles of Carrie on *Homeland* suggest that female bodies "work as physical representations of the conflicts among aggressive [Unites States] foreign policy, extensive domestic surveillance operations, and the rhetoric of civil liberties" (129). Bevan focuses her analysis on Carrie's mental illness and continued battles with a bipolar diagnosis, which inspire her career breakthroughs yet simultaneously cause her colleagues to question, belittle, and undermine her legitimacy as a CIA analyst, operative, and station chief (146). Carrie is portrayed throughout the series as sexually promiscuous, and she uses her sexuality to exert power and control over her work. The depiction of such incidents on *Homeland* is consistent for Bevan with "hackneyed associations among women, espionage, and trading sex for secrets" (146). Bevan argues that ultimately the "symbolic value of Carrie's body culminates [with] her discovery that she is pregnant with Brody's child and her decision to keep the baby and raise it as a single mother despite her reservation about balancing work with home life" (146). Reflective of Walters and Harrison's conceptualization of the aberrant mother as brazenly sexual, Carrie manipulates sex into a game of espionage and control in which motherhood is the consequence rather than the ideal that Carrie must endure amid her professional obligations.

After discovering she is pregnant, Carrie continues to participate in numerous activities that can potentially harm her unborn child, such as undertaking international field work and extensive drinking and smoking. In a conversation with a colleague after Brody's death and while contemplating a promotion to Istanbul station chief before giving birth, Carrie admits her hesitations regarding motherhood. Referring to her unborn child as a "bad situation" that she "didn't think through," Carrie confesses: "I can't be a mother. Because of me. Because of my job. Because of my problem" ("The Star"). Carrie's hesitations imply that motherhood is potentially incompatible with the demands of her job while she concedes the socially constructed stigmas associated with her mental illness. Carrie is visibly disturbed by the movements of her unborn child in the final weeks of her pregnancy and is exasperated by her father's excitement and anticipation for the arrival of his granddaughter. Her sister, Maggie, provides Carrie with the necessary baby equipment, and Carrie's dismay at her new Björn baby carrier and rocking chair signify that she is unprepared for her daughter's arrival. When discussing her unborn daughter with her sister, Carrie expresses the desire to give the child up for adoption in order to move to Istanbul and accept the position as station chief. Maggie believes the pregnancy will help improve her sister's happiness, which reinforces dominant notions that motherhood is the essential purpose of female identity. As Maggie informs her sister: "I think she's going to ground you, make you focus, be healthy, and I think you will be astonished by the love you have for her" ("The Star"). Maggie's point of view denotes an underlying belief that all women possess the ability to effortlessly adopt a maternal identity following the birth of a child, regardless of their own unique personal histories. Carrie is visibly suffering from the pain of Brody's death, and her mental wellbeing is questionable. Her family, however, overlooks these apparent warnings, and their advice to Carrie, while intended to be well meaning, reinforces longstanding ideologies of a woman's innate biological ability to naturally love her child regardless of extenuating circumstances.

Ultimately Carrie's need for a lasting connection with Brody compelled her to inadvertently listen to her family and walk away from the one opportunity she had to concentrate completely on her career and forsake motherhood entirely. Despite earlier resistance to a committed relationship, she is now relying upon motherhood (which threatens all her career aspirations) to maintain a connection with the deceased Brody.

Media portrayals of mental illness in the news and cultural texts like *Homeland* play a formidable role in shaping both public and clinical perceptions (Fenimore; Herson). Carrie is one of the most prominent female characters on television diagnosed as bipolar who is also depicted as successful and confident in a masculine-dominated profession. This aspect of her identity is particularly important, since very few cultural texts address the role of preexisting mental illness in relation to motherhood and parenting. Mothers who are bipolar face both increased social and self-inflicted stigmas primarily due to internalized fears over their ability to properly care for their children. These well-founded fears of failing to act in accordance with the high standards expected of maternal figures debilitate a mother's own ability to request assistance when the possibility of state apprehension is a clear threat. Elizabeth Fish Hatfield argues that Carrie's pregnancy challenges and negotiates hegemonic social normalities regarding not only motherhood but also maternal mental health by "allowing life with a bipolar diagnosis to become part of the national conversation" (34-35). Carrie's pregnancy and struggles to embrace her maternal identity must not be seen as trivial plot points intentionally written to shock audiences, as some critics have suggested. Rather, the maternal storyline's presence in *Homeland* functions for Fish Hatfield to demonstrate the control Carrie exhibits over her multiple competing and contradictory identities and subjectivities as well as the repercussion such decisions have when they violate socially constructed notions of acceptable motherhood. Carrie is evidently aware of the multiple stigmas she faces and initially expresses her desire to place her unborn child up for adoption—a decision that contradicts ideals of acceptable motherhood but one that Fish Hatfield argues is understandable considering the "stereotypes about mothering with mental illness" (48). Regardless of how well Carrie adapts as a mother, she will continue to face some form of stigmatization or marginalization due to her bipolar diagnosis.

When it is first revealed that Carrie is pregnant, she is seen placing a positive pregnancy test in a drawer with approximately one hundred other tests. The scene infers that she is partly in denial over her personal situation, a reading supported by her disinterest in—and at times complete disregard—for the health of her unborn child. Although Carrie expresses no curiosity in her child other than the fact that Brody is the father, she also does not seriously consider abortion despite being asked by her obstetrician if that is an option she wishes to pursue. Carrie eventually decides to have the baby, which she names Franny, as a means to keep a part of the recently deceased Brody alive but leaves Maggie to care for her daughter. As Franny grows and her features become more apparent, however, they bear a striking resemblance to Brody with her red hair, freckles, and pale complexion. Franny is a visual reminder of Carrie's continuing grief over Brody's death. The decisions Carrie makes concerning both her pregnancy and the upbringing of her daughter demonstrate for Fish Hatfield Carrie's responsiveness to how "she operates within various stigmas including those surrounding mental illness and capability, and chooses the immediate stigma of not wanting her child over the potential future stigma of bad motherhood" (42). However, Carrie's decision to leave her newborn is met with hostility from her immediate family who judge her as an unfit mother. Maggie frames this choice within the rhetoric of bad motherhood, chastising her sister with defamatory remarks, such as "You bring a life into this world, you take responsibility" and "There's not even a diagnosis for what's wrong with you!" ("Trylon and Perisphere"). Despite being aware of her sister's mental illness, Maggie's comments lack any consideration for the stigmas her sister must negotiate or the agency Carrie is attempting to exert over her often competing identities as a bipolar CIA agent and new mother. *Homeland*'s pregnancy thereby presents an alternative representation of motherhood in a culture dominated by practices of intensive mothering. By transforming Carrie into a mother—albeit one who often acts against the unattainable demands placed upon those constituting such an identity—*Homeland* provides a unique visualization of a woman who privileges her career over any expression of maternal care regardless of how such decisions are judged and condemned.

Intelligence and Infanticide: Carrie Mathison's Complicated Maternal Subjectivities

In the season four premiere, the first episode following the death of Brody and the birth of her daughter, Carrie is employed as the Kabul station chief and tasked with overseeing drone operations in northern Afghanistan. Brief and awkward Skype conversations are the only contact she has with Franny, although her picture is displayed on Carrie's bedside table. Carrie orders a drone bombing of a wedding attended by forty Pakistani citizens based on corrupt information that was provided by the Islamabad station chief, who is later beaten to death in front of Carrie and Quinn. Carrie expresses no emotion after witnessing the brutal death of a colleague in the streets of Islamabad, casually reapplying her lipstick after returning to the American Embassy ("The Drone Queen"). Carrie is ordered to return to the US by CIA Director Lockhart to testify in front of a Senate intelligence committee. The only time Carrie expresses some type of emotion over what transpired in Islamabad is after Lockhart instructs her to remain in the US instead of returning to her post, in which he sarcastically notes: "Look at it this way: You get to spend time with your kid" ("Trylon and Perisphere"). This comment inadvertently implies—and which Carrie interprets—that motherhood is a form of punishment. Lockhart's reference to her maternal identity evokes fear, disappointment, and noticeable contempt in Carrie, who responds by formulating a plan of action that includes threatening the CIA director to maintain her overseas posting.

Her return to the US requires Carrie to engage in person with her newborn baby, Franny, whom Maggie is caring for while she is overseas. Standing on Maggie's doorstep, Carrie hears Franny crying, which provokes Carrie to frantically attempt to leave while declaring: "It's really late. I could stay in a hotel!" ("Trylon and Perisphere"). Maggie asks if she would like to hold her daughter, which Carrie is hesitant to do but reluctantly accepts, ineptly holding Franny by the armpits. The next day, Carrie watches Franny's nanny changing her diaper; she declines to help when asked, flinching at the thought of such an action. After refusing to care for Franny that night because her jetlag was too intense, Carrie takes her daughter the next morning to Brody's former home. Reflecting on her feelings for Brody and their previous relationship, Carrie admits to Franny: "You think I'm a terrible mom? I am, but he would've been even worse. He was happy you were on the way.... I tried to hold on to that and feel it too.... But with his being gone, I can't remember why I had you" ("Trylon and Perisphere"). Away from the disapproval of her sister and colleagues, Carrie is afforded an honest moment with Franny, when she owns her subjectivities and rhetorically addresses the prevailing question plaguing the audience—why she followed through with the pregnancy and kept the child. The scene highlights Carrie's self-awareness over how her actions are scrutinized against the ideals governing the standards of acceptable motherhood, although *Homeland* frames this reflexivity within the discourse of monstrous motherhood with no direct acknowledgement regarding how her bipolar disorder may be influencing her actions and thought process. The fourth season of *Homeland* was promoted as a narrative revamping of the program, and Carrie's mental illness is not directly referenced during the initial episodes, which focus on her maternal responsibilities—aside from a brief shot of Carrie swallowing an unidentifiable pill, which she says is a sleeping pill.

The next scene depicts Carrie giving Franny a bath and washing her visibly red hair that serves as a reference to Brody. Franny accidently slips in the bath and sinks into the water; instead of raising Franny up, Carrie hesitates, and then submerges her daughter deeper into the bath with the possible intent of committing infanticide. After a brief moment, Carrie realizes her actions and desperately lifts her daughter out of the bathtub to embrace Franny in a most tender way. Krischer effectively details this powerful scene:

> This is not an easy scene to watch. The director lingers on the baby in the bathtub, shifting back and forth from the unknowing infant to Carrie's trembling, confused face. The baby slips for a moment and Carrie sees her future—what it would look like without a baby. It's a brutal moment and Carrie allows the baby to sink. The point-of-view now is the baby's—underwater. For all we've seen Carrie go through, this character could never recover from drowning her baby. It might be the last taboo in our antihero(ine)-obsessed age: a mother killing her defenseless child.... Carrie doesn't go through with it. She lifts the baby up and comforts her daughter. But it's a moment of clarity for her: I'm a danger to this child. And for the viewer, it's a scene so disturbing that—even amid so many TV shows engineered for maximum shock—it feels like a moment of unprecedented, and productive, boundary-pushing.

For most audience viewers, this bathtub scene in *Homeland* fortified Carrie's identity as a monstrous mother through its association with other well-known public cases of mothers accused of infanticide. In particular, the act of infanticide by drowning is most commonly associated in public discourse with Andrea Yates. Initially convicted for drowning her five children in a bathtub, Yates was later found not guilty by reason of insanity and committed to a low-security mental health hospital. Yates—who previously was diagnosed with nervous breakdowns and postpartum psychosis—was subjected to intense media scrutiny, and her case helped raise greater awareness towards maternal mental health (McLellan). This deeply troubling scene reflected in *Homeland* is especially significant not only because of the concerns raised for Carrie's mental wellbeing but also because it acts as her catalyst in realizing she is a danger to her child. Rather than seek help, Carrie acts in accordance with the conventions of Walters and Harrison's aberrant mother by formulating a plan to be sent back overseas in a distorted way to protect Franny.

Cultural Intermediaries and the Creation of Carrie Mathison as an Aberrantly Monstrous Mother

Homeland has received intense media scrutiny from both viewers and critics and other cultural intermediaries. The character of Carrie continues to be a particular focus of popular reactions, best illustrated by the *Saturday Night Live* skit in which Anne Hathaway mocks Claire Danes's hysteric performance and the actor's tendency to rely upon tears and wide eyes during emotional scenes (Wessels). Television programs have a sizeable cultural reach, and their presence in other series devoted to satire as social commentary, such as *Saturday Night Live*, can potentially alter intended readings of the narrative. Jonathan Gray terms these examples as "paratexts," which assist in the creation of dominant meanings and interpretations of a particular artifact, such as a television program or film (6). It is necessary to account for the power of commentaries on *Homeland* and Carrie's personal struggle with her maternal identity because such pieces not only act as extensions of the program but also function as "filters through which we must pass on our way to the film or program, our first and formative encounter with the text" (Gray 3). Emmanuelle Wessels employs Gray's concept of paratexts to address how cultural intermediaries construct a dominant reading of Carrie as a pathological woman who cannot handle the pressures of her career endeavours, particularly since her feelings and body are central affective elements involved in her labour (514-20). Her reading of *Homeland*'s paratextual material provides a framework to understand how cultural intermediaries function to maintain the ideological boundaries of acceptable motherhood by denouncing Carrie's monstrous and aberrant maternal persona without distinguishing how her actions must be situated within larger social discourses of mental illness.

Representations of the bad mother in popular culture signify for Linda Seidel a cultural dichotomy of disgust and obsession promoted by a penetrating media landscape. Bad mothers are demonized and othered according to Seidel as an "aberration" yet are subjected to intense surveillance and interest by the media (xii). Seidel's argument can also be applied to the popular reaction to Carrie's maternal persona—or lack thereof—on *Homeland* that characterizes her as a monstrous mother. Audiences gleefully responded on the internet and social media during and after the airing of the controversial episode containing the infamous bathtub scene. For example, viewers announced on Twitter that: "After watching the Homeland premiere, I'm declaring Carrie Mathison 'Bad Mother of the Year'"; "Homeland s4 eps 1 and 2 were great. Carrie is, unsurprisingly, the world's worst mother so far. That poor baby..."; and "I so wanna smack Carrie for being an unfit mother" ("The Mother of All Bad Guys"). Comments in response to the entertainment website the *AV Club*'s review of the bathtub scene described Carrie as a "downright psychotic narcissistic villain" and that "she was a terrible, terrible mother even before she had a baby to drown in a tub," referring to her decision to drink and smoke while pregnant; another post noted that "I feel like they recognize what a problematic character Carrie still is to a lot of viewers.... At this rate, it won't be long before she's dangling the kid out the window, Michael Jackson-style" (qtd. in Saraiya). The scandal in which Michael Jackson held his infant child over the edge of a balcony is presumably referenced by this user to emphasize the stigmas surrounding Carrie's mental state (Vassagar). However, these comments reflect a general hostility towards Carrie that manifests as a voyeuristic pleasure in condemning her as monstrous mother without much consideration towards her wellbeing.

The interpretation of the bathtub scene as an example of Carrie's identity as a monstrous mother is also reflected within journalistic critiques of the episode. Writing for *Yahoo*'s entertainment section, Dave Nemetz categorizes Carrie's worst maternal moments in the episode depicting the bathtub scene, introducing his rather patronizing ranking by asserting:

> When we found out Carrie was pregnant last season on *Homeland*, we felt a bit nauseous ... and it wasn't morning sickness. We know Carrie by now: She's a self-centred, emotionally unstable woman who's never had a healthy relationship.... Not exactly an ideal candidate for motherhood. And yet we may have underestimated just what a bad mom Carrie is, based on her interactions with baby Franny. She made Betty Draper look like Clair Huxtable. She made Livia Soprano look like Jane Cleaver.

Nemetz further mocks Carrie for her inability to properly feed Franny her bottle, for changing Franny's diaper on the kitchen table, and for driving with Franny seated in the front seat of the car. The rhetorical comparison of Carrie to television's iconic horrendous mothers is intriguing as it works as an intertextual reference to underscore her abysmal place on an imagined hierarchy of monstrous fictional mothers. *Vulture*'s Price Peterson continues to draw upon intertextuality to condemn Carrie's mothering in his review of the season four premiere:

> Working single mothers: How do they do it? In the case of *Homeland*'s Carrie Mathison, being a successful working single mother requires only white wine, sleeping pills, and living 7,000 miles away from your child. Hmm, upon reflection, it seems that perhaps Carrie Mathison is not actually a very good single mother and is in fact not doing it.

Peterson's reliance upon the phrase "doing it" is in direct reference to Allison Pearson's novel *I Don't Know How She Does It* (2002), which was adapted into a feature film in 2011 starring Sarah Jessica Parker. The book, released at a time in which the ideology of intensive mothering gathered potency in public discourse, chronicles Kate Reddy, a working mother attempting to balance her financial career while raising two children (Moir). Utilizing the language synonymous with *I Don't Know How She Does It* evokes an immediate comparison between Kate Reddy and Carrie and is intentionally designed to mock Carrie's capabilities as a mother, inferring to viewers that they should be disgusted by her actions.

What is missing from the dominant cultural commentaries that work to reinforce Carrie as a monstrous mother is any consideration of the influence of her bipolar diagnosis or that she may be suffering from PPD. Addressing the extreme reviews to the potential infanticide scene on Twitter, the arts website *Women and Hollywood* notes: "I have yet to read one tweet saying 'Did anyone listen to Carrie back when she was, like, I DON'T WANT THIS BABY. NO SERIOUSLY I DON'T.' Or "Homeland Season 4 Premiere: Drone Strikes & Postpartum Depression" ("The Mother of All Bad Guys"). In the comment section to Sonia Saraiya's review of the episode on the *AV Club*, few responses highlighted the author's insensitivity towards Carrie's mental health; most notably, one user remarked that Saraiya's recap neglected to recognize that "postpartum depression is a real thing," to which another user agreed: "I think it was weird for Sonia to casually dismiss that as something that Carrie would never do, when in fact I think it's potentially something that could happen to ANY mother." The season four finale of *Homeland* makes a brief reference to Carrie's possible PPD in a scene where Carrie meets a friend of her recently deceased father, Billy, during an outing with Franny in the park. Billy is aware of Carrie's challenges resulting from her new maternal identity, mentioning that her father frequently talked about Carrie: "He knew you'd come back for her.... I know you had troubles at first, which my wife did, too, so we talked on that" ("Long Time Coming"). In addition to considering infanticide, Carrie's irritability, coldness, and detach-ment after witnessing her colleague beaten to death in Islamabad can conceivably be attributed to PPD and also possibly posttraumatic stress disorder from the atrocities she has witnessed during her career. Despite the newfound conversations considering both mental illness and PPD in public discourse, particularly regarding celebrity mothers who have spoken openly about their struggles after giving birth, sensitivity to these issues have been largely absent from popular commentaries on *Homeland* despite the openings for larger social discussion offered by Carrie's own maternal experience.

Conclusion: Negotiating Maternal Identities and *Homeland*'s Subversive Potential

Carrie's maternal identity crisis alongside her mental illness and professional commitments as a CIA officer remain a complex storyline for the entire *Homeland* series. After a terrorist attack resulting in mass causalities at the American Embassy in Islamabad, Carrie's perspective on her maternal identity begins to change. During a Skype session with Maggie, she asks to see Franny and expresses sincere joy at the sight of her daughter, reaching to pat Franny through the screen of her computer and holding back tears. In the aftermath of the events in Islamabad, Carrie withdraws from the CIA and moves to Germany with Franny. She walks her daughter to school in the mornings and celebrates her birthday, actions that are a blatant contrast to Carrie's earlier attempts to reconcile her maternal identity. Later seasons of *Homeland* continue to depict the ways in which Carrie's commitment to her profession places Franny in potentially grave danger. She genuinely begins to love her daughter yet is hospitalized when she suffers a mental breakdown due to maternal guilt after nearly running Franny over in a school parking lot when frantically responding to an emergency situation with an operation. At a custody hearing, witnesses speak to the severe trauma Franny has experienced due to Carrie continuing to place her daughter in scenarios that threaten her life, and this tormented mother eventually adheres to an agreement that gives guardianship of her daughter to Maggie with bimonthly weekend visitation rights. Carrie's actions on *Homeland* are consistent with both Walters and Harrison's trope of the aberrant mother and cultural understandings of maternal monstrosities. In the end, Carrie does not express any normative maternal regret or shame about missing central moments in Franny's life and is removed from the mundane minutiae of parenting by choosing to prioritize her obligations to issues of national security.

Homeland's representation of motherhood as depicted through Carrie's struggle to fulfill her maternal obligations is an intriguing portrayal that challenges dominant ideologies of intensive mothering, in which mothers prioritize their children over professional or personal endeavours (Hays). The entertainment blog *Women and Hollywood* praises *Homeland*'s narrative decision to transform Carrie into a mother, commentating in their review of the maternal storyline: "Everyone around her is over the moon about the idea of her becoming a mother. I love that *Homeland* is going there; intentionally or not, it's a fantastic example of how some women who really don't have a maternal bone in their bodies are societally encouraged to do it anyway" ("The Mother of All Bad Guys"). *Homeland* exposes the prevailing belief presupposing all women are not only capable but eager to accept motherhood into their preexisting identities without any expression of reluctance or uncertainty despite a cultural discourse that presents the illusion of choice. Although Carrie's maternal actions can be categorized as monstrous, *Homeland* continues to confront dominant yet highly dangerous tropes of mothers successfully balancing their career with familial obligations while devoting considerable attention and resources to their children. The fact that Carrie cannot achieve this balance because she is experiencing PPD or a lapse in her mental wellbeing while simultaneously prioritizing her patriotic responsibility over Franny does not instantly transform her into a monstrous or aberrant mother. *Homeland* provides a highly destabilizing representation of motherhood; however, the overwhelming inability for viewers and commentators to appropriately address Carrie's maternal struggle alongside her experiences as a bipolar woman conceivably suffering from PPD demonstrates the need for greater attention directed towards how mental illness and motherhood are visualized within popular culture. Carrie is a highly complex individual, and the numerous layers that compose her character offer unique opportunities to help normalize maternal personas unafraid to struggle or outright reject their maternal identities.

Works Cited

Bevan, Alex. "The National Body, Women, and Mental Health in *Homeland*." *Cinema Journal*, vol. 54, no. 4, 2015, pp. 145-51.

Castonguay, James. "Fictions of Terror: Complexity, Complicity and Insecurity in *Homeland*." *Cinema Journal*, vol. 54, no. 4, 2015, pp. 139-45.

Douglas, Susan J. and Meredith W. Michaels. *The Mommy Myth: The Idealization of Motherhood and How It Has Undermined Women*. Free Press, 2004.

"The Drone Queen." *Homeland: Season 4*, written by Alexa Gansa, directed by Lesli Linka Glatter, Showtime, 2014.

Fenimore, Wanda Little. "Bad Girls From Eve to Britney." *Mental Illness in Popular Culture: Essays on the Representation of Disorders*, edited by Lawrence C. Rubin, McFarland & Company, 2012, pp. 146-64.

Fish Hatfield, Elizabeth. "Motherhood and Mental Health: Carrie Mathison's Homeland Pregnancy." *Mediated Moms: Contemporary Challenges to the Motherhood Myth*, edited by Heather L. Hundley and Sara E. Hayden, Peter Lang, 2016, pp. 33-52.

Gray, Jonathan. *Show Sold Separately: Promos, Spoilers, and Other Media Paratexts*. New York University Press, 2010.

Hays, Sharon. *The Cultural Contradictions of Motherhood*. Yale University Press, 1996.

Herson, Kellie. "Transgression, Embodiment, and Gendered Madness: Reading *Homeland* and Enlightened through Critical Disability Theory." *Feminist Media Studies*, vol. 16, no. 6, 2016, pp. 1000-13.

Krischer, Hayley. "Why the Bathtub Scene on Last Night's 'Homeland' Was So Uniquely Disturbing." *Salon*, 6 Oct. 2014, www.salon.com/2014/10/06/why_the_bathtub_scene_on_last_nights_home land_was_so_uniquely_disturbing/. Accessed 16 June 2021.

"Long Time Coming." *Homeland: Season 4*, written by Meredith Stiehm, directed by Lesli Linka Glatter, Showtime, 2014.

McLellan, Faith. "Mental Health and Justice: The Case of Andrea Yates." *The Lancet*, vol. 368, no. 9551, 2006, pp. 1951-54.

Moir, Aidan. "Branding the Bump: Mediating Motherhood and Celebrity Culture in Popular Media." *Journal of the Motherhood Initiative for Research and Community Involvement*, vol. 6, no. 1, 2015, pp. 50-66.

"The Mother of All Bad Guys: 'Homeland' Returns." *Women and Hollywood*. 9 Oct. 2014, womenandhollywood.com/the-mother-of-all-bad-guys-homeland-returns-d682cf3b9309/. Accessed 16 June 2021.

Negra, Diane, and Jorie Lagerwey. "Analyzing *Homeland*: Introduction." *Cinema Journal*, vol. 54, no. 4, 2015, pp. 126-31.

Nemetz, Dave. "'Homeland' Premiere: 7 Times Carrie Was an Awful Mom (Including One Really, Really Bad One)." *Yahoo!*, 6 Oct. 2014, www.yahoo.com/entertainment/bp/homeland-premiere-carrie-baby-215615280.html. Accessed 16 June 2021.

Peterson, Price. "*Homeland* Season 4 Premiere Recap: Bad Mom." *Vulture* 6 Oct. 2014, www.vulture.com/2014/10/homeland-recap-season-4-premiere-drone-queen-trylon-perisphere.html. Accessed 16 June 2021.

Podnieks, Elizabeth. "Popular Culture's Maternal Embrace." *Mediating Moms: Mothers in Popular Culture*, edited by Elizabeth Podnieks, McGill-Queen's University Press, 2012, pp. 3-32.

Saraiya, Sonia. "*Homeland*: 'The Drone Queen'/'Trylon And Perisphere.'" *AV Club*, 5 Oct. 2014, www.avclub.com/homeland-the-drone-queen-trylon-and-perisphere-1798181713. Accessed 16 June 2021.

Seidel, Linda. *Mediated Maternity: Contemporary American Portrayals of Bad Mothers in Literature and Popular Culture*. Lexington Books, 2013.

"The Star." *Homeland: Season 3*, written by Alex Gansa and Meredith Stiehm, directed by Lesli Linka Glatter, Showtime, 2013.

Steenberg, Lindsay and Yvonne Tasker. "'Pledge Allegiance': Gendered Surveillance, Crime Television, and *Homeland*." *Cinema Journal*, vol. 54, no. 4, 2015, pp. 132-38.

"Trylon and Perisphere." *Homeland: Season 4*, written by Chip Johann-essen, directed by Keith Gordon, Showtime, 2014.

Vassagar, Jeevan. "Horror Greets Jackson's Baby Dangling Stunt." *The Guardian*, 20 Nov 2002, www.theguardian.com/world/2002/nov/20/1. Accessed 16 June 2021.

Walters, Suzanna Danuta, and Laura Harrison. "Not Ready To Make Nice: Aberrant Mothers in Contemporary Culture." *Feminist Media Studies*, vol. 14, no. 1, 2014, pp. 38-55.

Wessels, Emmanuelle. "*Homeland* and Neoliberalism: Text, Paratexts and Treatment of Affective Labor." *Feminist Media Studies*, vol. 16, no. 3, 2016, pp. 511-26.

Chapter 7

Karla Homolka under Maternal Surveillance: A Critical Analysis of Mainstream and Social Media Portrayals of a Released "Monster" Who Became a Mom of Three

Rebecca Jaremko Bromwich

Introduction

Karla Homolka is Canada's most notorious female serial killer, widely understood as a "woman monster" (Vronsky). She rose to infamy in the 1990s for her role, with serial rapist and killer Paul Bernardo, in sexually torturing and killing three young women, one of whom was her sister. The horrific details of the killings, recorded on video tapes that formed part of the evidentiary record at Bernardo's trial, were the subject of a publication ban in Canada and became notorious throughout North America.(*Washington Post*). Paul Bernardo was found guilty after a four-month-long trial in 1995, was ruled a dangerous offender, and has remained in prison until today and will likely die there. Homolka, in contrast, was released after twelve years in prison, and then upon her release in 2005, she went into hiding. In 2012, Homolka was located by investigative journalist Paula Todd on the Caribbean island of Guadeloupe, living with her second husband, Thierry Bourdelais, who is the brother of her criminal defense lawyer (Todd). In April of 2016, media reports revealed that Homolka was living in Montreal, with her husband and three children, and that she had been volunteering at her children's school (Delean).

This chapter presents a critical discourse analysis of how public statements and media coverage of Homolka's presence in Montreal have intersected with problematic tropes of the monstrous mother. It critically inquires into ways the trope of the monstrous mother is questioned, reinforced, reinscribed, or refuted in these media and public texts, and examines the implications of how Homolka is represented as mother. Homolka's case, as it has been since she was first implicated in the killings, an extreme example, is an instance where it is difficult, and perhaps insensitive, to suggest that the social condemnation, othering, and monsterification of her is inappropriate.

Karla Homolka served twelve years in custody, after being sentenced in 1993 for her part in the horrific murders of at least three young women: Leslie Mahaffy, Kirsten French, and her own sister, Tammy Homolka. Over the course of the infamous trial of her spouse and accomplice, Paul Bernardo, that followed, the public and media were transfixed by her dangerousness, and as Jennifer Kilty and Sylvie Frigon have persuasively argued, paid far less attention to the con-textual reasons why she acted as she did (Kilty and Frigon).

Paul Bernardo was sentenced to life in prison with no chance of release for twenty-years and was declared a dangerous offender. In exchange for testifying against Bernardo at his trial, Karla Homolka received only a twelve-year-sentence for manslaughter. This plea bargain has been characterized as a "deal with the devil" (Williams; CBC), particularly since after her conviction was entered, videotapes were discovered that revealed Homolka had taken an active role in the killings (Frigon). Upon her release in 2005, Homolka went into hiding, only to be discovered by an investigative journalist, Paula Todd, in the Caribbean, in 2012 (Todd; Ha). After a brief surge in media attention, Homolka flew below the public radar for five years. However, in 2017, Karla Homolka emerged into the spotlight again, despite her strongly expressed objections, because media reports revealed her to be living near Montreal, in Chateauguay, Quebec, with her husband and three children, all born since her release (Delean). Self-proclaimed vigilantes have established groups and pages on social media to track Homolka's movements.

This chapter examines contemporary media and social media texts (2016–2018) that represent Karla Homolka as a mother. It discusses how, with few exceptions, these texts confirm and present Karla Homolka as a monstrous subject, a "devil," a "cunt," and a "monster"—a person who is fundamentally othered and presented as irredeemable. This chapter then goes on to critically analyze the implications of this discursive configuration of Karla Homolka as monster for other mothers in Canada and elsewhere. Most significantly, it is my argument that these representations of Homolka as monster are themselves dangerous—dangerous to her children and to her as they legitimate and incite violence against them and dangerous to readers in that they perpetuate overly simplistic stereotypes about women and mothers as monsters as well as their female and maternal subjectivities. I contend that without denying the monstrosity of her past acts, representations of Homolka as monstrous and "other" are troubling and dangerous in that they fail to appreciate how her case needs to be understood as an instance of how the human potential for harming, as well as helping, others is in us all.

The Study

This study is a critical discourse analysis of public documents produced in relation to the case of Karla Homolka's emergence in the Montreal area, in the suburb of Chateauguay. I used texts from 2016–2018 to analyze the discursive figurations of Homolka as a mother presented within them. To undertake this analysis, I looked critically at how the texts constructed gender, motherhood, and virtue or vice. I was specifically looking for the presence or absence of the construct of a monster.

The documents studied in this research were produced in two discursive sites: news media texts and social media. I looked at mainstream news media articles from April 2016 to June 2018, searching with the keyword "Homolka." Other texts studied are postings on the Facebook group Watching Karla Homolka.[1] This Facebook group has

5,849 members at the time of writing and hundreds of postings. The material examined for the purposes of this study is defined as public documents produced in relation to the known re-emergence of Karla Homolka in Quebec.

In undertaking this study, I am seeking to critically unpack dominant discourses about mothers as portrayed as monsters and how the discourses deployed in the sites studied affect the imaginable possibilities for maternal subjectivities. This study attempts to understand socially produced meanings of mothers as criminals using Karla Homolka's case as a particular event, in which confluences and tensions between ideologies and assumptions become visible (Johnson).

This study probes what Lauren Berlant calls the "caseness" (663) of Karla Homolka from 2016 to 2018. The analysis involved determining how various figures of Homolka are constructed. I work with the concept of figuration (Laurentis)—a process by which a representation is given a particular form. As Claudia Castañeda argues "a figure is the simultaneously material and semiotic product of certain [discursive] processes," where is a figuration is "a specific configuration of know-ledges, practices and power" (3-4). Accordingly, I qualitatively studied texts from media sources and social media sites to determine what figurations of Karla Homolka emerge in these cultural domains between 2016 and 2018.

Critical discourse analysis (CDA) is a methodological framework for conducting research into how discourses function as instruments of power and control; it looks at social structures and processes involved in text production. CDA is an analytical way to make visible relationships of causality that are otherwise opaque and to highlight links between texts and broader social and cultural power relations and discursive processes (Fairclough).

Findings

As Kilty and Frigon, as well as Belinda Morrissey (2003), among other scholars have noted, general popular characterizations of Karla Homolka have always been as a "monstrous" figure in Canada's criminal history. A middle class white girl with no prior criminal involvement, she was often seen in media portrayals dating back into the 1990s as "inexplicable" and "enigmatic" (Kilty). As Morrissey explores, it is overly simplistic and unsatisfactory to understand Homolka as a compliant victim of Bernardo. The videotapes and her own accounts of the marriage and murders evidence her agentic involvement, but they also do reveal Bernardo's violence towards Homolka. Kilty and Frigon critically explore how Homolka simultaneously occupies contradictory discursive spaces as both "in danger and dangerous... both the devil and the damsel in distress" (*The Enigma* 21). Homolka transgressed not only morality but also understandings of femininity (45).

The key finding in this critical discourse analysis is that the dual and contradictory construction of Homolka as both in danger and dangerous—as documented by Kilty and Frigon over the course of her case prior to 2016—shifted to a focus entirely on her dangerousness in the vast majority of the more recent popular constructions of Homolka as a mother. Homolka, once the subject of debate about whether she was a victim or villain has shifted in popular discourse: She is now clearly represented as dangerous, specifically to the children of the community in which she now resides.

Nowadays, twenty years after the crimes that made her notorious, mainstream news sources now overwhelmingly characterize Homolka as dangerous and monstrous; no articles that I looked at in this study refer to her as endangered or at risk at the time of the crimes. Homolka is characterized as a "psychopath" without refutation. She is called a "twisted," "monstrous" "serial killer"(Hawkins). In the 2017 *Global News* report that broke the story about her volunteering at a Montreal-area school, she is referred to as "one of Canada's most notorious killers." A 2017 *Toronto Star* story from the same quotes lawyer Tim Danson's characterization of her as follows: "I think she's dangerous and I certainly wouldn't take the chance with my kids to be around her." A 2017 article from the *Montreal Gazette* from the same timeframe concludes with a statement from the same lawyer as follows: "'She is a psychopath, and there is no cure for psychopathy,' Danson said. "And there could be a sequence of events that could come into play that could trigger her psychopathy'" (qtd. in Magder). Although the dominant portrayal of her former husband Paul Bernardo has long been that he is a monstrous, twisted serial killer and psychopath, at the time of the crimes, there was a tension between competing narratives of Homolka as a villain and a victim of domestic violence, with the former becoming dominant and continuing to dominate more than twenty years later.

In the Facebook group Watching Karla Homolka, she is graphically and relentlessly reviled as a "psychopath," "monster," "waste of skin," "cunt," and "disgusting piece of shit," and participants regularly post photographs of her at places in Chateauguay. They publicly track the whereabouts of Homolka together with comments that threaten and wish for harm to come to her. Not just in the uncensored world of social media but also in mainstream media texts is Homolka frequently configured as "still dangerous," as a "convicted killer," and as "a psychopath" (Warmington). In one particularly memorable turn of phrase, *Toronto Star* commentator Rosie DiManno called her a "psycho sexual vulture turned soccer mom" (DiManno). Homolka is no longer, anywhere in the documents I was able to retrieve, portrayed as a damsel in distress.

While there are no readily apparent contemporary configurations of Homolka as in danger, a certain minority of texts have suggested that she should be reincorporated into Canadian society. When former New Democratic Party leader Tom Mulcair suggested Canadians should consider forgiving Homolka, this was met with harsh criticism from media commentators and the public (Warmington). Kilty though has asked the public to forego harassing or spying on Homolka for the sake of her three young children, and, indeed, to protect the community by allowing her to integrate into it ("Watching Karla"). This article stands apart from virtually all others, particularly in the following quote:

> Allowing the stigma that Homolka will eternally carry to affect how we treat her children is a community failure and runs the risk of irrevocably damaging the mother-child relationship. While Homolka remains enigmatic in her dual identity as both victim and victimizer, it is important to consider that after 25 years, being a mother of three is now her most significant identity. Permitting Homolka to reintegrate and fade from our gaze will not only help protect her relationship with her children, it will prevent re-traumatizing the community with each media story that recounts the lurid details of this case.

Although a few texts do seek to reframe Karla Homolka as a mother and member of the community—a person whose mother-child relationship is worthy of community protection—the configuration of

Homolka as monster is dominant and seldom contested. Indeed, comments on Facebook frequently refer to visiting revenge upon her by killing one or more of her children.

My review of mainstream media texts and Facebook posts about Karla Homolka confirms that the dominant discursive configuration of Homolka is a construction of her as monstrous following the framework put forth by Jeffrey Jerome Cohen. This woman continues to be represented as a folk devil that demonstrates the social mores that cannot, and must not, be transgressed.

Analysis

The central finding of this critical discourse analysis of contemporary discursive configurations of Karla Homolka in the media, both mainstream and social media texts, is that the overwhelmingly dominant portrayal of her is as a monster. This finding can be better understood if analyzed with reference to Cohen's framework of understanding the discursive and social purposes of monsters. Cohen argues that the social purpose of monstrosity is cautionary. Monsters function as a warning and a demonstration to others:

> Every monster is ... a double narrative, two living stories: one that describes how the monster came to be and another, its testimony, detailing what cultural use the monster serves. The monster of prohibition exists to demarcate the bonds that hold together that system of relations we call culture, to call horrid attention to the borders that cannot—must not—be crossed. (13)

Configurations of Karla Homolka as monstrous in media representations of her serve the discursive and social purpose of reinforcing currently held definitions of vice and virtue. Certainly, even beyond Canada, Homolka has become a significant symbol of what is beyond redemption and unacceptable in our social order. In writing this, I find myself conflicted: on the one hand, I want to analytically resist this demonization of a person, and, on the other, this particular individual has earned condemnation in ways that I find personally morally legitimate.

The monstrous configuration of Karla Homolka in media discourses can also be analysed with reference to Adrienne Rich's notion of motherhood as both experience and institution, as she articulated it in her germinal text, *Of Woman Born*, and it is especially useful to read this representation in the context of that text's final chapter, "Violence: The Heart of Maternal Darkness." In this chapter, Rich explores ambiguities and potentialities intrinsic to maternal subjectivities that are "troubling." When Rich asks, "What woman has not dreamed of going over the edge?" (263), she makes a radical call for empathy. With this call, she begins a reflection for future maternal thinkers to consider that "instead of recognizing the institution of violence of patriarchal motherhood, society labels those women who finally erupt in violence as psychopathological" (Rich 263). I would argue that the current dominant representation of Homolka as violent and psychopathological—while failing to contextualize her past acts—is itself actively dangerous, laying a foundation for others to act violently against her and her children.

Paradoxically and ironically, then, the discursive configuration of Homolka as a monster is in itself dangerous. In explicitly and implicitly calling for her to be "hounded," "lashed," "punished," (DiManno), and killed, as well as tortured by the deaths of her own children, discursive configurations of Homolka as a monster lays discursive groundwork that legitimates violent acts against Homolka. Furthermore, the discursive configuration of Homolka as a monster also puts others at risk of arrest and criminalization. Those participating in vigilante and voyeur campaigns to surveil and harass Homolka run the risk of incurring criminal charges for harassment or uttering threats. Charges might legitimately be laid under s. 264 of the Criminal Code of Canada in relation to harassment and s. 264.1 in relation to uttering threats. Furthermore, all who participate in those online groups might be charged for aiding and abetting in the offence pursuant to s. 21 of the Criminal Code, which provides for party liability or even with conspiracy pursuant to s. 465 of the Code if the threatening or harassing conduct amounts to an indictable offence.

As the backlash against Mulcair's "forgiveness" remark shows, any empathy with Karla Homolka is a disturbing notion for most Canadians; her crimes are at the centre of our collective horror and moral outrage. Indeed, I have found it difficult to even work on this analysis and this chapter because any understanding of Homolka that moves beyond condemnation to additional considerations is socially taboo. She is defined as monstrous in popular culture, and this monstrosity has solidified over time. Yet in her contemporary embodiment as a middle-aged, middle-class, white mother, she also presents as a mundane, even privileged, figure: Homolka's mainstream motherhood challenges us because it engages the concepts of stability of identity as well as maternal subjectivities and intentionality.

Homolka's current primary identity is constructed as dangerous to her community and Canadian society for her camouflage within the dominant mainstream—she walks among us. Paradoxically, just as her criminal case represents an edge case pushing thinking about the agency of women in new directions, so too does her existence as a mother challenge stereotypical and widely held understandings about mothers. If she can exist among us and be capable of such evil in her past, this has implications about how maternal virtue is thought about, revealing that so-called good mothers are more complex than is regularly assumed.

Although the dominant configuration of Karla Homolka continues to be as a monstrous figure in social media and mainstream media portrayals, she continues to also be present as an edge case that challenges conventional understandings of maternal identities. For the posts on the Watching Karla Homolka Facebook group, for example, it takes discursive work for texts to reconcile her conduct, and apparent experiences, as a mother—which are very compliant with normative or average behaviour, doing such things as volunteering at a school, going to a grocery store, and waiting in a doctor's office—with her discursive configuration as a monster. Despite being widely assumed to be a monstrous, evil figure, Karla Homolka appears to be living in compliance with mainstream understandings of middle-class, white motherhood. The fact of her continued existence living in an identity of mundane, suburban maternality within the dominant social group opens doors for wider understandings of diverse maternal subjectivities and specifically troubles punitive ideas about criminality.

An intersectional feminist analysis of representations of Homolka as mother, which configure her unambiguously as monster, reveals these representations to be troubling. By completely othering her, configurations of Homolka as monster lay the foundation for aggressive, criminal, and even violent behaviour by members of the community.

Ironically, and horrifyingly, her failure, in the 1990s, to treat the victims of her murders and sexual assaults with Bernardo with any humanity or compassion becomes echoed in the texts produced by those who seek to watch her. By failing to consider or empathize with any aspect of herself or her mothering, these representations confirm and reinforce multiple layers and interlocking systems of power that further marginalize mothers who have been criminalized or incarcerated, whether in the present or in the past. Even in the face of discursive constructions of her that continue to portray her as a monster, Homolka's persistence in maternal averageness troubles notions that people who do terrible things cannot change and suggests that, at least sometimes, people with problematic—and even horrifying—histories can go on to live mundane suburban lives. Understanding her story more empathetically might provide men, women, and mothers in particular with helpful and necessary insight into the dark potentialities human beings share. I would argue that representing Karla Homolka with more compassion is both a frightening and culturally necessary thing to do.

Conclusion

This chapter has presented a critical discourse analysis of documents from mainstream media texts as well as Facebook posts from the online group Watching Karla Homolka. The analysis has revealed that contemporary configurations of Karla Homolka no longer present a tension between her dangerousness and existence in danger but overwhelmingly present her as a dangerous monster. Even so, they are complex, as a few texts do actively resist tropes of the monstrous mother.

I have argued that the public fascination with Karla Homolka reinforces ideas about what is socially condoned and what transgresses morality and femininity. When social media and mainstream media texts configure Homolka as a monster, they reinscribe and reinforce the social, moral, and gendered boundaries of acceptable femininity and acceptable maternity. As I have noted in this chapter, it may indeed be that her case troubles critiques of those boundaries and reinforces the moral legitimacy of the discursive process of constructing representations of certain people as monsters. Thereby, although these representations do social work that we should all support in condemning murder and sexual assault, they also reinforce the confining and rigid traditional boundaries of discourses of motherhood. At the same time, the present existence of Karla Homolka as a suburban, middle-class mother—in all visible respects now compliant with institutional expectations of motherhood—troubles common understandings of subjectivity, agency, and identity. This situation has resonances with what Sharon Pollock said with reference to her 1982 play about convicted killer Lizzie Borden: "All of us are capable of murder given the right situation" (qtd. in Wallace and Zimmerman 123). In the face of media configurations of her that represent her as a monster—and in the face of irrefutable and uncontested evidence to which she has confessed that in her past, she did monstrous things— Homolka has been able to now, at least apparently, live differently.

This chapter has absolutely not sought to recuperate the virtue of Karla Homolka, either in the contemporary context or in the past. In no uncertain terms, I condemn the acts for which she was convicted. Without taking any position on what Homolka now deserves, however, there can be no question, as Kilty writes, that her children are not at fault for what transpired all those years ago and are at strong risk of harm from the negative attention. Furthermore, social media configurations of Homolka are clearly indicative of voyeurism. There is vigilantism on the part of those obsessing over her case. Troubling aspects of the public fascination with her that are, I would contend, fed and legitimized by discursive configurations of her as monstrous. In this chapter, I have argued that these representations of Homolka speak to the importance of context, both to her conduct and to that of others; the ugliness and cruelty of these representations begin to mirror the cruelty of her own crimes.

At this stage, several decades after her conviction, and more than fifteen years since her release, self-help vigilantism that finds its basis in a configuration of Homolka as a monster ironically presents danger to the vigilantes themselves. Should they take action against her, this is likely to only lead to more charges, more people in prison, and more crime. Paradoxically, and tragically, public fixation on the configuration of Homolka as a monstrous mother is what likely poses the greatest current risk of harm to her children. Representations of Homolka on social media are troubling in ways that define the watchers at least as much as they define Homolka, and in ways that put those watchers at risk of arrest themselves. I am reminded of the iconic quote from Friedrich Nietzsche: "He who fights with monsters should look to it that he himself does not become a monster ... when you gaze long into the abyss the abyss also gazes into you" (Nietzsche 146).

I would concur in Nietzsche's analysis that in order to avoid becoming monsters, we must admit and feel, at least analytically, the truth of certain dark things about ourselves. This has resonances with Rich's admonition that empathy towards mothers who do monstrous things can help us better understand ourselves. On a personal level, the imperative for empathy with those who do things that are unforgivable is of particular personal significance for me in my role as a crown attorney, who prosecutes individuals, including women who are mothers, for their crimes. The case of Karla Homolka and the Facebook group tasking itself with watching her provides a case study for contemplating this tension: What is monstrous in Karla Homolka as a mother, as a sister, as a wife, as a person, is a human problem. She has done terrible things, but perhaps she is not so unlike us. Maybe what is most frightening about the acts of Karla Homolka for which she was convicted, which is revealed by her current life, is that she is, after all, a person who is quite ordinary. It would be culturally productive to reimagine Karla Homolka outside of a victim-villain binary and not as a monster. I would argue that Canadians have much to gain towards assuring our own ethical conduct from considering how she is not a monster outside of humanity but an example of the complexity of mothers' subjectivities—the potential of mothers, the potential of all of us acting in our own lives, for doing harm as well as good.

Endnotes

1. www.facebook.com/WatchingKarlaH/

Works Cited

Berlant, Lauren. "On the Case." *Critical Inquiry*, vol. 33, no. 4, 2007, pp. 663-67.

Castañeda, Claudia. *Figurations: Child, Bodies, Worlds.* Duke University Press, 2002.

Cohen, Jeffrey Jerome. "Monster Culture (Seven Theses)." *Monster Theory*, edited by Jeffrey Jerome Cohen, University of Minnesota Press, 1996, pp. 3-25.

Criminal Code of Canada SC 1985, c. 46.

Delean, Paul. "Châteauguay Parents on Edge after Hearing Karla Homolka Is among Them." *Montreal Gazette*, 20 Apr. 2016, montreal gazette.com/news/local-news/school-board-reassures-parents-after-rumours-of-karla-hamolkas-return-spread-in-chateauguay. Accessed 20 June 2021.

DiManno, Rosie. "Karla Homolka Should Be Hounded for the Rest of Her Life." *The Toronto Star*, 2 June 2017, www.thestar.com/news/gta/2017/06/02/karla-homolka-should-be-hounded-for-the-rest-of-her-life-dimanno.html. Accessed 20 June 2021.

Fairclough, Norman. *Critical Discourse Analysis: The Critical Study of Language*. Longman, 1995.

"Key Events in the Bernardo/Homolka Case." *CBC News*, 17 June 2010, www.cbc.ca/news/canada/key-events-in-the-bernardo-homolka-case-1.933128. Accessed 20 June 2021.

"Convicted Serial Killer Karla Homolka Volunteering at Montreal School." *Global National News*, 31 May 2017, globalnews.ca/news/3491735/karla-homolka-school-montreal/. Accessed 20 June 2021.

Ha, Tu Thanh. "Karla Homolka Lives in Guadeloupe and Has Three Children, New Book Reveals." *Globe and Mail*, 21 June 2012, www.theglobeandmail.com/news/national/karla-homolka-lives-in-guadeloupe-and-has-three-children-new-book-reveals/article 4360378/. Accessed 20 June 2021.

Hawkins, Erik. "Who is Karla Homolka from the Canadian Ken and Barbie Serial Killers?" *True Crime Buzz*, 19 Dec. 2019, www.oxygen.com/true-crime-buzz/karla-homolka-luka-magnotta-dont-f--k-with-cats-paul-bernardo. Accessed 20 June 2021.

Johnson, Rebecca. *Taxing Choices: The Intersection of Class, Gender, Parenthood and the Law.* University of British Columbia Press, 2002.

Kilty, Jennifer. "Watching Karla, 27 Years Later." *Winnipeg Free Press* 7 May 2016, www.winnipegfreepress.com/opinion/analysis/watch ing-karla-27-years-later-378490126.html. Accessed 20 June 2021.

Kilty, Jennifer, and Frigon, Sylvie. "Karla Homolka—From a Woman in Danger to a Dangerous Woman". *Women and Criminal Justice*, vol. 17, no. 4., 2017, pp. 37-61.

Kilty, Jennifer and Frigon, Sylvie. *The Enigma of A Violent Woman: A Critical Examination of the Case of Karla Homolka*. Routledge, 2016.

Laurentis, Teresa de. *Figures of Resistance: Essays in Feminist Theory*. Teresa de Laurentis, 2007.

Magder, Jason. "Parents Who Criticized Karla Homolka Say Greaves Academy Asked Them to Leave." *Montreal Gazette*, 17 May 2017, montrealgazette.com/news/local-news/greaves-academy-parents-who-criticized-karla-homolka-say-school-asked-them-to-leave. Accessed 20 June 2021.

Morrissey, Belinda. *When Women Kill: Questions of Agency and Subjectivity*. Routledge: London and New York, 2003.

Nietzsche, Friederich. *Beyond Good and Evil*. Translated by Walter Kaufmann. Random House, 2000

Rich, Adrienne. *Of Woman Born: Motherhood as Experience and Institution*. Norton and Company, 1986.

Todd, Paula. *Finding Karla: How I Tracked Down an Elusive Serial Killer and Discovered a Mother of Three*. Canadian Writers Group/The Atavist , 2012.

Vronsky, Peter. *Female Serial Killers: How and Why Women Become Monsters*. Berkley Books, 2007.

Wallace, Robert, and Cynthia Zimmerman, editors. *The Work: Conversations with English Canadian Playwrights*. Coach House, 1982.

"This Story Can't Be Told in Canada. And So All Canada Is Talking About It..." *The Washington Post*, 23 Nov. 1993.

Warmington, Joe. "NDP Leader Tom Mulcair Suggests Forgiveness for Karla Homolka. Hell No." *The Toronto Sun*, 1 June 2017, torontosun.com/2017/06/01/ndp-leader-tom-mulcair-suggests-forgiveness-for-karla-homolka-hell-no. Accessed 20 June 2021.

Williams, Stephen. *Karla: A Pact with the Devil*. Random House Canada/ Seal Books, 2004.

Chapter 8

"A Victim Twice": Maternal Violence in the Poetry of Ai

Jessica Turcat

The poet Ai, known for her unflinching dramatic monologues, published eight books of poetry and won the 1999 National Book Award for Poetry. Her books don short titles that splay recriminations across their jacket covers: *Cruelty* (1973), *Killing Floor* (1978), *Sin* (1986), *Fate* (1991), *Greed* (1993), *Vice* (1999), *Dread* (2003), and her final book, published posthumously, *No Surrender* (2012). Violence is laced throughout Ai's poetry, and many critics argue that it is the central theme that spans her five decades of publications. In the article "I Have Killed My Black Goat: Violence in Ai's Poetry," Leslie McGrath describes the unrelenting violence in her poems as Ai's "medium as much as clay might be a sculptor's" (33). No specific segment of the human population in Ai's poetry escapes unscathed; every demographic is unhinged by violence. The moment when the reader wants to close her book, refusing to turn another page, thinking that the horror meted out on the next line is too much to bear—that is where Ai's poetry declares its home.

Ai repeatedly forces her readers to witness the horrors that children endure at the hands of their mothers. These monstrous mothers starve, beat, and molest their children. They personify subjects that most authors, even the nerviest poets, never attempt to confront. However, when applying a feminist analysis focused on the monstrous actions, one can trace a cyclical history of gender-based violence that these mothers, particularly working-class mothers, suffer, endure and ultimately try to overcome by resisting their own victimhood, often at the hands of the male characters portrayed alongside them.

Since her work is almost exclusively written in the form of persona poems, Ai can reach far back in history, meld an array of women's voices, and give new perspective to their nightmarish experiences. Instead of asking "What factors make one write such horrors?" the more culturally relevant question that must be addressed in order to be *au fait* with Ai's poetry is "What factors make one commit such horrors?" This feminist maternal analysis of the poet Ai's rendition of the monstrous mother situates motherhood as both experience and institution, as presented in Adrienne Rich's *Of Woman Born*. Rich elaborates on how maternal violence is a product of patriarchy:

> Because we have all had mothers, the institution affects all women, and—though differently—all men. Patriarchal violence and callousness are often visited through women upon child-ren—not only the "battered" child but the children desperately pushed, cajoled, manipulated, the children dependent on one uncertain, weary woman for their day-in, day-out care and emotional sustenance, the male children who grow up believing that a woman is nothing so much as an emotional climate made to soothe and reassure, or an emotional whirlwind bent on their destruction. (282)

Ai's monstrous narrators decry their roles as mothers and women within patriarchy by spurring on abusive acts and perpetrating abuse themselves, at times with the argument that what they are doing is for the benefit of the child. Some of Ai's monstrous narrators even opt out of becoming mothers altogether by choosing to end their pregnancies. This chapter will characterize abortion as defined in Rich's *Of Woman Born* in the following manner: "Abortion is violence: a deep, desperate violence inflicted by a woman upon, first of all, herself. It is the offspring, and will continue to be the accuser, of a more pervasive and prevalent violence, the violence of rapism" (274). When reading the entirety of her work, the poet Ai reminds us that we are all damaged humans, all bastards, born of resilient but often desperate women and that if we live long enough to be mired in our own lies and betrayals, it is only because even before our first silent stirrings, our mothers chose to save us, to let us live.

One commonality that emerges while analyzing these monstrous mothers is the direct connection between their own plights—involving the violence to which they have been subjected throughout their lives and the violence that they inflict or allow to be inflicted upon their offspring. This parallelism between mother and child makes these narratives all the more poignant. Even though Ai's characters are presented as spectacles of abjection, because of their failure to act out and embody cultural ideals associated with their sex, they represent real women—real children—caught in a cycle of violence that few have the courage to illuminate. Rich contends: "Instead of recognizing the institution of violence of patriarchal motherhood, society labels those women who finally erupt in violence as psychopathological" (267). Ai's poetry does not reduce these narrators to desultory psychopaths. Even though they may be ignorant of the larger matrices of oppression in which they act out their maternal violence, by underscoring the cyclical nature of generational violence within the lives of these women, one is better able to recognize the patterns within "the institution of violence of patriarchal motherhood." This chapter provides a close textual reading of seven poems by the poet Ai that depict monstrous mothers and illustrates how, in each case, the woman has been "a victim twice"—by experience and institution—and further examines how that woman employs violence later in life to ward off her own victimhood, resisting being a victim in order to gain control over her sense of self. Through this analysis, violence is emphasized not merely as a rhetorical device used to evoke an emotional response in the readers but rather as a necessary consequence of representing the voices of victims often overlooked in society because of their doubled positioning as victims and abusers, although the individual women routinely refuse both labels.

In Ai's sixth book, *Vice: New and Selected Poems*, the 1999 National Book Award Winner, the poem "False Witness" portrays a mother addressing her six-year-old daughter, who according to the mother is a "cruel mistress" destined to make men suffer (lines 31-32). The mother narrates how she coaches her daughter in the "art of seduction" (45) by encouraging and willingly participating in the incestuous rape of the girl with the girl's father, even to the point of molesting her with a stick. Although this is one of Ai's most notable poems on maternal violence, "False Witness" is not the first poem in which the poet Ai delves into such subject matter. In fact, the dramatic monologue "Salome," published nearly a decade earlier in *Sin*, also presents a mother and father emotionally and sexually abusing their fifteen-year-old daughter, who narrates the poem. Ai relies on biblical allusions throughout the poem, which ends with the daughter being decapitated by her mother. Similarly, "False Witness" ends with the monstrous mother choking the daughter to "childhood's end" (95). This could imply that the mother has killed her daughter or that the illusion of innocence (i.e. childhood) that the daughter experienced up until that point has ended. Either way, the extreme violence in the poem leaves the reader questioning how a mother could perform such horrors on her own child.

When considering the savage ending of "False Witness," McGrath raises the following questions: "How can this mother not feel guilt about extending the chain of incest? How can she not see that she is trying to kill a part of herself with which she cannot come to terms?" (38). The mother does, however, express some wavering about the violent actions with the statement: "At first, I didn't even want you to be as debauched / as I had been, when my father first came into my bed, / but instead of suffering, you thrived" (34-36). The first part of this statement illustrates that at least initially the mother had wanted a different reality for her daughter. Ai's presentation of this monstrous mother is complicated by the narrator's admittance to her own victimization as a girl who bore incestuous rape by her own father. McGrath's final question raised—"At what point did she cross the line between innocent victim of incest and perpetrator of unconscionable violence toward both her husband and daughter?" (38)—seems to be impossible to answer even for the narrator who explains that she sifts through her memories in order to "try to find the woman / who became a mother / with no other thought than of revenge" (41-43), which suggests that her desire for revenge is in part due to the abuse that she endured as a child. The narrator warns her daughter: "I won't be a victim twice" (56). Despite the mother's attempted resistance to being forced into the position of victim again, she is already portrayed as faced with the double violence of childhood incestuous rape and of institutionalized motherhood. The mother's involved circumstance would inevitably be sensed by the daughter, for as Rich argues, "A mother's victimization does not merely humiliate her, it mutilates the daughter who watches her for clues as to what it means to be a woman" (246-47). Perhaps that is why the mother actively resists her return to the position of victim while addressing the daughter.

The cyclical nature of generational abuse presented in the poem is quickly undercut by the addition of the following question from the mother: "Am I lying to myself to ease my guilt?" (38). The admission to a possible semblance of guilt on the mother's part becomes linked with the question of whether or not the narrator is lying about the abuse she suffered at the hands of her father while growing up. This uncertainty is a critical aspect to understanding the multiplicities at work, as evidenced by the fact that the woman's identity as a "false witness" is emphasized as the title of the poem. The reader is left questioning the validity of the woman's statements, much like most of society does when a news story involving maternal violence emerges in our cultural consciousness. Every word she utters is scrutinized. Indeed, the monstrous mother is forever labelled and judged as a false witness, and no consideration is given for her personal or cultural positioning as a victim.

Several of Ai's poems present the familial home as a place where abuse thrives between generations, as family members repeatedly commit violent acts and repeatedly cover up those crimes for members within the household. The poem "The Secret" (*Dread*), narrated by a young girl who can only talk to her dolls and teddy bear, underscores how silence between family members operates to hide violence within the family home. The mother has killed the baby brother, Danny, by striking him on the head with a glass decanter, and the daughter is faced with the aftermath, as she watches the monstrous mother unravel and the father attempt to cover up the traumatic occurrences. The poem "Ice Cream Man" (*Greed*) also illustrates the haunting cyclical nature of abuse. When the narrator, the Ice Cream Man, seduces a little girl named Sherry, he slips into detailing the sexual acts that his "mommy and Stan, [his] brand-new daddy" force him into performing. The most detailed example of the cyclical nature of generational abuse is portrayed in "Reconciliation," one of Ai's longest poems, which is divided into four sections: "Birth Mother," "Oedipus, The Son," "Motherhood," and "Fatherhood." The poem functions as a conversation between four family members (birth mother, son, adoptive mother, and adoptive father) and depicts a pattern of ongoing control using emotional, physical, and sexual forms of abuse, punctuated by references to alcohol abuse. A close analysis of the four sections of this poem reveals how through the entanglement of generational violence and victimhood, the monstrous maternal figure emerges within the intimate space of the familial home.

The poem begins with the biological mother speaking to her son about the domestic violence between her and the son's biological father. The cyclical nature of domestic violence (also known as intimate terrorism), from which it can be nearly impossible to break free, is emphasized by the way the mother describes herself in the following reflection: "I was a blue and black bruise / without the will to choose another way of living" (28-29). Through her narrative, it is revealed that after the son's birth, the mother leaves him at an orphanage and, once again, returns to the abusive relationship. Years later, after the biological father has died, the mother tracks down her son and finds him drunk at a bar. Upon seeing him, she declares: "I knew those eyes / and I hated you. Inside my love was a hate / as fierce as it had ever been for [the abusive birth father]" (61-63). After this recognition, the birth mother punches her son. It is as if the similarities (the eyes, the drunkenness) between the son and the father triggers the mother's hatred, and violence immediately ensues. In the article "The Method of Ai," Yusef Komunyakaa depicts the familial situation presented in many of Ai's poems: "The characters hurt each other out of fear of being hurt, and often they are doubly hurt" (12). Although the son had done nothing to warrant the mother's aggression, he is still met with her reactionary violence because he physically resembles her abuser. Thus, the victimized mother directs her anger for the birth father towards the son.

The son also endures physical abuse from his adoptive mother. In the second section of the poem "Oedipus, The Son," he narrates how, at sixteen years of age, his adoptive mother slaps him and squeezes his genitalia:

I'm too surprised to move, or even breathe,
until she squeezes me there.
I fall to my knees,
then onto my side, curled in a ball.
Even when the pain has eased,
I lie staring at the maple trees,

whose green leaves are turning gold.
Finally, I'm numb in a way that makes me whole,
makes me her son,
because she'd goaded me into it at last
and now that I am,
she wants to tear me to pieces
like those rags she uses
to wipe my dad's spilled drinks from the floor. (84-97)

The poet Ai, not one to shy away from using explicit diction, relies on the euphemistic "there" when referring to the son's penis and scrotum. The specific imagery that the narrator does not include betrays as much as the lengthier descriptions provided. Since the dramatic monologue is narrated by the son, the use of "there" distances him from the bodily abuse inflicted by his adoptive mother. Based on this purposeful omission, it can be argued that the son is still so traumatized by the event that he chooses to avoid using explicit language while articulating what happened that afternoon. Later, the son goes into his adoptive mother's bedroom and has sex with her, an act that she encourages by exposing her nipples and, as the son observes, "she lifts her head, smiles and lies back" (104). Afterwards, the son grabs his suitcase and leaves the house. He recounts that he took his "mother's body / not out of love, or even hate, / but merely out of self-defense" (135-37). The son's reference to his adoptive mother's desire to tear him to pieces as well as his admission that he was acting in self-defence indicate that the sexual act with his adoptive mother is not consensual but rather a form of abuse. At merely sixteen, the son runs away from home in order to escape future abuse, but he remains haunted by what happened, since his section starts with his realization that "all my runaways lead / to my adoptive mother" (71-72).

The third section of the poem, "Motherhood," is told from the perspective of the adoptive mother, who directly addresses the son. Her chiding tone mocks and even threatens the son with inflammatory statements like: "Love is your mother" (159) and the lengthier explanation:

only mother love can save you, son
in a way that can't be measured, or understood.
It is a charm that only mothers possess,

even foster ones,
a spell that won't let go of you
until you give in, or are destroyed. (195-200)

Even though she did not endure pregnancy and birth, the adoptive mother is still portrayed as having been victimized by both the experience and institution of patriarchal motherhood. Unlike the other characters, particularly the male characters, throughout all of these monstrous mother poems, the women are routinely engaged in domestic chores; the adoptive mother in "Reconciliation" cleans spilled drinks and sets the table for family dinner. She is serving the husband and son, fulfilling her expected duties of patriarchal motherhood within the private domain of the family home. Yet she is met with abuse. The adoptive father is verbally abusive and blames her for both his and his son's alcoholism. She recounts how she suffers verbal abuse from the son too: "You tell me I'm a whore / like your real mother. All women are" (184-85). It is from her narrative that the reader learns what factors precipitate her slapping her adoptive son; it was in response to his verbal abuse. At the conclusion of her narrative the adoptive mother asserts, "I *am* your mother, son / and it is awful. It is bliss" (231-32). The juxtaposition between the words "awful" and "bliss" exemplifies how she is conflicted by her role as mother, even while emphasizing her relationship to the adoptive son. This is especially antithetical in light of the fact that she just had sex with her adoptive son—a taboo for biological and adoptive mothers in any society.

As "Reconciliation" unfolds, it becomes apparent that the son is held by two monstrous mother figures: his birth mother and adoptive mother. Yet both women are portrayed as doubly victimized by their roles within patriarchy. Although their monstrous acts of aggression against the son cannot be systematically excused, the poet Ai presents them in such a way as to force the reader to look at the factors that led to the abuse in the first place. As Rich argues, this powerful effect on women's lives cannot be understated: "Motherhood without autonomy, without choice, is one of the quickest roads to a sense of having lost control" (268-69). By presenting the women as victims of various social and cultural patriarchal pressures, their acts of violence within the family unit become linked with attempts to gain or assert power and control, comparable to the way perpetrators of intimate partner violence strategically dominate their victims. Yet even the adoptive father is not portrayed as a stereotypical out-of-control, raging alcoholic wifebeater, which is a familiar trope in popular cultural depictions of intimate partner violence.

The fourth and final section of the poem "Fatherhood" includes a surprising amount of tenderness, as the adoptive father wrestles with his own cowardliness when contemplating his desire to leave his adulterous wife. McGrath, in her analysis of the violence present in Ai's poetry, underscores the link between love and violence:

> When we think of intimacy, we tend to think of love and its physical correspondent, sexual satisfaction. Intimacy in Ai's work is achieved not through sex but through violence. The targeting, pursuit, seduction, vanquishment, and—later— remembering of a love affair all have their concomitants in acts of violence, particularly the intimate violence which Ai depicts so masterfully. (35)

Despite his abusive portrayal, the adoptive father's love for his wife becomes apparent by the end of the poem. Through his monologue, directed at the adoptive son, the father corrects his son's previous use of the word "whore" to describe the adoptive mother; instead, he says she is a queen "who uses men to do her bidding" (276). The "bidding," with which the father is faced in the final section of the poem, is driving his wife to Chicago after she comes to him pregnant, two months after the sexual encounter with their adoptive son, and in need of an abortion to be safe from scandal. The father bribes a nurse and takes the "chunk of discarded meat" (247) home in a jar small enough to hold "raspberry preserves" (312). The father uses the pronoun "it" four times in the nine lines detailing the aborted fetal tissue (240-48). Again, just as the son avoided specific details when recounting the adoptive mother's physical abuse, the use of the euphemistic pronoun "it" by the adoptive father places distance between him and the reality of the situation that he faces. The father further emphasizes the hurt he feels by stating "the nameless thing I'm burying / so deep in my heart no one but her can ever find it / and she will never try" (314-16). By the end of the poem, it is obvious that the adoptive father will not leave his wife, the adoptive mother. Even more striking, given its title, the poem offers little in terms of reconciliation between the family members. The obvious conclusion being that the cycle of abuse will continue, the characters will remain hurting and being hurt.

Though the figure of the monstrous mother appears in all of Ai's books, it was not until a 2010 interview with Janet Varnum, fifteen days before she died, that the poet Ai revealed the following: "['Child Beater'] was my first poem about abuse. I was able to draw somewhat on my mother, who was quite a threatening figure, actually. 'If your aunt offers you candy,' she would say, 'don't take anything or I'll kill you,' And that woman really believed in whipping, and I was able to draw on that" (119-20). In "Child Beater" (*Cruelty*), there is no father figure who is exposed as an abuser, only the mother serving as narrator while she inflicts cruelty on her daughter. This differs from the earlier examined poems, "False Witness" and "Reconciliation," in which Ai presents monstrous mothers who openly examine their own positioning as victims at the hands of patriarchal violence. In "Child Beater," however, only the mother is presented. The mother starves her daughter and forces her to crawl on the floor to eat and drink from dog bowls, all while she is beating her with a leather belt and preparing to choke her with a dog's chain leash.

In "Child Beater," the mother makes comparisons between herself and her daughter throughout—a narrative device similar to that in "False Witness." While strangling the daughter in "False Witness," the mother denies any similarities between her own self and her offspring: "I stare at you, looking for a sign / that you and I are kin, / but you are an imitation of the diamond that I am" (89-91). Even with this denial, it is apparent that the narrator is forced to confront her physical relationship with her daughter. Rather than calling attention to the sexual abuse by their fathers that they both suffered, the mother in "Child Beater" reflects on the similarities between her body and her daughter's by commenting: "Her body, somehow fat, though I feed her only once a day, reminds me of my own just after she was born" (7-8). The mother moves from reflecting on how the distended stomach of her daughter's emaciated body resembles her postpartum body to how her pregnant body felt with the daughter inside of her: "I still can't forget how I felt. / How heavy it feels to look at her" (9-10). The burden of carrying her daughter in pregnancy still weighs on the mother seven years later. Rich emphasizes this connection in the following manner: "Mothers and daughters have always exchanged with each other—

beyond the verbally transmitted lore of female survival—a knowledge that is subliminal, subversive, preverbal: the knowledge flowing between two alike bodies, one of which has spent nine months inside the other" (220-21).

Although the mother does not openly admit that she is acting out of revenge, as does the mother in "False Witness," one could argue that, at least to some extent, the mother's violent actions against her daughter are in retaliation for the toll that the victimizing experience of pregnancy and motherhood took on her. Rich analyzes this common yet often unexpressed occurrence:

> Typically, under patriarchy, the mother's life is exchanged for the child; her autonomy as a separate being seems fated to conflict with the infant she will bear. The self-denying, self-annihilative role of the Good Mother (linked implicitly with suffering and with the repression of anger) will spell the "death" of the woman or girl who once had hopes, expectations, and fantasies *for herself*—especially when those hopes and fantasies have never been acted-on…. Even a woman who gives up her child for adoption at birth has undergone irreversible physio-logical and psychic changes in the process of carrying it to term and bearing it. (161-162)

The narrator in "Child Beater" exemplifies a mother who "can't forget" what she exchanged for her child and transfers her own suffering and anger onto her daughter.

This form of violent retribution also appears in the dramatic mono-logue "The Mother's Tale," which was first published in *Sin* (1986). The fact that the poem begins with the mother stating, "Once when I was young" (1), emphasizes how she is thinking back to incidents in her youth, before she was saddled with children, while her son, Juanito, is preparing for his wedding. The mother again reiterates, "I was young, free" (13), before raising the question: "But Juanito, how free is a woman?—/ born with Eve's sin between her legs, / and inside her" (14-16). The narrator could be referencing the sexual desire that women possess, but "Eve's sin" was not of a carnal nature. Rather, in accord-ance with the Genesis creation account, Eve was punished for her defiant disobedience of God's instructions in order to pursue her own personal desire for knowledge. When reading this passage with consideration for the bodily knowledge that women inherit through the experience of pregnancy and childbirth ["between her legs, / and inside her"], one must consider another patriarchal institution— religion—alongside the institution of motherhood: "In Judeo-Christian theology, woman's pain in childbirth is punishment from God.... Since the curse laid on Eve in Genesis was taken literally well into the nineteenth century, the mother in labor had to expect to suffer; but what was even more significant, it was assumed until the last three decades that she must suffer *passively*" (Rich 117).

As the poem continues, the mother instructs her son: "You must beat Rosita often.... And she must be pregnant always" (26,31). Given the religious rhetoric employed throughout the poem, it can be argued that pregnancy is viewed as another form of punishment executed by the husband against his wife. The mother continues:

> if not with child
> then with the knowledge
> that she is alive because of you.
> That you can take her life
> more easily than she creates it,
> that suffering is her inheritance from you
> and through you, from Christ,
> who walked on his mother's body
> to be the King of Heaven. (32-40)

Here, "knowledge" is framed as a weapon to be used against the soon-to-be wife. In *Eve and Adam: Genesis 2-3 Reread*, Phyllis Tribble argues the following: "Subjugation and supremacy are perversions of creation. Through disobedience, the woman has become slave. Her initiative and freedom vanish. The man is corrupted also, for he has become master, ruling over the one who is his God-given equal. The subordination of female to male signifies their shared sin" (80). With Tribble's interpretation of the Genesis myth, all humans are condemned and in need of salvation. Christianity presents both male and female, husband and wife, as ensnared by their gender roles: "Suffering is her inheritance from you" ("The Mother's Tale" 38). Although the husband is positioned as the one who provides and potentially takes his wife's life, the instruction is doled out through the monstrous mother. Rich reminds her readers: "The institution of motherhood cannot be touched or seen.... It must go on being evoked, so that women never again forget that our many fragments of lived experience belong to a whole which is not of our creation" (281). Indeed, the future mother-in-law bolsters the institution of patriarchal motherhood, stripping any bodily knowledge and creative power the pregnant woman may possess and placing the control in the hands of her son as a future husband. The only outlook for Rosita, according to her future mother-in-law, is an inheritance of suffering from the husband and, in turn, Christ. As Rich explains, "The absence of respect for women's lives is written into the heart of male theological doctrine, into the structure of the patriarchal family, and into the very language of patriarchal ethics" (274). Both family and religion function as intimately connected institutions that relegate women to subordinated positions, both inside and outside of the home, in their current lives and their so-called promised afterlives. However, religion is sometimes presented as a salve for the suffering characters in Ai's poems, particularly for the female characters.

In "Motherhood, 1951," one of Ai's later autobiographical poems that references "Baby Florence,"[1] the female narrator turns to Saint Patrick in a plea to drive the snakes from her house as legend claims he did from Ireland. The pregnant female narrator takes solace in the religious doctrines and recounts: "They say I am protected from harm / Because the Virgin Mary put her heel / Upon a snake's head and crushed it / For the sake of all pregnant women" (59-62). As the poem progresses, the narrator kills a snake "that crawls about the room / without fear of discovery" (55-56) and while doing so goes into labour. Thinking back to the incident, the mother connects her own plight with that of the snake she killed, only to realize that "she was an expectant mother too" (126) as "a tiny bunch of eggs spill[ed] out of her" (125). Although the mother proves that she is capable of violence by killing the snake, she is not portrayed as monstrous. The mother seemingly feels guilt for killing the pregnant snake and afterwards she dreams:

... I'm dead
And hundreds of baby snakes are gathered at my wake.
They crawl all over my body
And I try to shake them off,
Until I realize they're part of me. (102-06)

In addition to distressing over the "hundreds of baby snakes" that she prevented from being born, the mother repeatedly expresses concerns about protecting and providing for the children and members of her own family. The nuns at Saint Mary's Hospital, where she is taken after collapsing in labor, claim that she has performed a miracle and that she should be canonized. By portraying the mother's violence towards a living creature (the pregnant snake) as an act of motherly love, Ai's conclusion is even more striking as the mother reveals how she chose to let her child(ren) live. The poem closes with the declaration: "Mothers must decide to save / Or execute their children" (129-30). The decision to "execute" is placed solely in the hands of the mother. The narrator presents the decision of mothers as an either/or choice ("to save / or execute"), emphasizing her own decision "to save" her child(ren). This juxtaposition distinguishes this "loving" narrator from the "monstrous" narrators in other poems who present "execution" as a form of salvation. The fact that the poet Ai presents mothers with polarizing views on their role as mothers—yet both as capable of violence—requires readers to question what constitutes motherly love and when does such love include the decision to execute.

"Fate," the title poem for Ai's fourth book (1991), also examines religion as a patriarchal institution that influences women's decision whether or not to execute. The narrator in "Fate" faces "the judgment of men and God" outside an abortion clinic (8). Towards the beginning of the poem, the narrator watches an antiabortionist throw a rock at a woman "who cannot defend herself" (7) and reflects, "We have always been the receivers / of what is given without love or permission" (9-10). Just as Rich in the final chapter of *Of Woman Born* titled, "Violence: The Heart of Maternal Darkness," frames abortion as an offspring of the "violence of rapism" (274), the narrator of "Fate" underscores that, historically, women have been on the receiving end of unloving and unpermitted sexual acts against them, often resulting in unwanted pregnancies. Thus, the "Fate" that is emphasized in the poem is the desperate and often overwhelming circumstances that some pregnant women face—a victimized fate that is singularly female:

A man may beget a child in passion or by rape, and then disappear; he need never see or consider child or mother again. Under such circumstances, the mother faces a range of painful, socially weighted choices; abortion, suicide, abandonment of the child, infanticide, the rearing of a child branded "illegitimate," usually in poverty, always outside the law. In some cultures she faces murder by her kinsmen. Whatever her choice, her body has undergone irreversible changes, her mind will never be the same, her future as a woman has been shaped by the event. (Rich xiv)

Having been raised a Catholic and having attended Catholic school until seventh grade, Ai presents abortion as inextricably entangled with the broader debate about women's position in society, where reproductive rights continue to be thwarted by right-to-life religious agendas. In her article "Abortion and Organ Donation: Christian Reflections on Bodily Life Support," Patricia Beattie Jung summarizes:

Many on both sides of the abortion debate continue to romanticize pregnancy and motherhood. This romantic myth blinds many to the real problems and devastating conflicts pregnant women frequently face. It blinds others to the work, delayed gratification, suffering and sacrifice constitutive of even planned, ordinary pregnancies. Romanticism about motherhood reflects a failure of persons on both sides of the abortion debate to take the experience of women seriously. (297)

The poem "Fate" requires the reader not only to address the mother's decision "to save / or execute" as detailed in "Motherhood, 1951" but also to examine the social and economic conditions that affect women's ability to determine their reproductive lives. As Rich details: "Throughout history numberless women have killed children they knew they could not rear, whether economically or emotionally, children forced upon them by rape, ignorance, poverty, marriage, or by the absence of, or sanctions against, birth control and abortion" (263). The poem concludes with a litany of questions from the narrator, who ultimately echoes the mother's decision presented in "Motherhood, 1951" but further emphasizes the realities faced by women who make the decision to abort:

Are some children born to suffer,
because we say so?
If I hadn't let go my own son,
had held on to him only in the abstract,

not the fact,
maybe I'd have spared us all the decision
to have, or not.
I'd have stretched out by the table
laid with speculum, tenaculum, dilators, forceps,
the abortionist's humble tools,
to have my womb vacuumed as clean
as a vacated room. (66-77)

Although the narrator is positioned as the one in control—the one who makes the decision "to have, or not," by going to the abortion clinic—she is victimized by a "crowd screaming *Baby killer*" (89).

"Fate" is not the only poem to address the realities of abortion. The autobiographical dramatic monologues "Relativity" (*Dread*), narrated by the daughter, and "Disgrace" (*No Surrender*), narrated by the mother, both reference the mother attempting to self-abort by falling downstairs "to get rid of" ("Disgrace" 130) her unborn daughter but only succeeds in scaring herself "into this reluctant motherhood" ("Disgrace" 132), as the baby continues "growing inside her / like the truth she could not hide" ("Relativity" 30-31). Although one might easily read these mothers' desires to abort as merely another manifestation of the monstrous mothers' egoism and selfishness, Jung asserts: "Elements of what is authentically human can be expressed both in the decision to abort and in the decision to bear the burdensome child. Self-love and other-love are both normatively human forms of love. What makes the choice tragic is precisely the fact that neither available option can express human love in its fullness" (297). Ai presents women who follow through on their decision to abort as well.

In *Cruelty*, published the same year as *Roe v. Wade* (1973), Ai unabashedly tackles the subject with a poem simply titled "Abortion." In it, the narrator of the poem, the husband, details how he knows that his woman has "done it" (4), self-aborted, because her "stomach is flat as an iron" (3). Rigoberto González, in his article "The Poet Ai: A Critical & Personal Appreciation," writes:

It's important to note that [the abortion] was the woman's choice—she warned her lover she'd do it. What's not clear is whether this was an act of revenge, an act of desperation, or a necessity because of economic hardship. The end result, however, is that the woman has managed to take control of a situation in her favor since the lover affirms his loyalty. (65)

Although the woman has taken control by making the choice to abort, in doing so she is forced to confront the unveiled developmental reality of the aborted fetus. The tension rises as he adds, "You warned me you would / and left the fetus wrapped in wax paper / for me to look at. My son" (4-6). Yet even this act could be interpreted as empowering for the woman, for as Jung argues: "Paternalism, however beneficent in origin, robs women of the opportunity to face their situation and their decision truthfully, with integrity, courage, and self-respect" (291). Although the silent woman in "Abortion" appears to be in control, even the conscious decision not to become a mother relegates her to victim-like status. It is only through the self-inflicted violent act of abortion that the woman secures her status within the home. Although the woman has survived the abortion while garnering the favour of the man of the house, her husband, she still potentially faces severe consequences, since in accordance with Rich's depiction of the act: "The first violence done in abortion is on the body and mind of the pregnant woman herself" (272). The poem does not address the potential psychological and physical ramifications of abortion that many women face. Additionally, the woman is now precariously positioned within society, as Rich argues: "Women who refuse to become mothers are not merely emotionally suspect but are dangerous. Not only do they refuse to continue the species; they also deprive society of its emotional leaven—the suffering of the mother" (164). Yet this ten-line poem offers no insight into the aftermath of her action. The woman, not in spite of but through her violent act, is presented as taking control, attempting to overcome victimhood, which Rich ultimately argues is the most critical for women:

The most important thing one woman can do for another is to illuminate and expand her sense of actual possibilities. For a mother, this means more than contending with the reductive images of females in children's books, movies, television, the schoolroom. It means that the mother herself is trying to expand the limits of her life. *To refuse to be a victim*: and then go on from there. (250)

Despite their violent acts, and despite the violent cultural and personal environments in which they operate, the refusal of victimhood by women narrators emerges as the central recurrent figure throughout Ai's poetry. Even Ai's poems portraying monstrous mothers "illuminate and expand" the possibilities for women and mothers by showing that, even though they are doubly victimized by the experience and institution of patriarchal motherhood, they ultimately refuse to be defined by their circumstances. In her own way, each woman refuses to be "a victim twice."

In addition to her depiction of women and mothers in her poetry, certainly, the poet Ai accomplished this goal of "expanding the limits" in her personal life. In a 1978 interview with Lawrence Kearney and Michael Cuddihy, she recounts how she would preface her readings with a statement that she had never been pregnant and had never had an abortion because people would assume that she had composed *Cruelty* by drawing from her personal experiences and with autobiographical intent. The poet Ai further reflects that it was "pretty naïve" to assume her poetry was confessional: "It's the tyranny of confessional poetry—the notion that everything one writes has to be taken from the self. Which for me isn't true. If anything, my poems come from the unconscious—I'm irrevocably tied to the lives of all people, both in and out of time" (qtd. in Kearney and Cuddihy). However, on several occasions, often in personal interactions, the poet Ai was known to allude to the biographical nature of the dramatic monologue and the inspiration that she drew from her own life. In the aforementioned 2010 interview with Varnum, the poet Ai asserts: "Children who are abused I think are in a terrible state where you love the person who's been cruel to you.... But some people have an amazing ability to recover. I don't know what the answer is to that. I always thought of myself as that kind of person, you know, that can recover" (122). Perhaps it was the act of writing poetry, a life-long passion that began at age twelve, which allowed Ai to keep her own terrors in their respective place and go on with her life. Perhaps by exploring fictionalized violence and victimization on the page, the poet Ai was able to become the kind of person who could recover from her own horrific experiences. In the end, we, the readers, are left with a life's work that not only serves to illustrate the capacity of human cruelty but also the capacity to overcome victimhood and regain a sort of triumphant sense of self.

Endnotes

1. "Florence Anthony" was Ai's given birth name, which she legally changed in 1973. She continued to publish under the name "Ai" for the rest of her life. Her final book, *No Surrender*, includes several poems with autobiographical references and one poem titled "Baby Florence."

Works Cited

Ai. *The Collected Poems of Ai*. Norton & Company, 2010.

Cramer, Steven. "*Fate* by Ai." *Poetry*, vol. 159, no. 2, 1991, pp. 108-11.

González, Rigoberto. "The Poet Ai: A Critical & Personal Appreciation." *Cimarron Review*, no. 173, Fall 2010, pp. 61-73.

Jung, Patricia Beattie. "Abortion and Organ Donation: Christian Reflections on Bodily Life Support." *The Journal of Religious Ethics*, vol 16, no. 2, Fall 1988, pp. 273-305.

Kearney, Lawrence, and Michael Cuddihy. "Ai Interviewed by Lawrence Kearney and Michael Cuddihy." *Modern American Poetry*, 2015, www.modernamericanpoetry.org/content/ai-interviewed-lawrence-kearney-and-michael-cuddihy. Accessed 20 June 2021.

Komunyakaa, Yusef. "The Method of Ai." *The Collected Poems of Ai*. Norton & Company, 2010.

McGrath, Leslie. "I Have Killed My Black Goat: Violence in Ai's Poetry." *The Writer's Chronicle*, vol. 47, no. 1, Sept. 2014, pp. 33-39.

Tribble, Phyllis. "Eve and Adam: Genesis 2-3 Reread." *Andover Newton Quarterly*, vol. 13, March 1973, pp. 74-81.

Rich, Adrienne. *Of Woman Born: Motherhood as Experience and Institution*. Norton & Company, 1976.

Varnum, Janet. "An Interview with Ai." *Cimarron Review*, no. 173, Fall 2010, pp. 88-122.

PART III
MOTHERS MADE
MONSTROUS

Chapter 9

The Monstrosity of Maternal Abandonment in the Literature of Women Writers from the American South

Jennifer Martin

Can a mother who abandons her children for personal pursuits be anything but monstrous? Three Southern women writers of the early 1990s interrogate society's expectations for mothers and the boundaries which women move across in the perceived transition from mothers to monsters. These canonical texts—Gail Godwin's *Father Melancholy's Daughter* (1991), Doris Betts's *Souls Raised from the Dead* (1994), and Dorothy Allison's *Bastard Out of Carolina* (1992)— explore mothers who are bombarded by both the national conservative wave following the Reagan Era and Southern mothering expectations. These women ultimately choose to flee their children rather than to attempt to reconcile conflicting maternal ideals and the realities of their personal desires. Although maternal abandonment is not an idea that is unique to the 1980s and 1990s in the United States (US), this study considers the societal forces that existed during the Reagan Era which contributed to Southern women choosing to abandon their offspring. The authors trouble the notion of monstrous mothers by revealing an interior to these fictional mothers that confuses where placement of empathy should lie. On the one hand, the authors show compassion for the woman who recognizes her unhappiness and ineffectual ability to mother and chooses to leave her children in loving hands to pursue other outlets for identity building. On the other, the writers also show compassion for the children, whose needs are often in conflict with those of the mother and who perceive abandonment as rejection by the mother leading to emotional and physical distress. These texts highlight the struggle by women to obtain a balance between maternal ideals and their personal needs—demonstrating the collateral damage to both women and children because of the multiplicity of conservative mother-hood ideals in the American South. The fleeing mothers of these texts who fail to comply with the often changing and evolving motherhood standards can hastily be identified as monstrous, yet a deeper look reveals a more complex understanding of these women.

Although there is a monolithic idea of perfect motherhood—a woman selflessly dedicated to her children and household with no thought of her own needs—these texts show that the actual application of this concept is fluid. For instance, Betts's Mary in *Souls Raised From the Dead* wishes that Christine, her mother, "lived out a perfect mother's role" (187). Mary dreams that

> She would wake up and be nine again to find that Christine had become her Girl Scout-troop leader and her fourth-grade helper mother, and her Damascus Sunday-school teacher and a P.T.A. refreshment mother as well as the pretty front-seat mother who periodically would lean back to touch the slumberer [Mary] and whisper, "Isn't Mary wonderful?" (Betts 188).

Mary's idea of perfect motherhood is full of specific and time-consuming labour demands on her mother leaving Christine as a submissive participant in Mary's life. Goodwin's Margaret in *Father Melancholy's Daughter* wants her mother, Ruth, to return as her play-mate who creates inventive games for the two to play and to engage in special secrets with her daughter, such as her understanding of the witch that Margaret believes hides in her closet. These activities detract from Ruth's ability to pursue her artistic interests. In Allison's *Bastard Out of Carolina*, Bone, Anney's daughter, cannot fantasize about any of these middle-class activities, since her impoverished position has not exposed her to Girl Scouts or to mothers who create games for the entertainment of their daughters. Bone simply wants Anney to leave her stepfather to end the abuse he inflicts on her, but Anney does not want to be denied her relationship with her husband. The fluidity and unstated assumptions of what constitutes a good mother create an impossible bind for these mothers because the expectations by which they are judged are in a constant state of flux depending on which of her judges—her children, her community, her family, or even herself—is determining her worthiness.

The abandoned children in these texts describe the pain they suffer as a result of maternal desertion. Frances Greenslade in her introduction to *Absent Mothers* writes, "Although the absent mother may appear in many stories as a plot device or as a symbol of the separation of mother and child, their frequent occurrence reveals the anxiety that both mothers and children harbor over this separation" (3). Although the standard of goodness that these fictional women are accountable to uphold is fluid, it is clear in the texts that the desertion is viewed negatively by both their children and the community surrounding the mothers. There is a community desire to contain these women in their maternal positions to avoid disrupting the patriarchal structures that control Southern society. So not only do mothers and children have anxiety about separation, but the larger community also struggles to maintain the social order by condemning women who choose alternative narratives for their lives.

The historical climate when these stories were written and published informs the struggles faced by the fictional mothers. Shari L. Thurer in *The Myths of Motherhood* writes of the 1980s and 1990s in the US: "A wave of cultural nostalgia swept Ronald Reagan into the White House and precipitated a vigorous attempt to turn back the clock and reinstate the traditional family" (289). Marjorie J. Spruill in *Divided We Stand*, her study of the 1977 National Women's Conference in Houston, notes the rise of two oppositional women's movements: the women's rights movement and a conservative women's movement. She writes: "Whereas in the early 1970s both Republicans and Democrats supported the modern women's movement, by 1980 the GOP had sided with the other women's movement, the one that positioned family values in opposition to women's rights" (2). Spruill contends that the National Plan of Action that was adopted at the Houston meeting did not "represent a consensus among American women on what federal policy should be. Solidarity among feminists was not the same as solidarity among American women" (8). Phyllis Schlafly emerged as a leader in the conservative women's movement. She supported the ideology that a

woman should not be driven to work outside of the home by the ideologies of the second-wave feminist movement. Instead, she endorsed
that a good woman embraced her role as a full-time wife and mother.

Even before the Reagan years in the US, the decisions women made
about mothering were scrutinized, particularly the way that motherhood was practiced by Southern white women whose mothering was
informed by the burden of Southern history, including the practice of
slavery that preceded the American Civil War. Southern writer Lillian
Smith's *Killers of the Dream*, published in 1949, describes a baseline for
considering the mothers in the fictional texts by Southern women
writers of the 1990s by critiquing the misery of white mothers. She
focuses on the unhappiness Southern mothers faced due to the many
restrictions on their opportunities to pursue interests outside the home.
Smith writes of these mothers: "Their own dreams destroyed, they
destroyed in cruelty their children's dreams and their men's aspirations.
It was a compulsive thing. Rarely were they aware of the hate compell-
ing them to do it. Most of them felt they were doing 'right'" (150). The
white, middle-class women Smith observes were trapped in their roles
as mothers due to the lack of viable alternatives available to them as
adult women in the American South. Long before Betty Friedan penned
The Feminine Mystique and pointed to the "problem that has no name,"
Smith critiqued the boredom and lack of opportunity for Southern
women to do anything but mother.

In the 1970s, with the rise of the women's movement across the US,
motherhood did not operate as a site of unity and shared experience
which would unite women. Instead, in many cases, motherhood became a battleground that pushed women into oppositional camps. In
Germaine Greer's *The Female Eunuch*, first published in 1970, she
asserts that the traditional roles for women as championed by Schlafly
and her followers are oppressive and deplete a woman's sense of self-
worth. Greer stakes her feminist claim: "A woman who has a child is
not then automatically committed to bringing it up.... A group of
children can be more successfully civilized by one or two women who
have voluntarily undertaken the work than they can be when divided
and tyrannized over by a single woman who finds herself bored and
imposed upon" (263). She continues: "If necessary the child need not
even know that I was his womb-mother and I could have relationships
with the other children as well" (264). Greer champions an idea of

mothering that is so foreign and contrary to mothers who relish the notion of a special mother-child bond and their roles as traditional, stay-at-home mothers that it is little wonder that at this point in history the two sides found themselves with no middle ground. These contradictory messages left many women without a clear understanding of what their own expectations about mothering should be and how they could perform successful mothering in a climate where the private act was regularly under public scrutiny.

Even while motherhood presents an embattled space for women, there are opportunities for mothering to empower women. Andrea O'Reilly in *Mother Outlaws* notes that since the late 1970s, "the oppressive and the empowering aspects of maternity, as well as the complex relationship between the two, has been the focus of feminist research on motherhood" (59). She identifies themes arising from feminist mothering studies: "The first theme is concerned with uncovering and challenging the oppressive patriarchal institution of motherhood. The second focuses upon the formulation and articulation of a counter discourse of mothering; one that redefines mothering as a female defined or, more specifically, a feminist, enterprise" (59). The fictional mothers examined in this chapter suffer from the oppressions of motherhood steeped in patriarchal structures but do not have the resources to gain empowerment through mothering—presenting a counternarrative to motherhood informed by feminist mothering thought. These Southern women writers are pessimistic that empowerment for women through the traditional, patriarchal culture of motherhood can exist and demonstrate how the societal impediments in the South prevent women from achieving a personal form of mothering that engages with her own needs as well as the needs of her children.

Dorothy Allison, in an interview with Susanne Dietzel, elaborates on her impressions of the controlling tropes of Southern motherhood:

I don't know any Southern writer who doesn't begin with mama. You know, she's like the air you breathe and it's a little dangerous because in fact there is this concept of the Southern mother in literature. To get serious attention is to give a kind of reverence; you have to write against the stereotype. And the stereotype is frightening. The stereotype is inhuman. The stereotype IS the mother who starves herself to feed her children, you know. And then the other stereotype is the mother who eats her children alive if they do not quite measure up to what she wants them to be. And you're always caught up between those two things if you're a Southern writer. (Claxton 45)

Allison illuminates the binary that has been established for Southern mothers by identifying two of the prevalent motherhood stereotypes in the South. The so-called good Southern mother is the completely passive woman with no interests beyond nurturing her children. In contrast is the mother who is willing to destroy her children should they disappoint her or stand in her way. Southern tradition privileges the sacrificial mother and fears the other mother to the point of deeming her monstrous.

Gail Godwin, the only writer in this group who is not a mother herself, speaks of her own mother, Kathleen Godwin, who ignored traditional roles for women and in the 1940s, divorced her husband and moved to Asheville, North Carolina, to raise Gail with the help of her mother. Godwin says: "My mother was the most glamorous person I knew. I was not completely sure of her, the way I was sure of Monie, my grandmother, who in our household performed the tasks associated with motherhood while Kathleen Godwin went out in all weathers to breadwin for us like a man" ("My Mother"). It is Monie, Godwin's grandmother, who takes on the tasks associated with nurturing a child that allows Kathleen to leave the home to pursue her interest in writing. Kathleen's work outside the home required an intense workday schedule. She rose before dawn, "dabbed perfume behind her ears and, checking her stocking seams in the full-length mirror, dashed off to her job, returning after dark in elated exhaustion, wearing the smoky, inky smells of her larger world" (Godwin, "My Mother"). Godwin's mother remarried in 1948, and Godwin recalls, "She spent the next 39 years of her life masked as a submissive wife" ("My Mother"). Godwin's fiction demonstrates her sympathies for bifurcated mothers like her own mother who was both a professional and a submissive wife.

Godwin's *Father Melancholy's Daughter,* told in first-person narration by the protagonist, Margaret Gower, highlights the turmoil that a mother who fails to uphold Southern standards of mothering can bring to her child. Margaret, a recent college graduate, writes the text as a series of memories of events that shaped her life. When Margaret was six years old, Ruth, Margaret's mother, leaves with a friend from her past for a weekend stay that extends into months. During this time, Ruth is killed in a car accident. Godwin, in an interview held while she was writing the novel, says, "What I am doing, it seems, in getting these two women together [Ruth and her friend], even though it destroys the father and splits the child down the middle, is getting something important back together: two warring sides of the same woman" ("My Mother"). In this novel, Godwin continues to consider her perception of the bifurcated mother that began with observations of her own mother. Margaret struggles to understand her mother as she is torn between her needs as a child wishing for a mother and her gradual awakening to the subversive forces in her Southern community that contributed to her mother's distress and need for escape.

Godwin confuses our sympathies as readers as Margaret's narrative reveals truths about the bleakness of Ruth's life. The catalysts for Ruth's desertion are embedded in the stories Margaret tells of their life. The picture that Margaret draws of the restrictive social circle of Romulus, Virginia, surrounding the role Ruth had to fulfill as wife to Walter Gower, rector of the small Episcopal Church in the community, offers clues about Ruth's motivations. Just before her mother's departure, she discusses a dress with Margaret that her daughter wants to buy. However, the dress has many buttons that Ruth realizes Margaret will not be able to manage on her own. Margaret remembers Ruth's response: "'Well, just remember, I'm not doing it for you [buttoning the buttons]. I've got enough buttons of my own to worry about.' My mother [Ruth] had this way of talking. She would say something that sounded simple and harmless in her light, melodic drawl, but underneath you often got the feeling she was saying something quite different at the same time" (Godwin 8). Godwin, writing for *Ms.* magazine, says in "The Southern Belle" that Southern women who are groomed to be belles must "acquire the art of indirect speech that will help her to keep life running smoothly" (52). Ruth has perfected this double talk of saying something apparently harmless but intending to throw daggers with her understatement. Ruth's "buttons" include the restrictive church society, her husband's constant withdrawal into the "black curtain" of his depression, and the pressures of being the consumed mother who is defined by her child.

The expectations of church and community concerning Ruth's

performance of wife and mother contribute to Ruth's flight. Godwin generates sympathy for Ruth's situation through Margaret's description of the judgmental women of Walter's church. For Ruth, the community of churchwomen who keep her under surveillance is oppressive. As Margaret relates her memories of her mother, she says, "Miriam Stacy, a drab, self-righteous old maid who lived with her mother, was the person who had told my mother she looked more like a college girl than a rector's wife and had caused Ruth to pull her hair back with a tortoiseshell clip" (Godwin 28). Ruth must suppress her free spirit— even to the point of how she wears her hair—in order to accommodate the vision of wife and mother held by the community.

Ruth's rebellion against the Romulus community began in small ways and sometimes involved her daughter and husband. Margaret details the game she played with her mother every Wednesday with the cars of the women attending the mid-week church service: "It was a highly subversive game: you had to show you knew whose car each was by revealing something, not necessarily flattering, about the owner, or by imitating the way that person talked" (Godwin 28). Margaret remembers this "secret war of insolence against this steadfast handful of ladies" with her mother "leading [her] willingly into rebellion against Daddy's Wednesday flock" (Godwin 28). As a child, Margaret is satisfied that these silly moments shared with her mother are enough to free Ruth from the oppression she feels under the constant scrutiny of these controlling women. Margaret's position as a young child when this memory occurred prevents her from understanding the intense unhappiness her mother experiences in that moment. As the reflexive adult penning her tale, Margaret demonstrates a new understanding of the oppressions on her mother's life in Romulus by recalling these events that seemed harmless as they occurred but demonstrated her mother's pain. Through Margaret's writing, she is awakened to her mother's distress with her life as the rector's wife and mother. Godwin allows for an empathetic reading of Ruth who is trapped in a life where she must constantly suppress her true self by wearing a mask of congeniality and acceptance of her role. It becomes obvious that Ruth could never be happy performing the role of perfect mother to Margaret under the patrolling eyes of the church community, and Margaret's gradual understanding of this through her restorative writing allows the reader to also empathize with Ruth's situation.

Mary, the daughter and protagonist of Betts's *Souls Raised from the Dead*, like Margaret, expresses her pain at being abandoned by her mother, Christine. In the novel, Betts directly challenges cavalier ideas about motherhood embraced by feminists in the 1970s, such as Greer. Christine abandons her family to pursue a career, leaving Frank alone to parent their daughter. Sara Ruddick asserts that "anyone who commits her or himself to responding to children's demands, and makes the work of response a conservable part of her or his life, is a mother.... Consequently, it is not difficult to imagine men taking up mothering as easily and successfully as women—or conversely, women as easily declining to mother as men.... A birthgiver may transfer to others the maternal responsibility of caring for the infant she has created" (xii). Despite the ease that Ruddick claims in the transference of mothering responsibilities, in the case of Christine, it is not a simple conveyance of power because her refusal to accept mothering responsibilities is rejected by her family and the community. Frank willingly raises the daughter he cherishes, but Mary does not view him as maternal and wants her mother to participate as well. Her society expects that Christine will willingly step out of her new life to come to Mary's side when her daughter is ill, but Christine has no desire to return. Thus, Christine is ostracized by the community in order to discipline her for her lack of adherence to the Southern mothering ideal.

Betts complicates our understanding of Christine by demonstrating Frank's shortcomings in their relationship, which provide evidence and sympathy for Christine's desertion of the family. Frank recognizes that his feelings towards Mary outweigh any feelings he has had for another human. As he anxiously waits by her hospital bed after a fall from a horse, he thinks: "This kind of love—it was all hazard. Never with any woman had he been so vulnerable. Not Christine when they were first married, certainly not Cindy Scofield on an occasional Saturday night now. Never with his parents. Not with one single friend. Caring so much can't be good for people. Men especially. It leaves us too exposed" (Betts 29). Mary may have crept into Frank's unemotional heart, but he admits it is a place Christine was never admitted. Frank represents all that society values—a man dedicated to his offspring who holds a good job as a highway patrolman and comes from a family dedicated to traditional values. By the standards of Southern society, he is the type of husband all women should aspire to marry. However, his inability to lose himself in love to anyone other than his daughter creates an emotional barrier that Christine finds counter to her needs in a relationship. Despite Frank's emotional shortcomings, he and his community consider that Christine is singularly at fault in the demise of their marriage and her decision to leave both Frank and Mary behind. Through Frank's emotional distance from women, Betts allows space for sympathy for Christine who felt trapped, unappreciated, and isolated as a wife and mother.

Christine exemplifies what Sarah LaChance Adams in *Mad Mothers, Bad Mothers, & What a "Good" Mother Would Do* considers maternal ambivalence—the condition faced by mothers who wish to both nurture and reject their children. Adams notes that women like Christine are not unusual: "My research shows that such feelings [a mother's simultaneous desire to both nurture and reject her children] are fairly common and are the result of valid conflicts that exist between mothers' and children's interests" (4-5). She further argues that "Ethical ambivalence is morally productive insofar as it helps one to recognize the alterity of others, attend to the particularities of situation, and negotiate one's own needs and desires with those of other people" (Adams 5). Yet Betts proposes an instance where the moral productivity of ambivalence is in question by making Christine the key for Mary's recovery from her potentially fatal kidney disease. At the crux of the novel is the question if Christine owes Mary the gift of life a second time by compromising her own healthy body in order to donate a kidney.

Betts's depiction of Christine and the reaction of the society she inhabits to her version of ambivalent motherhood offers the opportunity to test Adams's claims. The Chapel Hill society in which Christine lives assumes that a mother's love and desire to protect her child must be natural and that Christine is somehow lacking and wrong not to willingly give of herself anything that Mary needs. Christine's version of motherhood forces consideration of where the duty of a woman to a child ends. Adams admits: "In some cases it is impossible for both mother and child to get what they want and/or need. They interfere with each another, and their feelings are discordant" (36). The situation with Christine and Mary necessarily pits Christine's needs against Mary's needs and only one can succeed in this zero-sum game of Betts's creation.

Mary's feelings about her mother are conflicted. Mary, like Margaret, craves the affection of her absent mother and is willing to provide openings for Christine to participate in her life as a mother. Dr. Benjamin Spock, who published wildly popular trade books on child-rearing during the 1990s, weighed in on the importance of parental involvement for a child's wellbeing: "Parental lovingness is absolutely essential, and its influence is on the favorable side as long as it is a sensible and balanced love. It is also true that parental neglect, in the sense of indifference to the child's welfare, is always detrimental" (Spock 144). The community Betts creates in *Souls Raised from the Dead* endorses Spock's idea that parental neglect will harm Mary. Betts demonstrates the tensions between the idea of the sacrificial mother and second-wave feminist self-actualization. Through Mary's death, Betts voices the warning that parental neglect, even neglect wrapped in the guise of feminism, is indeed detrimental.

Whereas Mary views her mother as vital for her growth into a woman, Frank only views Christine as a vehicle for child creation and nourishment. Frank tells Mary: "She [Christine] had you. Even I can't stay mad at Christine when I remember she could do that one wonderful thing, could have you, Mary. Mary Grace? Your mother could mess up everything from then on" (Betts 67). Frank is not truthful in what he claims. He expects much more from Christine than simply giving birth to Mary. He expects Christine to walk away from the career she has created and become a kidney donor to Mary. Frank's patriarchal view of Christine as only a vehicle to serve Mary, which contributed to Christine's alienation as a mother, contributes to a sympathetic reading of her character in the novel.

The Southern society that Frank, Mary, and Christine inhabit has distinctive expectations for the behaviour of a mother—even for a mother who abandons her child. Dr. Seagroves, Mary's doctor, discounts Frank's rant that Christine would not be a willing donor for Mary with the simple statement: "She's a mother" (Betts 152). As a product of a traditional Southern society that associates motherhood with constant sacrifice, Seagroves believes Christine will naturally provide anything her daughter needs, even an organ.

Jill, Frank's love interest, concurs with Seagrove's conclusion: "She'll [Christine] do it [organ transplant donor] when the time comes, Frank, anybody would" (Betts 153). In light of Jill's decision to place her child from an unplanned pregnancy with an adoptive family and evade the responsibilities of motherhood, it is interesting that she believes another woman should make further sacrifice for her child. In fact, Jill is so ashamed of her past pregnancy and its outcome that she chooses not to share this part of her past with Frank. Yet she determines that Christine should do what Jill was not able to do for her own child—sacrifice her time and health for the wellbeing of her offspring. Through the character of Jill, Betts shows the boundaries that are permissible for a mother to abandon motherhood within this Southern society. For Betts, Jill is a character worthy of empathy because she responsibly gave her child up for adoption. Since Jill plans to complete veterinary school and pursue an "allowable" career for a horse-crazy woman, her motherhood abandonment is simply stated as fact and never debated or judged in the text. In contrast, Christine left the preteen Mary to pursue a career selling makeup and is judged harshly by Betts's Chapel Hill community in the novel for the frivolity of her pursuits and her abandonment of a daughter who wishes for her mother.

Georgia Broome, Christine's mother, has a class-related stake in the situation. She has been subjected to the Thompsons' brand of class privilege all of her life. She tells Christine: "Them Thompsons have always thought us Broomes was trash. Don't you go proving them right, you hear me?" (Betts 253). Mothers of the respectable middle class are expected to act in certain ways. Hesitating to offer a potentially life-saving organ to a child is certainly not part of the middle-class mothering script. Tired of the Thompsons' belittlement of the Broomes' circumstances, Georgia is driven to attempt to convince Christine to donate her kidney in order to allow the Broome family to ascend to middle-class respectability. Georgia also embraces a notion of sacrificial motherhood that transcends social class, as she tells her daughter: "You're not a natural mother, that's all there is to it" (Betts 253). A natural mother would not hesitate to try to save her child. Since Christine cannot easily perform this selfless act, she is denied social approval.

Christine's emotional and physical absence from her daughter fails for everyone in the novel. In the moment after Mary's death, Christine begs to reverse her decision to avoid donating her kidney to her daughter: "Something volcanic was happening inside Christine. It burst out in sobs and shivers and broken, gasping screams. 'I'll do it. OK? Yes! She can have it! Take the goddamn kidney! Hurry up!'" (Betts 310). Not only does her daughter die in that moment, but also all hope of an independent life for Christine free of the burden of mother-hood dies with her. Frank, while responding to a fatal car accident, considers his former wife: "The dead mother made him think of Christine, now back at the River Haven Mobile Park, who sometimes called Frank late at night, sometimes drunk. At first he hung up on her. He knew that another mother, Georgia [Christine's mother], turned off her own phone every night when the clock struck twelve to keep from hearing Christine cry" (Betts 338). Christine is a dead mother. She refused to offer any more of herself, both physically and emotionally, to Mary and, because of this, possibly contributed to Mary's death. Christine's desire for independence is at such odds with the motherhood ideal that it has catastrophic results for all involved.

The argument that Betts weaves through the novel is counter to second-wave feminist ideas that women can successfully work outside the home and raise children. In a 1958 letter to her friend, Louise Abbot, Betts says: "I fear it [a magazine they are discussing] leans toward feminism at spots, which doesn't [sic] interest me worth a woot; Viva La Difference" ("Letter," Apr. 1958). A decade later, Betts writes to Abbot: "By not 'fighting for women's rights' I seem to receive them; who's flakey here?" and "Am I nuts in thinking a husband and wife can have a quality in their lives that nothing else duplicates, replaces, or touches?" (Betts, "Letter," Jan. 1967). Throughout her correspondence with Abbot spanning five decades, Betts continues to defend her views that a traditional marriage and prioritizing her family's needs over her own are paramount to her success as a woman. Betts harshly judges Christine's attempt to assert herself as an independent woman who values self-definition and independence over family. However, Christine has suffered from a man who does not appreciate her and wishes to control her. She is not interested in the daily monotony of motherhood. She attempts to enact her own form of feminism by pursuing a career and her interests outside of her family. Betts thwarts the ability to fully empathize with Christine by making Christine possibly complicit in Mary's death through her failure to donate her kidney to her daughter. Yet there is no guarantee that Mary's outcome would have been any different had Christine agreed to become an organ donor. At stake is if a woman owes her child control and access to the woman's body for the duration of the woman's life. Betts's novel indicates that a mother can never be independent from her duty to her child.

Like Godwin's and Betts's novels, Dorothy Allison's *Bastard Out of Carolina* interrogates a mother-daughter relationship. However, Allison's novel considers the difficulties of motherhood performance for an impoverished woman, Anney, as told by her daughter, Bone. Anney was fifteen and unmarried at the time of Bone's birth. As Bone recounts the story of her birth, gleaned from the stories her family had shared with her, she reveals that Anney established her pattern of mothering even in childbirth. As Bone tells about her real name, Ruth Anne, she says: "I was named for and by my oldest aunt—Aunt Ruth. My mama didn't have much to say about it, since strictly speaking, she wasn't there" (Allison 1). Anney had fallen asleep in the back of Uncle Travis's Chevy before he hit a car head-on sending her flying through the windshield onto the pavement. When Anney woke three days later, Bone had been delivered and named. Anney's struggle to perform a version of good motherhood is layered between events like this when Anney removes herself from Bone physically and emotionally. Anney's extreme poverty and her lack of education complicate her ability to provide the basics of protective motherhood to her daughter.

Allison's novel explores the issues of mothering outside of privileged and affluent Southern society. Privileged white mothers such as Godwin's Ruth have increased potential to become what society perceives as good mothers due to their access to respectability, community support, education, and money, but Anney is denied access to any of these markers of privilege that have the potential to alter the outcomes for her and Bone. Anney's lack of respectability and community support are apparent in the "illegitimate" tag on Bone's birth certificate. Anney equates the stamp with an indictment of her social position. Bone relates: "Mama hated to be called trash, hated the memory of every day she'd ever spent bent over other people's peanuts and strawberry plants while they stood tall and looked at her like she was a rock on the ground. The stamp on that birth certificate burned her like the stamp she knew they'd tried to put on her. *No-good, lazy, shiftless*" (Allison 3). In multiple attempts to defy the systems of respectable middle-class society that worked to maintain a barrier between the classes, Anney repeatedly goes to the courthouse to attempt to have Bone's birth certificate reissued without the "illegitimate" stamp across the bottom. In these exchanges, a form of class warfare unfolds.

Privileged class values are displayed by the male clerk and supporting staff of women at the courthouse. None of the courthouse staff have sympathy for the teenaged mother, Anney, and her offspring. The clerk tells Anney on her first visit after denying her wish for an unstamped birth certificate: "This is how it's got to be. The facts have been established." Bone opines, "He drew the word out even longer and louder so that it hung in the air between them like a neon reflection of my mama's blush—*established*" (Allison 4). One of the women from the office shakes her head and mouths to her compatriots, "Some people" (Allison 5). When Anney returns a year later with Aunt Ruth in tow, Bone says: "The look he gave my mama and my aunt was pure righteous justification.... His face was set and almost gentle, but his eyes laughed at them" (Allison 5). Ultimately, the courthouse burns, and Anney is able to get an unblemished birth certificate for Bone. Bone reveals:

> Folded into thirds was a certificate. RUTH ANNE BOATWRIGHT. Mother: ANNEY BOATWRIGHT. Father: UNKNOWN. I almost laughed, reading down the page. Greenville General Hospital and the embossed seal of the county, the family legend on imitation parchment. I had never seen it before, but had heard all about it. I unfolded the bottom third. It was blank, unmarked, unstamped. (Allison 309)

Anney offers this public record as a protection to Bone from the judgment of those with higher social standings, but Anney's neglect in protecting Bone from the physical assaults of Glen generate a conflicted understanding of Anney's maternal performance.

Daddy Glen is a sexual predator. Anney marries him after her fabled, kind husband dies unexpectedly. He grooms Anney and Bone to be complicit in his patterns of sexual and physical abuse. After a particularly gruesome attack where Glen beats Bone's bare bottom and legs with a leather belt behind a locked bathroom door, Anney slaps Glen and comforts Bone, yet despite having heard the beating and seen the results, Anney asks Bone, "Oh, girl, honey. Baby, what did you do? What did you do?" (Allison 107). Bone had done nothing and Anney knows this, yet she desires to be blind to Glen's abuse and to place the blame for the beating on her young daughter.

Anney is forced to choose between her lover and her daughter. Ultimately, Anney discovers Glen in the act of raping Bone after a severe beating that leaves Bone hospitalized. As Anney tries to leave with Bone, Glen begins to beat his head against the car door—placing Anney between her wounded daughter and her daughter's tormentor. Even in this moment, Anney cannot put Bone's health above Glen's needs. Bone reports that Anney "grabbed his head, wrapping her fingers over his forehead to block the impact of his blows.... She was holding him, his head pressed to her belly" (Allison 290-91). Bone reflects: "Rage burned in my belly and came up my throat. I'd said I could never hate her, but I hated her now for the way she held him, the way she stood there crying over him. Could she love me and still hold him like that?" (Allison 291). For Anney, a young high-school dropout with two children, the lack of stability in her own life has contributed to her belief that a man will provide the anchor to hold her life together.

Aunt Raylene understands Anney's bind between two loves: Glen and Bone. She says, "Bone, no woman can stand to choose between her baby and her lover, between her child and her husband.... We do terrible things to the ones we love sometimes" (Allison 300-01). Raylene is the voice of Anney's family. They understand Anney, and, despite the hurt she has inflicted on Bone, they do not perceive Anney as monstrous. Instead, they view her as a hurt and scared young woman trying to make her way in the world with the scant resources available to her. Even Bone admits: "Once I was born, her [Anney's] hopes had turned, and I had climbed up her life like a flower reaching for the sun. Fourteen and terrified, fifteen and a mother, just past twenty-one when she married Glen. Her life had folded into mine" (Allison 309). Bone realizes the drain she was on Anney as a baby. She visualizes herself using Anney as a support to gain sustenance for life. She even notes that Anney's life folded into hers. Anney's existence was extinguished as Bone grew. Both Aunt Raylene and Bone offer a position to view Anney sympathetically. Her youth and lack of education and resources make her especially vulnerable to a man of Glen's cunning. Allison troubles the idea of Anney as a monstrous mother by offering these observations of Raylene and Bone as the novel closes.

Godwin, Betts, and Allison interrogate the societal boundaries between good and monstrous maternal performance. In each text considered, the abandoned child is left with a caring and loving adult. Margaret and Mary have their fathers, who centre their worlds on the care of their daughters. Bone is left with Aunt Raylene, who offers Bone love and stability. Even though each child is left in a safe and caring environment, the children suffer from the absence of their mothers—evidence of the children embracing the societal conditioning that privileges mother love as a requirement for a contented childhood. Both the children and the community find fault with these uncontrollable women for shunning their responsibilities as givers and keepers of life. However, the situations these women face in their maternal performance reveal a space to consider these women as victims of a society that makes unrealistic demands on them and denies them any form of individual expression. The erasure of selfhood drives the women to abandon their children and seek self-building through other avenues. The strict controls on maternal performance in the American South force these women into difficult binds, where escape from motherhood oppression causes them to be viewed as monsters by their communities and sometimes by their children. Godwin, Betts, and Allison call attention to the difficulties in maintaining a sense of self during maternal performance, which makes these fictional mothers sympathetic. These novels demonstrate the need to further probe the social structures that bind women to a constantly changing script of motherhood and drive women to abandon their maternal roles. Perhaps mothering abandonment is not monstrous but is instead a reaction of women to the conditions of their lives.

Works Cited

Adam, Sarah LaChance. *Mad Mothers, Bad Mothers, and What a "Good" Mother Would Do: The Ethics of Ambivalence.* Columbia University Press, 2014.

Allison, Dorothy. *Bastard Out of Carolina.* Plume, 1992.

Betts, Doris. "Letter to Louise Abbot," April 1958, Folder 625 in the Doris Betts Papers #4695, Southern Historical Collection, The Wilson Library, University of North Carolina at Chapel Hill.

Betts, Doris. "Letter to Louise Abbot," 16 Jan. 1967, Folder 625 in the

Doris Betts Papers #4695, Southern Historical Collection, The Wilson Library, University of North Carolina at Chapel Hill.

Betts, Doris. *Souls Raised from the Dead*. Scribner Paperback Fiction, 1994.

Dietzel, Susanne. "An Interview with Dorothy Allison." *Conversations with Dorothy Allison*, edited by Mae Miller Claxton, University Press of Mississippi, 2012, pp. 40-52.

Godwin, Gail. *Father Melancholy's Daughter*. Harper Perennial, 1991.

Godwin, Gail. "My Mother, the Writer: Master of a Thousand Disguises." *The New York Times*, 11 June 1989, archive.nytimes.com/ www.nytimes.com/books/99/04/04/specials/godwin-writer.html. Accessed 20 June 2021.

Godwin, Gail. "The Southern Belle." *Ms.* July 1975, pp. 49-52, 84.

Greenslade, Frances, editor. *Absent Mothers*. Demeter Press, 2017.

Greer, Germaine. *The Female Eunuch*. Harper Perennial, 1970.

Hill, Jane. *Gail Godwin*. Twayne Publishers, 1992.

O'Reilly, Andrea. *Mother Outlaws: Theories and Practices of Empowered Mothering*. Women's Press Toronto, 2004.

Ruddick, Sara. *Maternal Thinking: Toward a Politics of Peace*. Beacon Press, 1989.

Smith, Lillian. *Killers of the Dream*. W. W. Norton & Company, 1949.

Spock, Benjamin. *Raising Children in a Difficult Time: A Philosophy of Parental Leadership and High Ideals*. W. W. Norton, 1974.

Spruill, Marjorie J. *Divided We Stand: The Battle Over Women's Rights and Family Values that Polarized American Politics*. Bloomsbury, 2017.

Thurer, Shari L. *The Myths of Motherhood: How Culture Reinvents the Good Mother*. Penguin Books, 1994.

Chapter 10

"What Is Incomprehensible": The Myth of Maternal Omniscience and the Judgment of Maternal Culpability in Sue Klebold's *A Mother's Reckoning* and Monique Lépine's *Aftermath*

Andrea O'Reilly

This chapter examines the memoirs of two mothers whose respective sons, Dylan Klebold and Marc Lépine, committed two of the most infamous school shootings in North America and then died by suicide: Columbine in the United States (1999) and the Montreal Massacre in Canada (1989). The Columbine High School massacre was a school shooting that occurred on April 20, 1999, at Columbine High School in Columbine, Colorado. Dylan Klebold and his friend Eric Harris killed thirteen people and injured many more. They both later died by suicide. The École Polytechnique massacre, also known as the Montreal Massacre, was a mass shooting at the École Polytechnique in Montreal, Quebec, Canada, which occurred on December 6, 1989. Twenty-five year old Marc Lépine began his attack by separating the male students from the female students, and after calling the women a "bunch of feminists," he proceeded to kill fourteen women and injured another ten women and four men. He then died by suicide. His suicide note blamed feminists for the failure of his life.

The memoirs by Sue Klebold—*A Mother's Reckoning: Living in the Aftermath of Tragedy* (2016)—and by Monique Lépine—*Aftermath: The Mother of Marc Lépine Tells the Story of Her Life Before and After the Montreal Massacre* (2008)—narrate what Klebold terms "coming to terms with the impossible" and Lépine describes as "her descent into nightmare," as each mother seeks to understand what caused her son to commit the massacre and die by suicide. The chapter explores each mother's journey toward understanding her son's crime and death through denial, despair, anger, grief, shame, and, eventually, healing. I examine the normative discourse of good motherhood and how it informs and shapes each mother's attempt to explain and comprehend how her son, in Lépine's words, "turned into a heartless murderer" (22). In particular, I address two salient beliefs of normative motherhood: First, good mothers raise good children and bad mothers raise bad children; and second, good mothers, as involved parents, should and must know their children. Klebold and Lépine, in their poignant rendering and remembering of mothering, deliver a potent critique and corrective to these conjectures of normative motherhood. The first section of the chapter on *A Mother's Reckoning* examines the myth of maternal omniscience, whereas the second section on *Aftermath* considers the judgment of maternal culpability. What readers learn in these memoirs of loss is that children may be unknowable and that mothers are not responsible for the actions of their children. Consequently, the memoirs astutely disrupt, dispute, and discredit mother blame as they are enacted in the myth of maternal omniscience as well as in the judgment of maternal culpability.

A Mother's Reckoning and the Myth of Maternal Omniscience: "Your Children May Be Unknowable to You"

Klebold's memoir opens with an introduction by esteemed psychologist Andrew Solomon, in which he directly confronts the prevalent and normative belief that "a bad kid is only a ... product of pliable nurture rather than immutable nature" (x). He continues: "We want to believe that parents create criminals because in supposing that, we reassure ourselves that in our own house, where we are not doing such wrong things, we do not risk this calamity" (xii). He concedes that he, too, initially believed that upon meeting Sue and Tom Klebold, he would discern the "innumerable, clear mistakes" of their parenting (xii): "I didn't want to like the Klebolds, because the cost of liking them would be an acknowledgement that what happened wasn't their fault, and if it wasn't their fault, none of us are safe" (xii). But upon meeting the Klebolds and "liking them very much," he realized that the "psychopathy behind the Columbine massacre could emerge in anyone's household" (xii). For Solomon, "the ultimate message of [Sue Klebold's memoir] is terrifying: you may not know your own children, and, worse yet, your children may not be knowable to you. The stranger you fear may be your own son or daughter" (xiii).

In his introduction, which frames and structures the reading of the memoir, Solomon confronts and discredits normative assumptions of motherhood—good mothers know their children, and good mothering creates good children. His exoneration of Sue Klebold compels the reader to likewise not blame the mother for the Columbine massacre. However, I argue that even though the introduction counters normative motherhood, the memoir itself serves to both reinforce and validate it. Although Sue ultimately comes to reject the normative supposition that equates bad children with bad parenting, her belief in the myth of the omniscient mother remains steadfast. In his introduction, Solomon comments that Sue "presents *not knowing* as a betrayal of her son and the world" (my emphasis, xvi), and when Solomon asks Sue what she would ask Dylan if he were in the room, she replies, "I would ask him to forgive me, for being his mother and *never knowing* what was going on inside his head, for not being able to help him, for not being the person that he could confide in" (my emphasis, xvii). Whereas the introduction challenges the normative assumption of good motherhood that children are knowable, Sue's words say otherwise: As a mother, she should have known, and in not knowing, she failed—or in her words "betrayed"—not only her son but also the larger society. Moreover, because Sue believes she is a good mother, this realization particularly devastates her. As a good mother, she should have known what Dylan was going through; she should have been able to help Dylan, thus preventing the Columbine tragedy and her son's suicide. Sue never questions the belief in the good all-knowing mother even as the introduction challenges it. Rather, Sue still believes in the truth and sanctity of this normative and mother-blaming myth of the omniscient mother. For Sue, the responsibility for the tragedy rests not with normative motherhood and its expectation of the omniscient mother but with her: She failed to be the all-knowing mother that she believed herself to be.

Indeed, the memoir valorizes rather than critiques many of the assumptions of normative motherhood—particularly what I have termed elsewhere as essentialization, naturalization, and idealization. In patriarchal motherhood, it is assumed (and expected) that all women want to be mothers (essentialization), that maternal ability and motherlove are innate to all mothers (naturalization), and that all mothers find joy and purpose in motherhood (idealization). Significantly, throughout the memoir, Sue positions herself as a good mother, specifically through these three central mandates of normative motherhood. The tension, if not paradox, of the memoir is that even though Sue believes in the myth of the essential, natural, and ideal mother and believes herself to be that mother, her practice of normative motherhood did not prevent the tragedy of Columbine. For Sue, this paradox is not caused by the mandates and myths of normative motherhood but by her failure to be that good mother, particularly an all-knowing one. However, I suggest that her own memoir undercuts the idealized myth of the omniscient mother, which Sue vehemently believes in and defends. Indeed, the memoir compels the reader to ask the following questions: If a mother who believes in and practices good motherhood cannot know her son, then who or what is at fault? Is it the individual mother or the normative discourse of motherhood that assumes that she can know her son? In its answer to these, *A Mother's Reckoning* powerfully critiques the normative mandate of the omniscient mother.

In making my argument, I do not suggest that normative motherhood caused the Columbine massacre; rather, I argue that many readers of the memoir, and Sue herself, believe a good mother could have and should have prevented the Columbine massacre. The essential, natural, and ideal mother of normative motherhood, it is assumed, could not have raised a son capable of such a massacre, and, more particularly, she would have known what was going on with her son and could have prevented the tragedy from happening. But as I discuss below, Sue was that good mother, but even as that good mother, she still raised a bad son and failed to know what her son was going through. For Sue, and for many readers of the memoir, this failure indicates Sue's poor mothering. In contrast, I argue that this dissonance between the aim and outcome of Sue's mothering—a good mother who raised a bad child—reveals not the shortcomings in Sue's mothering but the fissures in normative motherhood's ideology. If the principles of normative motherhood were true, the Columbine tragedy could not have happened, since Sue was a loving and involved mother. Sue's narrative of good motherhood thus underscores the fallacies of normative motherhood, particularly as it is conveyed in the myth of the omniscient mother.

Sue, as she explains in her memoir, "wanted to be a mother since she was a child" (60). She describes Tom, and herself, as "loving, attentive, engaged, active, involved and present parents" (xx, 62). As Sue elaborates: "My own 1950s childhood looked like the traditional postwar life depicted in the television shows of that day. Although the world had changed significantly (and I worked four days a week, instead of staying home full time, as my mother had with her three kids), that close knit suburban family was the one Tom and I followed in raising our own children" (62). Tom and Sue were "hands-on parents who limited the intake of television and sugary cereals … [They] monitored what movies [their] boys could see, and put them to bed with stories and prayers and hugs" (61). She and Tom were "confident parents," especially with their second child, Dylan. Sue believed that her many years of babysitting, her graduate training in child development and psychology, and her career in teaching prepared her for mothering: "Naively I believed the combination of knowledge and intuition honed by experience was sufficient to stand my own children in good stead. At the very least, I reasoned, we'd know where to turn if we encountered problems" (62). Sue always took "pleasure and pride in being an active and respected part of [her] community; in being thought of as a good mom" (44); she "had taken great pride in [her] sons, in the family Tom and [she] had built, and in being a good mother" (123). Sue is indeed the good mother of patriarchal motherhood.

About her son Dylan, whom they called "The Sunshine Boy," Sue says the following: "Dylan was the classic good kid. He was easy to raise, a pleasure to be with, a child who had always made us proud"

(61); "[he] wasn't a kid we worried and prayed over" (xx). He "always made [Sue] feel like a good mother" (12), and "[she] was grateful to be Dylan's mother, and loved him with [her] whole heart and soul" (xx). Sue also believed that those closest to her were "inoculated against suicide because [she] loved them or because she was an astute, sensitive, caring person who could keep them safe" (156). On the night of Dylan's prom, only seventy-two hours before the massacre, Sue thought about how her "youngest son always seemed to do the right thing" and how she had "*done a good job with this kid*" (29-30). And on the day of the Columbine tragedy, Sue "woke up as an ordinary wife and mother," who was "happy to be shepherding [her] family through the daily business of work, chores and school" (32). Indeed, as Sue reflects in her memoir: "If anyone had peeked inside our lives before Columbine ... what they would have seen, even with the tightest zoom lens, was thoroughly ordinary, no different from the lives unfolding in countless homes across the country" (xx). And as the SWAT team arrived at their home following the massacre, Sue thought, "*We are the last people on earth anyone would expect to be in this situation*" (11).

Sue is the quintessential good mother of normative motherhood: She is happily married and is an attentive, engaged, and devoted parent; her children are at the centre of her life and identity, and she is a know-ledgeable and loving mother. The question, then, that propels A *Mother's Reckoning* is how does one account for the Columbine tragedy? As Sue reflects, "I understood the world was united by a single question, which was to know why the shootings had taken place" (52). Most people—in accordance with the dictate of normative motherhood that equates bad children with bad parenting—blame the parents, particularly the mother. Before the Columbine tragedy, Sue would have likewise blamed the parents: "I completely understood why people were blaming us. I'd certainly be furious beyond measure with the parents of *that* child, had it been the other way around. I'd hate them. Of course I'd blame them" (44). Sue further comments:

> Didn't I wonder about a criminal's family whenever I heard about a terrible act of violence? *Didn't I think, What on earth did the parents do to that poor child so he could grow up to do something like that? A child raised with love, in a loving home, could never have done such a thing.* For years, and without a second thought, I'd accept explanations laying the blame squarely with the criminal's

family. Obviously, the parents had been oblivious, irresponsible, secretly abusive. Of course the mother had been a shrew, a smother, a doormat. (95)

However, Sue eventually rejects and resists this mother-blaming stance to explain the massacre and her son's suicide because the "caricatures of us [as parents] were not true—and the truth was far more disturbing" (44).

Sue recognizes that "the natural response to tragedy is to look for meaning. How could this happen? Who is to blame" (245). But parental culpability as the explanation for the massacre is "misleading, because it tie[s] up too neatly a far more confounding reality" (245):

> Like all mythologies, this belief that Dylan was a monster served a deeper purpose; people needed to believe they would recognize evil in their midst.... If Dylan was a monster, then the events at Columbine—however tragic—were anomalous, the equivalent of a lightning strike on a clear, sunny day. The problem? It wasn't true. As monstrous as Dylan's actions were, the truth about him is much harder to square.... The disquieting reality is that behind the heinous atrocity was an easygoing shy, likable young man who came from a "good home." (61)

This challenge to the stance of parental culpability and mother blame reveals that Sue does resist the normative assumption equating bad children with bad parenting to explain the tragedy of Columbine; however, her refutation still does not answer for Sue, or the reader, why Columbine happened.

In the preface to the memoir, Sue writes the following:

> Sixteen years have passed since that terrible day, and I have dedicated them to understanding what is still incomprehensible to me—how a promising boy's life could have escalated into such a disaster, and on my watch. I have interrogated experts as well as our family, Dylan's friends, and, most of all myself. What did I miss, and how could I have missed it? I have scoured my daily journals. I have analyzed our family life with the ferocity of a forensic scientist, turning over mundane events and exchanges in search of the clues I missed. What should I have seen? What could I have done differently? (xix)

Later in the memoir, she asks "how a child raised in [her] home ... whom [she] had taught to say *please* and *thank you* and to have a firm handshake [could have] killed other people and planned even greater destruction" (254). For Sue, the answer is simply but profoundly not being the omniscient mother of normative motherhood.

On Sue's first day back to work, a member of her team complimented the computer teacher for keeping the machines in good working order, to which he responded, "Well, you get to know the machines. After a while, it's like being a good parent" (118). While looking at Sue, the teacher then added, "When you're a good parent, you just sort of know what your kids are up to" (118). And even as Sue is appreciative and humbled by the many kindnesses shown by both friends and strangers, she still "felt sure they must be wondering. *What on earth did you people do to create such anger in a child? How could you not see what was happening?*" (48). Later in the memoir, Sue mentions a letter she received written in black marker with the words: "How COULD YOU NOT KNOW??!" (97). For Sue, it was the question she had asked herself day and night:

I had not imagined myself to be a perfect parent, by any stretch of the imagination. I did, however, believe my close connection to Dylan ... meant I would be able to intuit if something was wrong, especially if something was very wrong. I would never have told you that I had access to Dylan's every thought and feeling, but I would have said, with confidence, that I knew exactly what he was capable of. (97)

But she concludes that she would have been wrong. Here, Sue explicitly references the myth of the omniscient mother: the ability to intuit a child's feeling and to foretell their behaviour. In the chapter appropriately titled "Judgement," she reads the media coverage of the deposition and reflects: "There it was again; conscientious parents would have known what their sons were planning; our failure to know meant we were responsible" (267). But Sue also says the following: "Hurt as I was, I also understood. I too had believed a good parent should know what her kids were thinking. If the situation had been reversed.... I would have blamed them too" (267).

Sue's comment reveals a tension, if not a paradox, in her interpretation of the omniscient mother to explain the Columbine tragedy.

Sue's insertion of the word "had" (before the word "believed") in the above quote suggests that she no longer thinks a parent should be expected to know, yet the word "would" positioned before "blamed them too" implies that she does believe a parent should be blamed for not knowing. Earlier in this chapter, I discussed how Sue "presents *not knowing* as a betrayal of her son and the world" (my emphasis, xvi), and if she could speak to Dylan, she "would ask him to forgive [her], for being his mother and never knowing what was going on inside his head, for not being able to help him, for not being the person that he could confide in" (xvii). I suggest that when Sue writes the memoir, sixteen years after Columbine, paradoxically she no longer believes a parent should know, but she still believes that had she known, she could have prevented the tragedy. And in her to failure to know, she bears responsibility.

In other words, although Sue no longer positions the mandate of omniscience as prescriptive—a parent should know—she does still consider it as explanatory (i.e., had she known, the tragedy could have been averted). But for this explanation to function, it requires that a mother can know, which is what the omniscient mother myth assumes. Sue's own experience, however, suggests otherwise: Children may not be knowable. Indeed, the memoir is replete with innumerable examples and testimonies of the very "un-knowableness" of children. "Nothing, I saw," Sue explains, "made me think he was suffering from problems of any magnitude" (120). Sue was desperate to show people that Dylan had been loved and that she had been a good mother—"and that, despite our close relationship, I'd had no idea what he was planning or the slightest suspicion he was capable of such a barbaric act" (119). Sue later wonders, "How could Dylan have hidden a side of him so entirely different from Tom and me, from his teachers, his closest friends, and their parents" (147). Shortly before the massacre, Sue hugged Dylan and told him she loved him and was proud of him, but Dylan only looked down embarrassed and whispered his thanks. For years, Sue replayed this scene in her mind: "The memory of that hug is one of the most painful I hold ... the knowledge that, to this day, I have no idea what on earth Dylan could possibly have been thinking" (231).

Sue does concede that "There were hints that Dylan was troubled," and she takes "responsibility for missing them," but there was no "deafening klaxon, no blinking neon danger sign" (60). When Dylan was arrested for breaking into a van and stealing electronic equipment, his parents disciplined him, and Dylan was required to attend a diversion program. Sue also suggested counselling, to which Dylan responded: "I do *not* need counselling. I'll show you I don't" (196). Dylan received an early termination from the program, and the counsellor told Tom and Sue that Dylan "had done exceptionally well ... and he was convinced that [Dylan] was on solid ground" (217). This was ten weeks before the massacre. After Tom and Sue learned of the disturbing paper Dylan had written for his English class, they asked the teacher if they should be concerned, but the teacher assured them it was nothing to worry about. Although Sue had planned on reading Dylan's paper, she simply forgot about it: "This lack of follow through on my part was uncharacteristic, but indicative: I believed Dylan was a psychologically healthy human being. I never considered that the paper could be a reflection of deeply seated problems" (226). Sue later reflects, "It is not that I didn't know something was wrong, but I had no idea it was a life and death situation, I was just worried Dylan was unhappy" (226-27).

Significantly, Sue realizes that she could not have known what Dylan was thinking or planning because he did not want his parents to know:

> In retrospect, I can see how Dylan expertly allayed our concerns, whenever we raised them. I don't know whether he was managing himself, or us—whether he was hoping whatever was wrong would get better, or that we wouldn't notice how bad it was. He'd always been the kid we could rely on to do the right thing, the kid who wanted to take care of everything himself. So when he said he was okay, we believed him. (215-16)

Sue further explains that she and Tom "did not react with greater purpose when Dylan's life went off the rails *because he seemed to get himself back on track*" (175). And he showed no clear and present danger, as some children do: "We had not done everything right ... [but] even with these regrets, there was no obvious indications he was planning something destructive" (263). Sue stresses that if she had noticed something seriously wrong, she "would have moved mountains to fix it" (263). Yet she parented Dylan as the child she knew—"not the one he had become without [her] knowledge" (266). That Sue did not know what Dylan was thinking and planning because Dylan simply did not want her to know critiques and counters the myth of the all-knowing mother.

Through the personal testimonies of other families, as well as through expert advice, the memoir further disrupts the myth of maternal omniscience. Cindy, a friend of Tom's when he was growing up, sent them a letter, in which she shared how she was raped as a teenager and how it left her depressed and suicidal. She never told her parents and suffered in silence for several months until she finally told a friend, who supported her. Cindy writes the following: "This is what SHOULD have happened with Dylan. A friend, a peer should have been there for him. *Please know this. This friend could not have been* [his parents] ... The process of growing up and separation make it *extremely difficult* for children to seek out their parents...for help with these hidden, painful problems" (103-04). For Sue, "Cindy's letter validated for us how a child's personal devastation could go undetected by the most watchful parents, teachers, and peers, if they chose to keep it concealed" (104). Sue further reflects, "I would not have thought it possible for a kid to hide an event as earthshaking as rape, or thoughts and feelings as serious as suicidal ideation, especially from parents like the Worths" (104). Sue realizes that "each day brought a new shock to illuminate how painful—and dangerous—this belief of the all-knowing mother had been" (104). Sue cites an experiment cited by Adrian Raine from his book *The Anatomy of Violence*. Children aged four were asked not to peek at a toy, and whether they did or not was secretly filmed by the researchers. When a group of undergraduate students were shown the footage of the children giving their answers and were told to determine which were lying, the students were correct only 51 per cent of the time. And when police officers reviewed the video, they were correct only 41 per cent of the time. From this study, Raine concludes: "Parents you *think* you know what your kids get up to, but actually you don't have a clue with your own toddler" (218). For Sue, this is a cold consolation because until April 1999, she still believed that Dylan could not have deceived her (218).

Sue believes she could have prevented the tragedy, if she had known what Dylan was going through. Yet she also paradoxically understands that she could not have known what her son was going through. Sue was fooled, which shows how naïve and dangerous the belief in the myth of maternal omniscience is. I have taught this memoir in my bad mothers literature course on two occasions. At first, most students believed in the myth of maternal omniscience and argued that Sue should have known what Dylan was thinking and planning. However, when I asked the students about whether their parents knew what they were thinking and doing as a teenager, their response was "of course not!" In one student's seminar on the memoir, she shared with the class how she kept her depression, even suicidal ideation, from her father when she was a teenager. When asked why, she explained that she did not want to upset or worry her father, who was raising her as a single parent, nor did she want to disappoint him. The belief in maternal omniscience is naïve and dangerous precisely because it assumes that mothers can always protect their children from all troubles or tragedies. And when mothers fail to avert difficulties or disasters with their children, as they inevitably do, mothers are held solely and fully accountable and responsible.

In saying this, I do not discount Sue's argument that parents can be more attentive to indicators of depression; moreover, I share Sue's conviction that "asking 'why' only makes us feel hopeless," whereas "asking 'how' points the way forward, and shows us what we must do" (277). I lost my own father to suicide as a teenager and my own children struggled with depression as teenagers, so I agree that "a broader call to action and a comprehensive overview [on mental health] is long overdue and urgently needed" (xxi). However, even with knowledge or intervention, parents may not be able to protect or save their children. Eric, the other Columbine shooter and Dylan's friend, did see a psychiatrist, yet this did not prevent his role in the Columbine shooting. Moreover, in assuming that it is only mothers who can and should know their children, others—fathers, siblings, friends, teachers, coaches—are exempted from their responsibility in caring for children and are exonerated from accountability: Dylan's friends had "been as blindsided as [Sue] had been" (89), but no one blames Dylan's friends for not knowing what Dylan was thinking or planning, even though teenagers are often closer to their peers than family members. Finally, and most importantly, the myth of maternal omniscience—in assigning all responsibility for children's failings solely and only to mothers— justifies and legitimates the mother blame so rampant in patriarchal culture and so pivotal in the disempowerment of mothers. Sue writes the following in her memoir: "The only thing I knew for sure was that Dylan had participated in the massacre *in spite* of the way he had been raised, not because of it" (257). For me, what is truly incomprehensible is not, as Sue believed, "how a promising boy's life could have escalated into such a disaster" (xviiii); it is rather how the myth of maternal omniscience allows us to judge and blame this mother for a massacre committed by a son so fully and completely loved.

Aftermath and the Judgment of Maternal Culpability: "I Am Not Responsible for Your Decision"

Monique Lépine's memoir *Aftermath* likewise critiques and counters normative motherhood, but with this memoir, the focus is less the myth of maternal omniscience and more the judgment of maternal culpability, particularly as it is enacted in maternal self-blame. Although Sue blames herself for not being an omniscient mother who could have prevented the Columbine tragedy, Sue also presents herself as the good mother of normative motherhood, and, thus, the memoir challenges the assumption of maternal culpability. Sue was a good mother, yet she raised a bad son, exposing the belief in the all-knowing mother as fallacious and fictitious. In contrast, Monique does not present herself as the good mother; indeed, her memoir opens with "I have never been a happy and fulfilled wife and mother" (vi). In the opening pages of the memoir, readers learn that Monique is a divorced mother who was forced to return to work when her children were young and that "those first years of single motherhood were difficult" (3). "In a way," Monique explains, "my children lost both their parents as the father was not involved with the children and my full-time job kept me so busy, I only saw them on weekends" (3). Marc's younger sister, Nadia, died of a drug overdose at twenty-eight in 1996, seven years after Marc committed the Montreal Massacre and died by suicide. In the space of seven years, Monique had buried both her children. Moreover, *A Mother's Reckoning* reinforces Sue's status of the good mother through the introduction by an esteemed expert and in the idealized photo of her and Dylan on the cover of the book as well as with the normative family photos that open each chapter; in contrast, Lépine's memoir contains no family pictures and the cover is graced only with a black-and-white photo of a crumpled flower, an image suggestive of thwarted or damaged growth. In framing and positioning Monique as the bad mother as scripted by the dictates of normative motherhood, the memoir seems to suggest maternal culpability as the reason for the Montreal Massacre. However, I argue that what the memoir recounts is Monique's own dispute and discord with mother blame, particularly as it is internalized as maternal self-blame. Through Monique's journey from guilt to healing, she comes to reject the judgment of maternal culpability, as she writes in a letter to Marc that "*I am not responsible for your decision*" (177).

The memoir opens with Monique seeing the news of the massacre on television and "being appalled by the senselessness of the attack" (3). Later that evening at her weekly prayer meeting, she asked the group "to pray for the mother of the Polytechnique killer," and as she prayed, Monique thought "Poor woman, poor mother ... How can she possibly go on after such an ordeal?" (4). She thought this because she "too was having a lot trouble at that time with [her] own children" (4). Monique did not learn until the following day that the Polytechnique killer was her son Marc. When the police asked her to accompany them to the police station, Monique protested, "Why? I've done nothing wrong" (11). The police, Monique felt, "had little regard for what [she] might be going through" (11). As the police asked her question after question, Monique "was so terrified and dazed with grief that [she] couldn't concentrate [and] just blurted out the first things that came to mind" (12) After the "seemingly endless charade went on and on," Monique responded to the police's question about Marc's high school attendance with "Figure it out for yourself and go to hell" (13). Later in the conversation, the police asked her to talk to a psychiatrist, and when they requested that she stay at a hotel, Monique responded: "To a hotel! What hotel? I don't have money for a hotel" (14). Monique instead stayed with her pastor—"a place where [she] could hide away and feel safe" (15). Monique's self-presentation as emotionally unstable and as ill-mannered serves to reinforce her representation as the bad mother and the attendant supposition of maternal culpability.

Significantly, the opening chapter of *A Mother's Reckoning* concludes with Sue knowing that "the greatest mercy I could pray for was not my son's safety, but for his death" (17), whereas the opening chapter of *Aftermath* ends with Monique thinking, "I have always been afraid of the dark and that night especially so. I was afraid Marc would come back to kill me" (15). We are told later in the memoir that "Every night [Monique] was haunted by the same nightmarish scenario ... [her] son had decided [she] was the cause of all his problems and was coming to stab [her]" (23). Later when Monique returned to live in her condo three months after the massacre, "she was terrified at the prospect ... [as her] apartment [was] filled with [her] son's intangible presence" (39). She had convinced herself that Marc "was going to come back and kill [her]" (39). This nightmare and Monique's fear, I argue, represent her guilt in believing that she is responsible for the massacre. As Monique writes, "My shame, guilt, and above all, grief overwhelmed me" (16). When Monique wanted to attend the funeral of the victims to offer comfort, she thought, "The mother of a killer cannot do that, especially if she bears part of the responsibility and public blame." As her feelings of guilt grew, she asked herself whether she had "raised him properly" or whether she had given him "enough love and encouragement" (25). Yet as Marc's ghost followed her everywhere, Monique realized that this creature "no longer bore the slightest resemblance to the person [she] had brought into the world" (27). To start living again, she had to get him out of her head "by erasing his name and removing all traces of his existence" (27).

Although both Monique and Sue experience guilt for their son's crime, Sue's guilt is conveyed as regret or remorse for not helping Dylan and not being the omniscient mother, whereas for Monique, the guilt is internalized as maternal self-blame—for not being the good mother capable of raising a good son. Initially, Monique seeks to alleviate her guilt through banishing all memory of her son. Upon the recommendation of her social worker, Monique burns all photographs of her children: "It was a relief to make a definite, albeit symbolic break with the past. My children had been burned to ashes; my tangible memories of them would suffer the same fate" (142). In contrast, because her guilt is experienced as regret, Sue endeavours to hold Dylan's memory close: "In those very early days, a great deal of what I filled my diaries with was memories.... Trying to unravel the mystery would come later. In those first days, I wrote simply out of love" (59). In other words, because Sue experiences regret for not being the omniscient mother, she seeks connection with her son, whereas the self-blame Monique feels for being a bad mother forces her to distance herself from her son.

Since Monique blames herself for the massacre, her memoir, unlike Sue's, devotes many pages to her past to account for her failure as a mother. Monique imagines her children hurling insults at her: "You're too weak and ineffective! ... you're to blame for what happened to me." (79). In order to heal, Monique realizes, she will have to dig into her past to uncover why her "children hate her so much" (79). Readers learn she had three abortions with her boyfriend, who later became her husband, because he refused to wear condoms to prevent pregnancy. When she gave birth to her son, she discovered that another woman at the hospital had also just given birth to a child who was also fathered by her husband; she later learned from seeing her husband's income tax returns that he had two children with another woman. Her husband was negligent and violent with her and the children. One time, her husband picked up and threw Nadia into her crib; another time, he put the children to bed but neglected to remove their boots and snowsuits (53). When Marc was an infant, she worked as her husband's secretary for his business, and when she made mistakes in typing, he used "to slap [her] about the face and neck with his meaty hands" (52). He would then demand she retype the document, and if Marc were crying, he would refuse to allow her to attend to the child: "The longer his cries went unanswered, the more my baby withdrew into silence" (52). As Monique further explains: "Although I hated [my husband] more and more and more and more every day, I was still subservient toward this man, still ready to forgive him in order to save our marriage" (48)

Monique did eventually leave her husband because of the violence toward her son. One morning, Marc was singing to himself in his room and woke his father, who then slapped Marc in the face so hard "the marks lasted a week" (54). Monique longed to comfort her son, but his father would not allow her to "pamper him" because according to him, showing "any sign of love or affection to a boy only spoiled him" (54). At this moment Monique states: "I had had enough and filed for divorce" (54). However, upon the official separation, Monique was "literally thrown out onto the street," as her husband had taken out a second mortgage on their home and it along with all their personal possessions were seized. (55). Without child support from her ex-husband and after having been told by the government that if "she could not support [her] children, they would be ... taken ...and put up for adoption, (140), Monique returned to her career of nursing and had to sometimes leave her children with caregivers, whose sole motivation was money (161). Monique also, at times, placed her children with a surrogate family and saw them only on the weekends (140). As Monique explains, "I wished my children could have lived with me all the time, but then I would not have been able to work, which was the only way I could support them" (141). "I was not happy", Monique writes, "with the balance between my professional and my private life" (142). She continues: "I know that, to this day, many single mothers struggle with the same problem" (142). After her divorce, she "had many lovers—too many, in fact"; she was "very unstable, trying unsuccessfully to fill a huge emotional void" (95). Looking back, Monique is "ashamed of what [her children] must have thought" and "wonders if Marc, seeing his mother behave this way ... may have thought that all women were like that and none deserved respect" (96). Marc's life "was filled with instability and violence [and] in the twenty-five years he spent on this earth, he moved at least fifteen times, living in places as far-flung as Montreal, Puerto Rico and Costa Rica" (52).

Monique is evidently not the attentive and engaged mother demanded in normative motherhood, nor did she provide the constant care and stable family, as Sue did. However, Monique loved her children, and I argue she did the best she could, given the conditions and circumstances of her life. Upon the birth of Marc, she writes, "I wanted this child with all my heart" (43); she thought, "he was the most beautiful baby in the world" (46), and her "life with [the] new baby was good and sweet" (47). When Monique found six-year-old Marc in a closet, remembering his father's violence and terrified that a workman in their home would do the same, she took her son to a psychiatrist, although this would have been an uncommon practice in the early 1970s. The psychiatrist explained that "[Marc's] behavior was caused by the emotional trauma of divorce" but that "he would get over it in due course" (56). Since she had separated from her husband in 1971, she devoted herself to raising and providing for her children: "They were my all, my joy, my life" (70). Arguably, Monique could have done better or more for her children, but it was the children's father who abused and abandoned them, not Monique; she did the best she could as a divorced woman fleeing a violent marriage in the early 1970s.

Regardless, Monique accepts maternal culpability for many years following the massacre:

No matter how much I tried to put the blame for what happened on society, on their father who abandoned them at a young age ... I was forced back to the same conclusion: that I bore a large part of the responsibility. Looking back, all I could see were mistakes and shortcomings in everything I had done ... My children did not create themselves: I could not deny the fact that they must have inherited a share of me; my personality traits, angers, neuroses, and fears. In fact, the more I thought about it, the more convinced I was that they had become what I myself might have been, had I not somehow managed to control my darker impulses. (78-79)

Monique sought solace in religion for her guilt and strove to atone for it through charitable service to others. She volunteered with a young mothers' organization and attempted to "reconstruct [for the young mothers] a value system ... teaching them how to be good mothers" as her way of 'indirectly protecting their children, by enabling the little ones to receive the warmth and tenderness that had been so lacking for Marc and Nadia" (105-06). However, Monique says the following: "No matter how much I strove for it, I was unable to attain inner peace, or shake off my guilt. I had let my daughter die of an overdose. My son had committed a monstrous criminal act" (78).

After many years of healing, however, Monique refutes the explanation of maternal culpability, as she finally shares her story at a church assembly after many years of silence and seclusion. She concludes her address by boldly proclaiming her identity: "I am Monique Lépine, the mother of Marc Lépine" (111). Monique further reflects on her declaration: "That evening ... almost thirteen years to the day after the Polytechnique massacre, I shed the guilt and shame that had weighed me down for far too many years and took on a new identity" (111). Seventeen years after the Montreal massacre—and following the Dawson College shooting in Montreal in 2006, in which another young man killed one student and injured many more before committing suicide—Monique decided to tell her story in a televised interview: "I had come to believe that bringing my experiences to a wider audience would help people understand that mothers are not responsible for the acts of their children. I wanted them to know that ... life will go on, albeit differently, it is possible to endure terrible ordeals and come out the other side" (118). The day following the interview, and for the first time since the massacre, Monique met, at their request, the parents of Anne Marie Lemay, one of the women murdered by her son. The parents told Monique the following: "What happened was not your fault. We have always held you in our thoughts" (123). After her television appearance and the meeting with Anne Marie's parents, Monique "felt released from an incredible burden" (126)—the judgment of maternal culpability, which had defined and burdened her. She felt empowered to seek explanations for the massacre not in her own life but in the life of her son: "What had been going on inside Marc's head? I felt it was a crucial question. Perhaps the process of looking for an answer would finally bring to a close my own inner journey, begun immediately after the shooting so many years ago" (126-27).

The final pages of the memoir are, thus, devoted to Marc's story, as Monique seeks to understand what happened. Monique met with several of Marc's friends so as to "bring to light the memories of him that they had never shared" (128). She learned from his friends that Marc had anger management problems, suffered from low self-esteem (132), and was abnormally shy (153). Listening to these stories, Monique speculated whether her children's difficulties may have stemmed from what psychologists call "attachment disorder," whereby an unloved child becomes emotionally damaged and has difficulty developing relationships with others. Monique wonders whether "that was what happened to Marc and Nadia, if the abuse they suffered had doomed their lives from the start" (138-39). Monique learned as well that Marc "had preconceived notions about women ... [which] grew into outright prejudice" (131). Marc never shared such opinions with his mother; had he done so, "she would have certainly never have agreed with him" (131). Monique, then, wonders the following: "If Marc's hatred toward women was unconsciously directed at me because he thought of me as a feminist, perhaps he thought if I had played a less liberated, more traditional role, I would have loved him more" (161-62).

However, these moments of returning maternal self-blame are challenged and corrected with the words of one of Marc's friends: "Marc loved you very much ... [it was] the lack of a father figure and the memory of his father's violence [that] were both decisive factors in what [he] did" (134). And although Monique reprimands herself for not being an omniscient mother—"Not a day goes by when I don't blame myself for failing to realize my son was turning into a killer. How could I not have noticed how desperate his state was?" (129)—she realizes, as does Sue in *A Mother's Reckoning*, that "there are aspects of our children's inner lives that we can simply never know" (147). These feelings are further validated by a police officer who investigated the massacre and whom Monique later meets. The officer told her the following: "Some things in life just cannot be explained. Your son was probably mentally ill but nobody knew it. Was there any way to prevent this? That is the guilt we all share ... I want you to know that none of the officers blamed you. Perhaps no one else has said this to you, but I believe you were, and in many ways still are, a victim" (182-83). Another officer said: "In spite of our extensive inquiry, we will never know the whole truth.... We can't really say what was going on inside [Marc's] head" (195). In *Aftermath*, as in *A Mother's Reckoning*, public officials refute and discredit the assumption of maternal omniscience to confirm that a mother cannot be blamed for what she did not know. Indeed as Monique writes in her letter to her son: "After decades of struggling to understand, I have no idea what drove you to it" (177). Thus, Monique understands that she is not responsible for her son's decision. In detailing Monique's journey from guilt to understanding, *Aftermath* delivers an incisive and potent challenge and corrective to the myth of maternal omniscience as well as the judgment of maternal culpability.

Conclusion

Normative motherhood, as noted above, assumes and expects that all women want to be mothers (essentialization), that maternal ability and motherlove are innate to all mothers (naturalization), and that all mothers find joy and purpose in motherhood (idealization). However, the realities of mothers' lives tell a quite different story. In her memoir, Monique writes the following:

Children come into the world without any instruction booklet.... Women may think they are preparing themselves for motherhood by learning how to change diapers, warm bottles, but they are mistaken. A mother is a lot more than a nanny: She must be a nurse to treat injuries, a confidante to harbour secrets disclosed, and a psychologist to sort out disagreements—all without

220

necessarily having the qualifications to perform any of these tasks. (161)

Indeed, contrary to the assumptions and expectations of normative motherhood, the desire to mother and the ability of mothering is not innate in women, nor is joy inherent in motherhood. Both Sue and Monique loved their sons, and they did the best they could to raise them. Both Dylan and Marc loved their mothers, and, as evidence suggest, they never held their mothers responsible for the shootings or their suicide. Erik, Marc's friend, told Monique that "Marc loved you very much; he often said so" (134). In *A Mother's Reckoning*, during the "Basement Tapes" when Eric suggests that they say something about their parents, Dylan, we are told, "looks down at his fingernails and says, almost inaudibly, 'My parents have been good to me. I don't want to browse there'" (136). The script of mother blame dictates that the sons should hold their mothers responsible for how their lives turned out, but they do not. Marc loved and respected his mother, and Dylan knew his parents were good to him. If the sons refuted the explanation of mother blame, then we as a society should do the same. Indeed, this is the request of *A Mother's Reckoning* and *Aftermath*: We must interrogate the myth of maternal omniscience as well as the judgment of maternal culpability to realize that what is truly incomprehensible are not the tragedies of Columbine and the Montreal Massacre, but that the mothers were blamed for them. In other words, it is not the maternal that is monstrous in these memoirs but rather our patriarchal culture that deems the mothers so.

Works Cited

Klebold, Sue. *A Mother's Reckoning: Living in the Aftermath of Tragedy.* Crown Publishers, 2016.

Lépine, Monique, and Harold Gagne. *Aftermath: The Mother of Marc Lépine Tells the Story of Her Life Before and After the Montreal Massacre.* Translated by Diana Halfpenny, Viking Canada, 2008.

O'Reilly, Andrea. *Matricentric Feminism: Theory, Activism, and Practice.* Demeter, 2016.

Solomon, Andrew. "Introduction." *A Mother's Reckoning: Living in the Aftermath of Tragedy.* Crown Publishers, 2016, x-xvii.

Chapter 11

Monster Mothers and Mother Monsters from *Dracula* to *Stranger Things*

Melissa Dinsman

A backlash against women's rights succeeds to the degree that
it appears not to be political, that it appears not to be a struggle at all.
It is most powerful when it goes private, when it lodges inside a
woman's mind and turns her vision inward, until she imagines the
pressure is all in her head, until she begins to enforce the backlash,
too—on herself.
—Susan Faludi, *Backlash*, p. xxii

"But did you ever stop to think, maybe she's the monster?"
—"Chapter 5: The Flea and the Acrobat,"
Season 1, *Stranger Things*

The Duffer Brothers' hit show *Stranger Things*, released on Netflix on 15 July 2016, is an obvious homage to sci-fi and horror movies—such as *Alien* and *Aliens*, *Carrie*, the *Star Wars* trilogy, and *Poltergeist*—as well as to buddy adventure films like *Goonies* and *Stand by Me*. But with this cultural nostalgia for cinema of the 1970s and 1980s comes a reminder of some dark impulses of that same moment around gender, which manifest in even older-fashioned tropes of mothers and mothering. *Stranger Things* presents its audience with three familiar types of so-called bad mothers: the negligent mother (Karen Wheeler), who seemingly has the ideal family but never knows where her children are; the sexual nonmother (Nancy Wheeler), whose promiscuity keeps her from fulfilling her current, and potentially future, caregiver role; and the working mother (Joyce Byers), who serves as the single but exceedingly determined mom from the other side of the tracks. These mother types, or tropes, are familiar to fans of 1980s cinema because they reflect the negative maternal images that once filled the screens, both big and small. These images, according the Susan Faludi, were part of a larger "backlash" against women and feminism during the Reagan and Bush administrations that infiltrated the newspapers and magazines (including *The New York Times* and *The Nation*), self-help books, and even Hollywood, with films, such as *Fatal Attraction* and *Overboard* presenting independent women as either psychotic enemies of domestic bliss or in need of converting to a more traditional mothering role. As Faludi writes, the 1980s were "a powerful counterassault on women's rights, a backlash, an attempt to retract the handful of small and hard-won victories that the feminist movement did manage to win for women" (xviii).

But the backlash against female advancement as seen in the 1980s was nothing new, with similar regressive shifts occurring in the decade following the end of World War II and at the close of the nineteenth century as a response to the emergence of the New Woman. In fact, in its obsessive presentation of women as inattentive, sexual, and even hysterical, *Stranger Things* seems to take its 1980s mothering tropes straight out of the 1890s, specifically Bram Stoker's gothic horror novel *Dracula* (1897). Thus Joyce (Winona Ryder) finds her working mother counterpart in the dangerously smart mother-to-all-men Mina Harker (a role Ryder played in Francis Ford Coppola's *Dracula*); Nancy (Natalia Dyer) reimagines Lucy Westerna, whose sexuality both shocks her friend and leads to death; and Karen (Cara Buono) serves as a sort of Mrs. Westerna, whose parental inattention puts her daughter in danger. In their transgressions of cultural norms, these three mother types are depicted as monstrous. But if mothers can be monstrous, monsters can also be maternal: Dracula symbolically breastfeeds Mina and the Mind Flayer protects Will Byers during his transformation. Finally, there is *Stranger Things*' young heroine Eleven (Millie Bobby Brown) and her disturbing merger of the mother and monster into one through her birthing of the Demogorgon, her telekinetic powers, her self-sacrifice to protect her friends, and her symbolic rebirth. As I will argue in this chapter, in the summer of 2016, only months before the United States (US) presidential election, old ways of depicting motherhood became new again and perhaps even more dangerous.

At its most basic level, the plot of *Stranger Things* shares some key similarities with its classic monster predecessor. Like Stoker's *Dracula*, in season one of *Stranger Things*, a half-humanoid, otherworldly monster is released into the Western world and attacks humans, one of whom is twelve-year old Will, who is abducted in the first episode. Will has a group of friends (Mike, Dustin, and Lucas), and a newly arrived girl (Eleven), who (like Stoker's Crew of Light) tries to uncover the truth about the monster in order to defeat it and rescue Will. The monster is, like Dracula, remarkably indestructible, and all attempts to use modern weaponized technology against it fail. The only person capable of defeating the monster is Eleven, a girl with telekinetic powers, who many in the fictional town of Hawkins, Indiana, also see as monstrous.

The term "monstrous" is generally used to explain things that are beyond our comprehension and therefore not classifiable or categorizable. Writing on "unnameable" monsters, such as John Carpenter's the Thing, Maria Beville argues that "we use the word [monstrous] to explain things that we cannot understand, and for the most part this applies to behaviour when it is seen to have transgressed the limits of what we ourselves imagine doing" (5). In both *Dracula* and *Stranger Things*, the ability to name the monster is essential for the survival of humankind. Once Dr. Van Helsing explains that the Count is a vampire, he is able to use occult weapons to defeat the monster. Likewise, in *Stranger Things*, where the word "thing" makes up half the show's title, Will's friends label the monster a Demogorgon from the popular quest game Dungeons & Dragons. By giving the "thing" a name, the kids are able to imagine the monster's motives and thereby create rules for its defeat. Thus categorization, even if not scientifically precise, helps the Hawkins kids understand the unknowable. According to Beville, through categorization, one makes the unknown no longer a monster: "Its excess, which is its monstrous nature, is sidestepped when it is classified, and when we are allowed to evaluate our levels of fear in relation to it from a position of safety and distance" (5). But while giving a monster a name may improve its knowability, it does not lessen the monstrosity of its actions. If "monstrous" means to "transgress the limits of what we ourselves imagine doing," then Dracula and the Demogorgon, both of whom prey on humans to replicate themselves, remain monstrous even after categorization.[1]

Beville's definition of the monstrous as transgressing social norms has significant implications for my discussion of feminine and maternal representations in regressive times. Both Stoker and the Duffer Brothers provide examples of women who challenge the traditional visions of motherhood for their respective eras. Although the critical response to *Stranger Things* has largely praised the representation of women, and in particular Ryder's portrayal of the mother as fighter, the show ultimately reproduces the gender dynamics of the movies it seeks to emulate and thus reimagines the Reagan era backlash against feminism for a 2016 audience.[2] The negligent, sexual, and working mothers may, in the end, help save the day, but they are also part of the reason people go missing or die. Such monstrous qualities in the mothers and potential mothers of *Stranger Things* reflect the retrograde feminism of the 1980s, but they also speak to a similar backlash against women occurring today.

The Negligent Mother

With the rise of feminist theory in the 1970s, Stoker's novel saw a significant increase in critical attention due to its representation of the late-Victorian New Woman. But critical consensus remains undecided as to whether Stoker presents a progressive or regressive view of working women and motherhood.[3] An early critic, Carol Senf, took up this question, defining the New Woman as one "who chose financial independence and personal fulfilment as alternatives to marriage and motherhood" and whose embracement of not only education and employment but also sex made her "a subject of controversy in journalism, fiction, and—presumably, at least—drawing rooms" (35). The New Woman, who stepped outside the private feminine sphere, was set up against the traditional domestic mother and suggested the instability of the status quo. As Laura Sagolla Croley writes:

> The largely middle-class New Women who valorized women's education and work outside the home, demonstrated that, like older versions of masculinity, the cult of domesticity and its

idealized version of motherhood might not prevail. More radical New Women, professing that women were entitled to the same forms of sexual expression as men, illustrated that even female chastity was not an irresistibly permanent norm. (95)[4]

Part of the disdain for the New Woman centred on what was perceived as a shirking of maternal duties. Critics of new womanhood argued that if middle-class women worked outside the home, then they could not fulfill their caretaking duties. Thus, the trope of the absent or negligent mother found new life in Victorian fiction, including, for example, Charles Dickens's *Great Expectations* (1861) and Thomas Hardy's *Tess of the d'Urbervilles* (1891).

In Mrs. Westerna, Stoker imagines a negligent mother with deadly consequences. Lucy's mother flits in the background of *Dracula*'s first half in which she preoccupies herself with her daughter's upcoming wedding to Sir Arthur Holmwood. When Lucy becomes ill from Dracula's bite, Van Helsing places garlic around her neck and at the entry points to her room to keep Dracula away, but he refrains from explaining his reasons to Mrs. Westerna, who suffers from a heart condition. Thinking she knows best for her daughter, Mrs. Westerna removes the garlic. Relaying the good news to Van Helsing that Lucy has improved, Mrs. Westerna claims credit for her daughter's sudden recovery:

Well, I was anxious about the dear child in the night, and went into her room. She was sleeping soundly—so soundly that even my coming in did not wake her. But her room was awfully stuffy. There were a lot of those horrible, strong-smelling flowers about everywhere, and she had actually a bunch of them round her neck. I feared that the heavy odour would be too much for the dear child in her weak state, so I took them all away and opened a bit of the window to let in a little fresh air. You will be pleased with her, I am sure. (Stoker 150-51)

Mrs. Westerna's maternal concern for her daughter, while authentic, proves to be naïve and ultimately harmful to Lucy's condition. By removing the garlic and opening the window, the mother invited the vampire into the home and "'all unknowing, and all for the best as she thinks ... los[t] her daughter body and soul'" (151). Regardless of Van

Helsing's decision to "'not tell her'" to "'not even warn her,'" Mrs. Westerna's inattentiveness to the doctor's treatment and her blindness to the clues to her daughter's ailment ultimately result in Lucy's death only a week later, when, looking to comfort her daughter, Mrs. Westerna stays with Lucy one night and is literally frightened to death by a grey wolf shattering the bedroom window pane with his head (151). As she dies, Mrs. Westerna rips the garlic wreath from Lucy's neck and falling, pins Lucy to her bed. Unable to move and no longer protected, Lucy is bitten one last and fatal time. That Mrs. Westerna loves her daughter is never questioned. But her negligence—in part due to Van Helsing's decision to withhold vital information from her— leads to Lucy's death as well as her own. According to Croley, Stoker "associates vampirism with deviant motherhood" (96). Although Croley is specifically thinking about the undead Lucy and the female vampires feeding upon children, we might also consider the negligence and inattention of Mrs. Westerna—a deviation from idealized mother- hood—as leading to the vampirism of her own child.

Such negative depictions of motherhood were nothing new. In her study of fictional eighteenth-century British mothers, Marilyn Francus points out that representations of good mothers were hard to find and that instead the negligent mother was set alongside the wicked mother as monstrous: "Eighteenth-century British narratives of mothers veered toward deviance and sensationalism, as wicked mothers, abandoning mothers, infanticidal mothers, pushy mothers, and evil stepmothers dominated the cultural landscape in ballads, fables, novels, plays, and court records" (10). As with the rise of the New Woman in the late-nineteenth century, Francus argues that these portrayals of motherhood were due to the perception that patriarchal power was weakening. Such fears continue to resurface into the twentieth century and find their culmination in the antifeminist policies of the Reagan administration in the 1980s.[5]

This particular backlash against feminism in the US began in the late 1970s among the evangelical right, moved into the White House in 1981, and was a part of popular culture a few years later. Inundated with antifeminist narratives from politicians, the media, and enter- tainment industries, women began to internalize the messaging and therefore "enforce the backlash, too—on [themselves]" (Faludi xxii). The backlash helped convince women that "women's 'liberation' was the true contemporary scourge—the source of an endless laundry list of personal, social, and economic problems" (Faludi xviii). Part of this internalization, however, was tied to class: middle and upper-class women were far more likely to eschew the label "feminist" than their working-class counterparts.[6] Such class distinctions made their way to television as well. Although shows like *Designing Women* and *The Golden Girls* carved out spaces for independent women, for the most part, mid-1980s sitcoms and dramas presented viewers with a female hierarchy that had suburban housewives on top, followed by career and single women (Faludi 148).

Stranger Things simultaneously replicates and disrupts this hierarchy through Karen Wheeler: the homemaker and negligent mother. Karen presents herself as a "traditional eighties housewife" (Logan). She expresses love for her children, consoles Joyce with a casserole, and proudly displays a reelect Reagan/Bush sign in the yard during season two. Karen manages the house and her children while her husband plays the stereotypical oblivious father. That Nancy and Mike are both kind and strong willed, and the fact that Mike sees his mother as a potential ally to the homeless Eleven, should suggest that Karen has parented successfully. On the surface, Karen is the 1980s mother that women were supposed to be. But Karen is also neglectful. She often has no idea where her children are, suggesting that her offspring might have gained their positive characteristics despite rather than because of her. In season one, episode seven, for example, Mike goes missing, and the Wheeler family is paid a visit by a government agency, which suggests that their son is in danger. The audience knows that Mike is currently looking for Will, thereby making him a target of both the agency that seeks him and the Demogorgon. Although Karen suggests that they look for Mike, she is easily dissuaded by her husband. In fact, Karen's inattention to her children's whereabouts throughout season one (evolving to her almost complete absence in season two and culminating in her admission during the penultimate episode of season three that she has no idea where her children are) results not only in their endangerment but also Nancy's sexual awakening.

The Sexual Nonmother

According to Ann Sumner Holmes and Claudia Nelson, the Victorian anxiety over female sexuality presented itself in two competing images of motherhood: the asexual, pure mother and the sexually "devouring, possessive, threatening" mother (3). Such divergent depictions were shaped by events such as the Contagious Diseases Acts in the 1860s and the branding of prostitution as the great social evil. As Holmes and Sumner write, "The gradual acknowledgement of the female libido gave rise to new anxieties about socially dangerous expressions of feminine sexuality, anxieties that were especially keen with regard to mothers" (4). Stoker presents these competing images of motherhood through Mina and Lucy, although Lucy fails to fulfil her motherly role in the traditional way. Even before her vampiric transformation, Lucy vocalizes a scandalous level of sexuality when she suggests that women should be allowed polygamous relationships. In a letter to her best friend Mina, she writes, "Why can't they let a girl marry three men, or as many as want her and save all this trouble? But this is heresy, and I must not say it" (Stoker 82). Her wish, ironically, comes to pass through blood transfusions. Once bitten by Dracula, Lucy requires a significant amount of blood to replenish what she has lost. The blood of her fiancé, Arthur, proves insufficient and unbeknownst to him, the veins of three other men must be opened. Following her funeral, Arthur states that he finds comfort in the knowledge that his blood had mixed with Lucy's:

> When it was all over, we were standing beside Arthur, who, poor fellow, was speaking of his part in the operation where his blood had been transfused to his Lucy's veins, I could see Van Helsing's face grow white and purple by turns. Arthur was saying that he felt since then as if they two had been really married, and that she was his wife in the sight of God. None of us said a word of the other operations, and none of us ever shall. (Stoker 187)

Thus, Lucy's wish for multiple husbands (one made more from the desire to spare her suitors' feelings rather than any real sexual impulse) is made a symbolic reality in the process of her vampiric transformation. But even though these transfusions were for medical purposes, Arthur's friends (and even the doctor who prescribed the treatment) seem to view them as sexual acts.

Once Lucy's transformation is complete, however, her implied sexual freedom is let loose upon London with deadly consequences. Reemerging from the dead as the "bloofer lady," Lucy, who died before becoming a wife and mother, preys upon the children of Hampstead, thereby becoming the "devouring, possessive, threatening" mother feared by Victorian society (Stoker 190). But vampire-Lucy reverses the role of the nurturing mother by sucking the life out of her child victims. Lucy also exhibits the aggressive female sexuality associated with the New Woman: "The sweetness was turned to adamantine, heartless cruelty, and the purity to voluptuous wantonness" (Stoker 221). Using her newfound sexuality, she attempts to seduce Arthur and feed her insatiable appetite. As a result, she brings about her own violent demise at the hands of her once lover, who drives a stake through her heart, and her friends Drs. Seward and Van Helsing, who cut off her head. For Senf, this scene "succeeds in destroying the New Woman and in reestablishing male supremacy" (45), whereas for Friedrich Kittler, Lucy's violent death serves as a warning to "women who do not live as wives and future mothers" (75). But this argument ignores both Lucy's desire to be a wife while alive and her attempt to replicate herself through children once she is dead. Rather than see Lucy's violent end as a result of only her nonmother status, it might instead prove useful to see Lucy's monstrous fate as a result of being forced into a traditional motherhood role by either societal pressures or the need to stay alive.

Unlike Lucy, who inadvertently gives up her virginity via blood transfusions and pays a fatal price, Nancy Wheeler survives the first three seasons of *Stranger Things*. Nancy's endurance marks her as a "final girl"—a term coined by Carol J. Clover to explain the sexist trope of the morally upright girl's survival at the end of a horror film. But Nancy upends the characteristics of the final girl by choosing to drink, party, lie to her parents, and have sex with her boyfriend, Steve Harrington. By allowing Nancy to survive, the Duffer Brothers challenge the historically sexist portrayal of women in sci-fi and horror. Molly Fitzpatrick argues that Nancy's endurance and rich "inner life" make her "the unsung feminist heroine" of the show. This, however, is an optimistic reading. Although Nancy challenges some of the stereotypes of women in film, her actions are not without fatal consequences. Nancy's decision to have sex with Steve and leave her best friend Barb alone leads to Barb being killed in the Upside Down by the

Demogorgon. Barb's disappearance has a long-lasting impact on Nancy and proves to be the catalyst for many of the decisions she makes throughout *Stranger Things'* first two seasons.

Although the Duffer Brothers add complexity to the representation of the teenage girl in horror films, they still emphasize her sexual choices. Like Lucy, the men who choose to help Nancy are often concerned with her sexual activities: when Nancy reports that Barb is missing, the police question her about her liaison with Steve; Steve misinterprets Jonathan Byers's comforting Nancy as a prelude to sex; and Jonathan takes photographs of Nancy and Steve in the act when out searching for his missing brother. Even though they break the final girl trope, the Duffer Brothers cannot escape society's long history of policing young women's bodies and the "anxieties about socially dangerous expressions of feminine sexuality" (Holmes and Nelson 4). Nancy's actions as a sexual nonmother also lead her to shirk her duties as a sister. Like her mother, Nancy is unaware of her brother's dangerous search for Will. But whereas Karen's neglect is framed as a failure in motherhood, Nancy's is depicted as a sign of a future failure. In her attempt to distance herself from her suburban mother and her explorations of her sexuality, Nancy is portrayed as lacking the maternal caretaker skill that would have helped keep Barb alive and her brother out of harm's way.

The Working Mother

Of all the women that figure in *Dracula* and *Stranger Things*, the working mother has the most success in defeating the monster, but this success comes as a result of her own transgressive qualities. In *Dracula*, Mina Harker's journaling, stenography, and typewriting are essential to the Count's defeat and also align her with the New Woman. As Charles Prescott and Grace Giorgio argue, "Writing represents for Mina an attempt to establish a strong sense of self, which in this charged historical moment carries the political resonance of the New Woman" (490). Although the workday skills Mina acquires suggest that Stoker approved of the advances women were making in the public sphere, especially in comparison to the horrific fate that awaited those women who transgressed sexual codes like Lucy, the reality is that Mina's motivation is not purely self-serving. In a letter to Lucy, Mina claims that she is learning shorthand because she "want[s] to keep up with Jonathan's studies" and that by enhancing her secretarial abilities, she will "be useful to Jonathan" once they are married (Stoker 78). Mina's motivations as expressed in this letter imply that her work outside the home is an extension of her wifely responsibilities.

Mina's duties also involve performing the role of mother even before she bears biological children. Despite Mina being a "clever woman" with a "man's brain," she is depicted as a mother to the Crew of Light and to her manuscript (Stoker 195, 242). After Lucy's death, Mina is expected to comfort a "hysterical" Arthur, despite still being in mourning herself: "I suppose there is something in woman's nature that makes a man free to break down before her and express his feelings on the tender or emotional side without feeling it derogatory to his manhood" (Stoker 238). Far from avoiding this role, Mina embraces it when she sits down beside Arthur and asks him to allow her to be of "some little service" during his grief (Stoker 238). Even Mina's secretarial skills can be read in light of her role as mother. Laura James, for example, argues that Mina's secretarial work should be read as part of her "wifely duties": "Mina's conflation of her typing duties and her expected role as family nurturer is wrapped up in her belief that through her transcription of Jonathan's journal she can protect him from further anxiety" (93). It is noteworthy then that much of Mina's typewriting takes place in the bedroom she shares with her husband, thereby conflating "sexual and textual reproduction ... within the marital bedroom" (James 94). But James stops her analysis before it reaches its maternal conclusion: the text, via its wifely production, is also Mina's child and her nurturing of it leads to Dracula's defeat.

Mina's mothering practice culminates at the novel's end with her transformation into the silent Victorian mother. This role is one that Van Helsing forces Mina to play even before she imagines herself a mother. After writing the text that puts the men onto Dracula's trail, Van Helsing proposes keeping Mina in the dark, effectively kicking her out of the Crew of Light because of her potential to become a mother: "'Even if she not be harmed, her heart may fail her in so much and so many horrors, and hereafter she may suffer—both in waking, from her nerves, and in sleep, from her dreams. And, besides, she is a young woman and not so long married; there may be other things to think of some time, if not now'" (Stoker 242). Van Helsing reasons that the monstrous may infect Mina (like it did Lucy), which would in turn become a stain on her future motherhood. This threat to Mina's ability to become a good Victorian mother "is already coercive enough to force her back into domestic passivity" (Prescott and Giorgio 503). Ironically, Mina's expulsion from the group leads to her vampiric infection, and it is uncertain in the end whether this has left any lasting mark on her or the child. What is made clear, however, is that Mina's awareness of her uncleanliness after her attack and her ability to remain pure of heart and mind enable her to reap the ultimate Victorian rewards: domestic peace and motherhood. Purity was, according to Holmes and Nelson, "a crucial component in ideal maternity;" thus, while sex was essential in the making of motherhood, the Victorians often viewed middle-class mothers as "essentially virginal" (2). By *Dracula*'s conclusion, Stoker has removed Mina from the story's action and her authorial role, giving Jonathan authorship of the final note. Mina has been saved not only through her ability to bear a child (a son of course) but also her desire to be a dutiful wife, which includes handing over the authorial powers to her husband. Because Mina's social transgressions are used in service to the family, they are presented as less threatening than Lucy's sexual independence. Rather than praise the New Woman, Stoker's novel suggests that female advancements are permissible as long as they reinforce traditional maternal values.

Mina's retreat from the public sphere and her subsequent reinforcement of Victorian cultural norms that saw an impenetrable division between working woman and motherhood would seem to find its counterpart in Karen Wheeler, the stay-at-home mom. But Mina, whose secretarial work was done for the benefit of a family she had yet to have, is much more akin to Joyce Byers, the single working mother from the other side of the tracks. Like Mina, whose mothering potential is given unwanted protection by Van Helsing, Joyce too finds her maternal instincts constantly questioned by a disapproving town. Yet like her predecessor, Joyce proves to be the most logical character of the show, using methods of deduction and the decoding of blinking Christmas lights to find her son, Will, in season one. As Clio Chang notes, "Although the outside world thinks Joyce is crazy, she is the most methodical of the bunch, which makes her frustration all the more palpable." Unlike Mina, Joyce has difficulty finding people to believe her; even Jonathan (her eldest son) and Jim Hopper (the police chief) only believe her once they find their own proof. Part of this is due to Joyce's frenzied (even hysterical) behaviour as she searches for Will, but the town's dismissal of Joyce is also very much tied to issues of class. Unlike Karen Wheeler (and even Mina), Joyce does not garner the same level of respect as middle-class mothers.

Writing about motherhood as the central theme of *Stranger Things*, Katherine Webb points out that Joyce does not reflect the usual image of motherhood in 2016: "Joyce isn't the model of a parent that's often reflected back to us as an example of what we should aspire to be. She's rarely home, always working, barely making ends meet." In fact, Joyce's maternal transgressions align her with the stereotypical depiction of a bad mother: "They're negligent. They hurt their children, intentionally or otherwise. Or, perhaps even worse, they create an environment in which their children can hurt others" (Webb). Although Webb goes on to argue that Joyce challenges the bad mother stereotype—she risks her own life by entering the Upside Down to save her son and also uses her mothering instincts to comfort Eleven—Joyce also fits it. In season one, her need to work means that almost twelve hours go by without her knowing that Will is missing; this negligence transfers onto Jonathan once Joyce becomes completely consumed by her search for Will. In season two, Joyce's concern for Will's wellbeing causes her to become overprotective, essentially smothering his social life. This metaphorical smothering foreshadows the physical suffocating of Will through excessive heat that Joyce along with Jonathan and Nancy are forced to perform in order to remove the Mind Flayer from Will's body. In what is essentially a torture scene, Joyce's bad mothering is depicted as unconditional love as she hysterically weeps and withstands being strangled by the hands of her possessed son in order to set him free.

The audience, however, is meant to have sympathy for Joyce. She is not the bad mother. She is the fighter-mother—forced to make horrible decisions and risk her own life in order to protect her children. This trope is common in 1980s sci-fi and horror films. As Molly Eichel writes, "These women, who exist in predominantly male-geared genres, are fierce, yet feminine, committing inhuman acts in the service of their offspring.... Hell hath no fury like a woman whose children are fucked with." For Faludi, however, the trope of the fighter-mother proves to be just as damaging to feminism as the narrative of the submissive housewife. Faludi points to the divergence between the films *Alien* and *Aliens* to help make her case. In *Alien* (1979), Ellen Ripley is the resourceful engineer who becomes the sole survivor (a more independent version of the final girl) of an alien attack. In *Aliens* (1986), Ripley is transformed into "the tough talking space engineer who saves an orphan child." She is "sympathetically portrayed, but her willfulness, too, is maternal; she is protecting the child—who calls her 'Mommy'—from female monsters" (116); 1980s Ripley no longer fights to save herself; she fights to save a child and her own potential to become a mother. Motherhood, therefore, becomes the primary acceptable reason for women to transgress gender norms—whether they are working or defeating monsters. Unlike the independent woman who eschews current or future parental responsibilities and must therefore be punished, mothers who embrace their monstrous qualities for the sake of their children are rewarded with the birth or return of their sons.

The Mother Monster in 2016

In *Dracula* and *Stranger Things*, the monstrosity of motherhood is made concrete by the maternal qualities of the monsters. Anne Williams argues that Dracula represents fear of the maternal, most specifically the "forgotten terror—fear of Mother Nature" (446). In his fight against the men of scientific enlightenment, Dracula, "a creature of the dark, madness, and of ancient superstition," is frequently associated with the "'Other' of Western culture, the female" (Williams 446). Barbara Almond also links Dracula with the maternal. In a psycho-analytic reading, she argues that the novel is about "mother-child bonding gone wrong," where Dracula (with his oral fixation) begins as the excessively needy "monster baby," which transforms women into "bad mothers" and ends as the "vampire mother" force feeding Mina ("Monstrous Infants" 222, 229). Emphasizing the maternal nature of the act, Dracula compels his new vampiric child Mina to drink from his breast: "his right hand gripped her by the back of the neck, forcing her face down on his bosom" (Stoker 285). In season one of *Stranger Things*, there is a similar fixation with orality and feeding, as the Demogorgon (whose entire face is a mouth) devours its victims. This dynamic evolves slightly in season two with the introduction of the

Mind Flayer (aka the Shadow Monster), who creates a symbiotic, hive-like relationship with plants, Demodogs, and Will, who it possesses by feeding itself into Will's mouth (a striking similarity to Dracula feeding himself to Mina). According to Almond, monsters fit into two categories: those that lack human connections and those that thrive off them (*The Monster Within* 52). Dracula, who replicates himself through his victims and maintains psychic connections with them, serves as an example of the latter. So too does the Mind Flayer, who protects Will from the Demodogs in order to use him as a spy. Though less obviously maternal than Dracula, the Mind Flayer still performs the same self-serving caretaker role.

However, it is through Eleven that *Stranger Things* offers a new and more intertwined version of the mother monster. Born Jane, Eleven was taken away from her mother at birth and raised in a government facility that cultivated her telekinetic powers in order to spy on the Soviets. Eleven, however, accidently opens a portal to an alternate reality (the Upside Down), which unleashes the Demogorgon upon Hawkins. After escaping from the lab, Eleven meets Mike and his friends, who rename her Elle. Her increasing powers terrify both the government agents trying to recapture her and her newfound friends, prompting Lucas to say, "But did you ever stop to think, maybe she's the monster?" Eleven shares many of the same qualities as Mina: She looks after her friends; she is connected to the monstrous "Other" world; and she has telekinetic powers. Like Mina, who acts like a radio receiver in order to pick up Dracula's signal (Stoker 312), Eleven broadcasts what she hears in the Upside Down over a speaker and switches the radio dial with her mind. But whereas Mina's powers are temporary—enabling her to shed her monstrous qualities and claim the coveted position of domestic mother—Eleven's powers are permanent (although at the end of season three, it seems she may lose them for a while). The monstrous is a part of Eleven. Upon admitting in season one, episode six (significantly titled "The Monster") that she opened the gate, Eleven exclaims, "I'm the monster," thereby verifying Lucas's fears from the previous episode. But if Eleven is a monster, then Elle represents the human side that coexists within her. Although Eleven transgresses the laws of physics as well as the gender expectations of little girls in the 1980s (her boylike appearance is frequently commented upon in season one), she shows that disobeying societal norms also enables girls to do great things. Thus, as the monster she crushes the brains of her enemies, but as the mother, she sacrifices herself to save her friends.

The three characterizations of motherhood discussed in this chapter feel quite contemporary, and the success of the Duffer Brothers when it comes to representing current gender politics is ambiguous. By capturing our nostalgia for the past, *Stranger Things* also holds up a mirror to our present moment and, in particular, the ways in which we view women and mothers. Turning to the work of Stuart Hall helps explain why popular culture also speaks to contemporary politics. As Hall famously writes, "Popular culture is one of the sites where this struggle for and against a culture of the powerful is engaged.... It is the arena of consent and resistance" (239). For Hall, popular culture is political, and it is within this space that we see our world reflected to us in ways that are both familiar and make us uncomfortable. Writing on *Stranger Things*, Chang notes the town's failure to believe Joyce Byers "feels all too familiar, and amounts to a thematic echo of real-world phenomena" in which assault victims "are often met with suspicion" when reporting the crime. Such a failure to believe victims, Chang argues, even became a political point during the 2016 election.

That feminism has been experiencing a backlash since 2016—when we witnessed an educated, experienced woman be repeatedly told she lacks the look and stamina to be president—is hardly surprising.[7] Even after the "blue wave" of the 2018 election, which saw a record number of women elected to public office, women hold only 127 out of the 535 voting seats in Congress. Likewise, women make up only 6.6 per cent of Fortune 500 CEOs, another record high set in 2019, and continue to fight for equal pay for equal work. These gains in power among American women, however small, are reflected in season three of *Stranger Things*. Karen, Nancy, Joyce, and Elle all evolve into more complex characters by the third season and often take the lead in making decisions regarding family, friendships, and the best methods to hunt monsters. Karen and Nancy even engage in a mother-daughter conversation about sexism in the workplace that feels particularly timely in the #MeToo era. This, however, is not enough to override the monstrous mother tropes that have proven themselves to be at the core of not only *Stranger Things* but also the material from which the show draws its inspiration. In its representation of women and motherhood,

238

Stranger Things both moves beyond the stereotypes of the Reagan years and reimagines them for the current generation. No longer can women escape the monster within (as with Mina or even Ripley in *Alien 3*). If we look to Eleven as the mirror for women and mothers today (she would be in her mid-forties in 2016) then the message is clear: The monster is us, and we should embrace it.

Endnotes

1. Although this chapter largely focuses on seasons one and two of *Stranger Things*, it is worth noting that in season three, released on July 4, 2019, the trope of monster replication via human victims is taken to a new extreme, as the Mind Flayer (first introduced in season two) creates an army of zombies/pod people ("The Flayed") out of the local Hawkins population. These zombified Hawkins residents ultimately melt and decompose and merge together to create a new unnamed monster.

2. See: Clio Chang in *The New Republic*, Elizabeth Logan in *Glamour*, and Molly Eichel in *AV/TV Club*.

3. Carol Senf, for example, claims Mina is a modern woman but not a New Woman because of her criticism of New Women, her professional aspirations, and her response to marriage (46). In contrast, Charles E. Prescott and Grace A. Giorgio argue that although Mina does not see herself as a New Woman, her actions suggest she is one. More recently, Laura James finds the middle ground and suggests that there are "ambiguities" regarding Mina's status as a New Woman (93).

4. Croley's Marxist reading of *Dracula* aligns the Count with the lumpenproletariat ("the poorest of the poor"), which included "gypsies, beggars, vagrants, petty criminals, madmen, [and] slum-dwellers" (85). Dracula symbolizes the threat of the unemployed lumpenproletariat to "middle-class norms" (87). Moral degradation, including promiscuity and a deteriorating domesticity, was seen as contagious to the working and middle classes (95).

5. Before Reagan was elected, he removed support for the Equal Rights Amendment from the GOP convention platform. During his years as president, he worked against abortion rights within the US and

instituted the "Mexico City Policy," which cut funding for international family planning programs. His policy of shrinking the federal government meant that departments that aided women also saw massive cuts, including the Equal Employment Opportunity Commission and housing programs that supported women and children escaping domestic abuse.

6. "In 1986, while 41 percent of upper-income women were claiming in the Gallup poll that they were not feminists, only 26 percent of low-income women were making the same claim" (Faludi xx).

7. A quick search for "feminist backlash 2016" pulls up a slew of articles with titles like: "2016 was the Year the Feminist Bubble Burst" (*Slate*); "The Backlash against Feminism Has Hit a New Low with Donald Trump" (*The Guardian*); "Fear of a Female President" (*The Atlantic*); "How to Survive an Anti-Feminist Backlash" (*The Nation*); and "The Feminist Backlash Isn't Helping Hillary Clinton with Young Women" (*Vice*).

Works Cited

Almond, Barbara. "Monstrous Infants and Vampyric Mothers in Bram Stoker's *Dracula*." *The International Journal of Psychoanalysis*, vol. 88, no. 1, 2007, pp. 219-35.

Almond, Barbara. *The Monster Within: The Hidden Side of Motherhood*. University of California Press, 2010.

Beville, Maria. *The Unnameable Monster in Literature and Film*. Routledge, 2014.

Chang, Clio. "Stranger Women: How 'Stranger Things' channels the female frustration of being disbelieved." *The New Republic*, 23 Aug. 2016, newrepublic.com/article/136229/stranger-things-channels-female-frustration-being-disbelieved. Accessed 21 June 2021.

Clover, Carol J. *Men, Women, and Chainsaws: Gender in the Modern Horror Film*. Princeton University Press, 1993.

Croley, Laura Sagolla. "The Rhetoric of Reform in Stoker's 'Dracula': Depravity, Decline, and the Fin-de-Siècle 'Residuum.'" *Criticism*, vol. 37, no. 1, 1995, pp. 85-108.

Duffer Brothers, the, creators. *Stranger Things*. 21 Laps Entertainment and Monkey Massacre, 2016–2017.

Eichel, Molly. "*Stranger Things'* Joyce Comes from a Grand Tradition of Badass Sci-fi Mom." *AV/TV Club*, 25 July 2016, tv.avclub.com/stranger-things-joyce-comes-from-a-grand-tradition-of-1798249817. Accessed 21 June 2021.

Faludi, Susan. *Backlash: The Undeclared War Against American Women.* Three Rivers Press, 1991.

Fitzpatrick, Molly. "In Praise of Nancy Wheeler, the Unsung Feminist Heroine of 'Stranger Things.'" *Splinter*, 16 Aug. 2016, splinternews.com/in-praise-of-nancy-wheeler-the-unsung-feminist-heroine-1793861231. Accessed 21 June 2021.

Francus, Marilyn. *Monstrous Motherhood: 18th-Century Culture and the Ideology of Domesticity.* Johns Hopkins University Press, 2012.

Hall, Stuart. "Notes on Deconstructing the Popular." *People's History and Socialist Theory*, edited by Raphael Samuel, Routledge and Kegan Paul, 2018, pp. 227-40.

Holmes, Ann Sumner and Claudia Nelson. "Introduction." *Maternal Instincts: Visions of Motherhood and Sexuality in Britain, 1875-1925*, edited by Ann Sumner Holmes and Claudia Nelson, MacMillan Press, 1997, pp. 1-12.

James, Laura. "Technologies of Desire: Typists, Telegraphists and their Machines in Bram Stoker's *Dracula* and Henry James's *In the Cage*." *Victorian Network*, vol. 4, no. 1, 2012. pp. 91-105.

Kittler, Friedrich A. "Dracula's Legacy." *Literature Media Information Systems*, edited by John Johnston, OPA, 1997, pp. 50-84.

Logan, Elizabeth. "The Moms of 'Stranger Things' Are So Important, but Nobody Ever Talks About It." *Glamour*, 26 Oct. 2017, www.glamour.com/story/the-moms-of-stranger-things. Accessed 21 June 2021.

Prescott, Charles E. and Grace A. Giorgio. "Vampiric Affinities: Mina Harker and the Paradox of Femininity in Bram Stoker's 'Dracula.'" *Victorian Literature and Culture*, vol. 33, no. 2, 2005, pp. 487-515.

Senf, Carol A. "'Dracula': Stoker's Response to the New Woman." *Victorian Studies*, vol. 26, no. 1, 1982, pp. 33-49.

Stoker, Bram. *Dracula*. Edited by John Paul Riquelme. 2nd ed., Bedford/St. Marin's, 2016.

Webb, Katherine. "Keeping the Lights On: 'Stranger Things' and the

Emotional Crisis of Motherhood." *Bright Wall / Dark Room*, vol. 43, 2016, www.brightwalldarkroom.com/2017/01/10/keeping-the-lights-on-stranger-things-and-the-emotional-crisis-of-mother hood/. Accessed 21 June 2021.

Williams, Anne. "Si(g)ns of the Fathers." *Texas Studies in Literature and Language*, vol. 33, no. 4, 1991, pp. 445-63.

Chapter 12

"The Terror of Mothering": Maternal Ambiguities and Vulnerabilities in Helen Phillips's *The Need* and Melanie Golding's *Little Darlings*

Andrea O'Reilly

I n the introduction to *Monstrous Mothers: Troubling Tropes*, Abigail Palko argues that patriarchal culture censures and polices women through the idealization of the good mother and the demonization of the bad mother and that mothers are an easy and favourite scapegoat—they become a proxy for our cultural fears and uncertainties. This collection, as with most scholarship on the monstrous mother, considers what Barbara Almond calls "the monster within: the hidden side of motherhood." With its emphasis on maternal subjectivity, this scholarship focuses on the monstrous feelings of the mother, particularly as they are expressed in maternal ambivalence, disappointment, and regret. However, little has been said on the monstrosity of mothering itself—the potential terror and horror the experience creates and causes for mothers. What happens when we shift our focus from the mother to the experience of mothering in theorizing the bad and monstrous maternal? What is revealed when what evokes terror and is made terrifying is not the mother but mothering itself? What renders mothering terrifying? How may the inevitable fears, anxieties, worries, and doubts women experience as they become mothers be represented, particularly when they are denied and discredited by normative motherhood? How may the terror of mothering be conveyed in women's writing? What may be learned from considering maternal terror? And how, in turn, does this shift from the terrible mother to the terror of mothering serve to trouble normative motherhood? This chapter takes up these questions in its reading of two contemporary novels: *The Need* by Helen Phillips (2019) and *Little Darlings* by Melanie Golding (2019).

The chapter considers how the two novels, through the genre of speculative fiction, evoke and examine the terror of mothering. *The Need* tells the story of Molly, a paleobiologist and mother of two young children who is visited and then stalked by her doppelganger Moll—a woman who emerges from the Pit, the dig site where Molly works, and whose two children were killed by a bombing at this site. In *Little Darlings,* Lauren, a new mother of twins, believes her children have been taken and replaced with changelings. Through the presence of changelings and doppelgangers and plots of home invasion and child abduction, the novels present and position mothering—not mothers— as terrifying. Synonyms for "terrifying" include "daunting" and "distressing," and indeed in the two novels, mothering is rendered such through the variabilities and vulnerabilities of motherwork. Maternal practice, as theorized by Sara Ruddick, demands that mothers protect their vulnerable children, but as both novels show, mothers also become vulnerable in this responsibility because they cannot always protect and preserve their children. The novels also explore and emphasize the inherent dualisms of mothering: sacred and mundane, terror and ecstasy, subjugation and inspiration, burden and gratification. In this, both novels show that it is these ambiguities of mothering rather than maternal ambivalence that cause the contradictions, incongruities, and uncertainties of mothering. Whereas *The Need* exposes the vulnerabilities and ambiguities through considering maternal practice, *Little Darlings* does so through an examination of becoming a mother.

Margaret Atwood defines speculative fiction as literature that "deals with possibilities in a society which have not yet been enacted but are latent" (qtd. in MasterClass). I suggest in using the genre of speculative fiction, Phillips and Golden expose the latent vulnerabilities and ambiguities of mothering to reveal what normative motherhood denies: It is mothering that is terrifying, not mothers themselves. Under normative motherhood, mothers are demonized and serve as repositories for cultural fears. However, in both *The Need* and *Little Darlings*, what is rendered frightening is not mothers themselves but what is expected and required of mothers in the institution of motherhood.

"It's Just Both These Things Completely at Once": The Bliss and Burdens of Maternal Practice in Helen Phillips's *The Need*

The Need, writes Kailey Brennan, "is a genre-bending thriller that explores the scary, intense, and sometimes comical experience of being a mother" and belongs, as noted by Alexander Alter, "to a growing body of surreal speculative fiction that uses horror tropes to capture the panic, self-doubt, and pressures that new mothers face." Alter goes on to argue that "for Phillips, writing about a supernatural threat felt like the most accurate way to explore the treacherous emotional terrain of motherhood and the lurking feeling that even the most mundane situations are fraught with peril." In an interview, Phillips explains that the idea for the novel originated from an evening when her husband was out for a few hours, and she was alone nursing the baby and heard a sound in another room: "I just had this flash. What would you do?" (qtd. in Iversen). Phillips elaborates:

> So much of that time in one's life—well, at least for me—felt very vulnerable. You're doing things you've never done before, and you're loving someone like you've never loved before, and you're also taking responsibility for keeping someone else alive, so all those anxieties were present and then just hearing something in the other room. So, I had a flash, like, I have to write about this feeling. I have to write about this feeling of being alone with your child, and there being a threat. It's just the most primal thing. (qtd in Iversen)

However, Phillips emphasizes that as her maternal thriller progresses, the reader realizes that the intruder is not the real threat: "The apparent enemy is not the actual enemy" (qtd. in Rachel Barenbaum).

Rather, as Phillips continues, "You realize that what you thought you needed to be scared of is not at all what you needed to be scared of; in fact, you need be scared of something far less conquerable than a specific nemesis" (qtd. in Barenbaum). And who or what is this far less conquerable actual enemy to fear in *The Need*? For Phillips, it is the reality of mothering—"the intensity of that love, the intensity of being responsible for another human's well-being, the intensity of knowing that you cannot protect your children from every threat" (qtd. in Wang). Indeed, as Phillips elaborates: "What is scary about the book is the idea that when you bring life into the world, something can happen to that life that you've brought into the world" (qtd. in Kelly). When asked by Frances Yackell about *The Need* being described as "motherhood as horror," Phillips comments: "I was trying to describe what some aspects of motherhood feels like and, I guess without trying to use elements of horror, they slipped in *naturally*" (my emphasis, qtd. in Yackell). In an interview with Kyle Williams, Phillips further says: "I was thinking of what it can feel like to have this responsibility to these vulnerable people, and to be so sleep-deprived so that you're in a kind of half-dream state all the time, and to have looming doubts about your own capacity to protect and raise your children ... this led me to the idea of a thriller." Thus, as Phillips emphasizes in her interview with Yackell: "I needed speculative fiction to make it work and the pacing of a thriller to make it work." Moreover, as Phillips argues: "Realism doesn't describe the surreal and bizarre bodily experiences of motherhood. When you're in the twenty-fifth hour of labor, and you're having hallucinations, that is surreal. Having sex for a few minutes, which then leads to life—what could be crazier than that?" (qtd. in Wang). Indeed, *The Need*, in its genre of speculative fiction and with its accompanying horror tropes and thriller plot, makes possible the articulation of the vulnerabilities and ambiguities of mothering to reveal the inherent and latent terror of mothering experienced by Molly, the protagonist, throughout the novel.

Reviewer Doug Gordan describes *The Need* as a "subversive thriller," whereas Hillary Kelley says that "motherhood as horror isn't a new genre but *The Need* sends it to a new place." I suggest what makes the novel subversive and takes it to a new place is how *The Need* through the genre of speculative fiction affords unique and startling explorations of "the permanent state of mild panic" caused by motherhood—"to spend every moment so acutely aware of the abyss, the potential injury flickering within each second" (18). The enemy in *The Need*, as Phillips explains, "is your own dread (as a mother) and the potential bad things that can happen to you and the ones you love. It's not something without but something within" (qtd. in Williams). In this novel, what evokes terror is the vulnerability of mothering itself. In her book *Maternal Thinking: Toward a Politics of Peace*, Sara Ruddick argues that mothering is characterized by three demands: preservation, growth, and social acceptance. "To be a mother," continues Ruddick, "is to be committed to meeting these demands by works of preservative love, nurturance, and training" (17). The first duty of mothers is to protect and preserve their children: "to keep safe whatever is vulnerable and valuable in a child" (80). "Preserving the lives of children," Ruddick writes, "is the central constitutive, invariant aim of maternal practice: the commitment to achieving that aim is the constitutive maternal act" (19). "To be committed to meeting children's demand for preservation," Ruddick continues, "does not require enthusiasm or even love; it simply means to see vulnerability and to respond to it with care rather than abuse, indifference, or flight" (19). For Molly, the mother in *The Need*, preservative love is described as the following: "From the beginning she had felt that her primary responsibility to them was to their bodies. Enabling them to grow from two cells into trillions of cells, into a body, and then ensuring that the body kept growing and growing" (112).

I argue that *The Need* enacts and expands upon Ruddick's theory of preservative love to explicate and elucidate the fears, frights, anxieties, and apprehensions of this maternal demand: "keeping safe whatever is vulnerable and valuable in a child" (80). The novel renders visceral the demand of preservation and reveals how terrifying the protection of a child can be for the mother, as Molly often reflects upon "these two lives for which she was (irrevocably, unbearably) responsible" (86). However, it is not only children who are vulnerable, as theorized by Ruddick, but mothers are also made vulnerable in this need to protect and preserve their children. As Molly reflects, "The need to go home ... and return to two small impeccable bodies. The excruciating need" (80). And as Moll says to Molly: "The umbilical cord runs both directions. The mother keeps the children alive and the children keep the mother alive" (253). "Need" is a multifaceted word in this novel, as Phillips elaborates:

I realized that I needed to call the novel *The Need* because the idea of need is woven throughout the book in so many different ways. [There is] the child's desperate, literal need for the mother, in utero and out of utero. And at the same time, the mother needs her children. She might be able to physically survive without them, but in a way she cannot survive without them. (qtd. in Yackell)

This need, in this novel so named, is the terror of mothering.

The novel opens with Molly at home with her two young children, Viv and Ben, while her husband is away; she is crouched and clinging to her children, as she hears footsteps in the house: "[Her] desperation for her children's silence manifested as a suffocating force, the desire for a pillow, a pair of thick socks, anything she could shove into them to perfect their muteness and save their lives" (4). Initially, Molly wonders if the sound of footsteps is simply caused by a problem of her own— "the minor disorientations that sometimes plagued her [since becoming a mother four years ago], the small errors of eyes and ears" (5). However, as each short suspenseful chapter unfolds, we learn indeed that there is an intruder whom we later learn is Moll: "the other version of Molly who came through the Pit. Her children are dead and she wants Molly's children" (109). When she hears Viv's scream, Molly thinks: "How could she be so stupid; she'd done the idiotic horror-movie thing, leaving the vulnerable flank unguarded" (15). And then wonders: "What could she do to make sure he would shoot her and spare the children?" (11). Molly is resolved "to make sure nothing horrific happens to [her children]" (34). As her daughter Viv steps towards the intruder, she hesitates "as though jerked backward by a magical thread, the thread of Molly's love, the umbilical cord tugging the child toward the mother, holding her back at the edge of a cliff" (42). When Molly finally confronts the intruder, she reflects, "the level of her vulnerability astounded her, destabilized her" and realizes "she had only her body, her words, with which to save her children" (43). Significantly, when Molly reflects on the need to protect her children, her milk "lets down" (34, 37, 43), signifying the visceral embodiment of the need to protect her children and the terror it causes.

The intruder scene signifies and evokes Molly's preexisting anxieties of motherhood and serves, as noted by Aviva Briefel, "as a manifestation of the deepest fears of not being able to protect your children" and in "immersing readers in this state of anxious suspense, the opening scene makes the psychic and physical toll of maternity visceral" (qtd. in Fallon). The novel's opening scene of a real and justified panic invokes the "permanent state of mild panic" experienced by Molly in the everyday mothering of her children. As Molly is "hurrying to see who had broken into their home," she likens this to "always hurrying to put groceries away"; she also realizes that her heart rate was elevated (because of the intruder) as it always was when she was the sole caretaker of her children (18). The perils of Molly keeping her children safe from the intruder recall those of her everyday mothering: "the risk of someone throwing up; the risk of someone crawling over and trying to touch the throw-up" (45). As the horror trope of the intruder signifies and cojoins with the terror of mothering, the thriller page-turning structure of the novel, as Phillips explains, is reminiscent of the experience of having young children: "There's a lot of urgencies—someone needs something and there's pasta on the stove and I need to make sure the pasta doesn't boil over on someone" (qtd. in Brennan). Moreover, as Phillips emphasizes, "Molly is a heroine in some kind of dramatic tale" (qtd. in Williams)—both as she protects her children from the intruder and in the everyday busyness of her mothering. The elements of both the horror and thriller genre, Phillips emphasizes, "was the best way to get at this fullness [of motherhood]" (qtd. in Brennan) and to show its inherent and latent vulnerabilities.

As *The Need* shifts the focus from the terrible mother to the terror of mothering, the emphasis becomes the ambiguities of mothering rather than maternal ambivalence to further transgress normative renditions of the monstrous maternal. In *The Monster Within: The Hidden Side of Motherhood*, Barbara Almond defines "ambivalence" as follows: "[It is] a mental state, in which one has both loving and hating feelings for the same person. It characterizes all human relationships, not just that of mother and child. Being able to tolerate both kinds of feelings, at different times, without having one feeling destroy the other, is a sign of good mental health" (8). Writing specifically on maternal ambivalence, Rozsika Parker defines it as "a complex and contradictory state of mind, shared by all mothers, in which loving and hating feelings exist side by side" (18). Almond argues that ambivalence itself "is not the problem but rather the guilt and anxiety that ambivalence provokes" (24). Mothers fear, in the words of Adrienne Rich, that "hate will overwhelm love" (81). In *Of Woman Born*, Rich relates that her children have caused her great suffering: "It is the suffering of ambivalence: the murderous alternation between bitter resentment and raw edged nerves and blissful gratification" (81). As Parker elaborates, maternal ambivalence "is well established in psychoanalytic literature but because cultural expectations and assumptions presume and demand that a mother love her children unconditionally and selflessly the mother who exhibits or admits maternal ambivalence is judged harshly and is the object of shame and disbelief by other mothers and herself" (18). "That mothers have mixed feelings about their children," Almond contends, "should come as no surprise to anybody; but it is amazing how much of a taboo the negative side of maternal ambivalence carries in our culture, especially at this time" (xiii). Indeed, normative motherhood assumes that maternal desire and maternal ability are innate to all women and require that all mothers find joy and purpose in motherhood. However, since these mandates prescribe, rather than describe, mothers' lives, mothers experience ambivalence in motherhood.

In *The Need*, it is the ambiguities of mothering and not maternal ambivalence that disturb and disrupt normative motherhood. Molly is not an ambivalent mother as is normally assumed in discussions of the monstrous maternal; rather, it is mothering itself that is fraught with contradictions, dualisms, and paradoxes. The novel as noted in the title of Kristen Iversen's review "perfectly captures motherhood's duality; its terror and ecstasy." Motherhood, as Phillips emphasizes, "expands and limits": "When you have children, you have this beautiful and terrifying responsibility to them. That fear it's inhibiting. It's motivating" (qtd. Iversen). Brennan elaborates: "Phillips explores the dualities of raising children, the loss of self a woman can go through yet the fierce love she feels for [her children]. She showcases the dread, joy, the fatigue, the monotony, the spiritual and physical connection and elation a mother can experience." Throughout the novel, Molly is "maddened by [her children] and melted by them, maddened/melted, maddened/melted, maddened/melted" (19). At work one day, Molly reflects: "Usually she was pleased to descend into the Pit, a little break from the rest of her life, no one requesting milk from her body or asking why pee is yellow. But today, as she made her way down, she missed the children vastly, painfully to the point of distraction" (41).

"Her children filled her home, outrageously with a force larger than they were, like angels or aliens" (92). One night as she watches her children sleep, she does so with "awe tinged with horror and disbelief" (86). When she enters her children's bedroom after her meeting with Moll, she describes it "like trespassing in a greenhouse containing rare tomatoes grown from her own flesh" (86). Molly describes holding her nursing baby in her arms "as ecstatic a physical experience as dancing into the night" (54). The morning after meeting Moll, she reflects: "There it was: bliss, the halo, the guilt of her richness. The ecstasy of the ordinary" (93).

Yet when Molly thinks about the upcoming week with her husband away, she realizes: "She was weary. She wasn't sure she had the stamina.... So many meals, so many diapers, so many tantrums between now and next Saturday" (45). The morning after her visit with Moll as the children are eating breakfast, Molly thinks: "They needed things. More yogurt. More jam. Spoon flipping onto the floor. Mess! Wet washcloth. But this one reeks. So: another Laundry soon.... A handprint here ... Don't touch. Come here ... No... Too messy. I'll clean it up. Not now. Too messy" (95). In meeting the demands of her children, Molly "let[s] her body be drained again and again and refilled again and again" (41). And as Molly describes her visit to the grocery store "as a small miracle to be here, in the normal light of the grocery store," where she simultaneously ponders upon "the expenses and excesses of the exhausted mother. What a thing it was, grocery shopping, so tedious and so crucial" (101). When Viv has a tantrum in the store, Molly feels hot and helpless and can only apologize as everyone watches with judgmental eyes. She wishes "she had methods for ushering Viv back into her tamed self. But she had never developed any methods. The beast within fought its way out while the mother watched in awe" (103). And later at Viv's birthday, described by Molly as a "tsunami," she makes herself "dizzy from it," and when she looks "at her overheated and overcrowded home, she could have sworn she was moving through a fever dream, a bright chaos" (122).

The ambiguities of mothering are further enacted and symbolized through breastfeeding in the novel. Phillips elaborates: "Lactation—like many other aspects of motherhood—is at once a burden and a treasure.... You are profoundly connected to your child. At the same time, you just can't go away for eight hours or do whatever you want....

You have to know where you are and who needs you" (qtd. in Barenbaum). In the novel, Molly "felt like her breasts were currently the common property of the family (sucked by the baby in hunger; sucked by the child in jest, in imitation of the baby; sucked by the husband in desire; sucked too, by the breastpump" (45). In one moment, Molly reflects upon "the burden of the milk" (14), and in another, she explains that she "gave in [to nursing her son] less to his nagging and more to *her own desire* to hold a person close and, effortlessly, give him what he most wanted" (my emphasis, 8). Breastmilk is also integral to the horror dimensions of the novel, which signify the ambiguous terror of mothering. Both the excitement of her work and the fear for her children causes Molly's milk to come down. Indeed, Phillips has called her novel "a lactation thriller" (qtd. in Crumb).

The novel's attention to the ambiguities of mothering over the ambivalence of the mother to explain and convey the complexities and contestations of motherhood is further emphasized through the novel's paradoxical positioning of the maternal as both human and animal, as both mundane and sacred. Phillips writes that she wanted to capture "the rhythms of daily life, the way the mundane and the sacred, the exasperating and the miraculous, the dread-inspiring and the awe-inspiring are all mixed together when one has children" (qtd. in Lindsay). She elaborates: "I am fascinated by the duality of life, by the way the most mundane moments can have cosmic implications" (qtd. in Lindsay). In another interview, Phillips comments: "Bearing a child and nursing a child made me feel like an animal. That is quite beautiful, and also quite strange and disturbing" (qtd. in Crumb). The novel is replete with descriptions of Molly's mothering as both animal and human, mundane and sacred. When Molly finishes pumping her milk, she reflects: "Partway the accomplishment of an animal, partway the accomplishment of a deity" (20), and when she puts the human milk in the fridge, she pulls out the cow milk (26). As her milk comes down at work, Molly thinks, "Reminder: Mother. Reminder: Animal" (13). Molly describes her return to home after work "as stepp[ing] into her alternate life, the secret animal life" (41). And after she pours cow milk for her daughter, Molly "experiences a flash of mother-to-mother gratitude. *Thank you Ma Cow for letting me steal your milk for my own offspring*" (17). When a man on a tour of the Pit says to Molly he will pray for her soul, "twin droplets of milk emerged from her nipples" (36). As she places her baby Ben in his crib, she describes him as "a milk-saturated baby in the position of Jesus on the cross, arms outflung" (54). Moreover, Molly details the cast of light in her daughter's bedroom "as the sacred upon the mundane: the glow of the nightlight rendered the toothbrush and the toothpaste and pajamas and the blanket golden, as though everything Viv touched took on a mystical sheen" (128). These passages—linking the human with the animal and the sacred with the mundane—further accentuate and amplify the paradoxical dualisms of mothering that cause it to be simultaneously miraculous and monotonous, celestial and visceral.

The dualisms of mothering are further reinforced through the interfaces of Molly's work and home identities. Indeed, as noted by Fallon, "Phillips handles the exhausted question of work-life balance and maternal guilt with a subtle but a devastating touch." However, Molly is not conflicted by her desire to work, and she is devoted to her job as a paleobotanist. Although the dual commitments to work and children certainly exhaust Molly, she is enriched and sustained by them both, and both are integral to her identity. When Molly's children arrive at her workplace one afternoon, Molly thinks, "It was one of those rare sweet relaxed moments of motherhood, this easy mingling of work and home" (28). Throughout the novel, the two are interwoven, as Molly reflects upon her life: "*The life of the mind, the life of the diaper. The life of crushed Cheerio. The life of the soggy kiss. The life of the sticky floor*" (57). The interfacing of her work and home identities is introduced with the opening chapters that rapidly shift from her workplace to her home and is symbolized by the breastpump frequently referenced throughout the novel. Phillips elaborates: "A breastpump is like from science fiction, and it's also this symbolic thing, bridging the gap between a working identity and a mothering identity via a machine, so it feels like a metaphor for what motherhood is like right now" (qtd. in Iverson). In the novel, the breastpump functions as a conduit between Molly's two identities. When Molly is pumping her milk, she describes "the simultaneous relief and frustration" (13), and another time, she thinks "she needed to deliver the milk to the minifridge and transform from one kind of person into another" (16-17). Although Viv, Molly's daughter, is initially horrified when she sees her mother pump her milk, she later considers the breastpump as a sort of pet (16). Thus, in

The Need, it is not maternal ambivalence—alterations between resentment and gratification as well as conflicts between work and motherhood—that is examined but rather the ambiguities of mothering itself. Mothering is paradoxical and dualistic: Mothering is both "terror and ecstasy; beautiful and crazy" (Brennan) and is "simultaneously bliss and subjugation" (qtd. in Greenblatt). Molly is happy to be with [her children] and exhausted to be with them" (56). Indeed, as Phillips emphasizes: "There is such duality in motherhood. It's the most enormous burden you can possibly take on, and it is the most straightforward path to ecstasy I've ever experienced. *It's just both these things completely at once*" (my emphasis, qtd. in Crumb).

The dualisms of mothering are most fully enacted and symbolized by the doppelganger Moll, who emerges from the Pit after her own two children are killed by a bombing, and who represents, as with the other artifacts found in the Pit, the potential and possibility of "other iterations of the universe" (75)—one in which Hitler is an artist and Molly's children are killed. Significantly, it is Molly's "sleep-deprived fugue state as mother of two" and her "post-Ben apocalyptic exhaustion" that cause her to become entranced by the found objects—ones her coworkers (and Molly herself before motherhood) would have discarded without a second glance. These "recognizable objects that were slightly yet fundamentally off" (31) are what reveal the alternate reality, and once displayed, they give rise to death threats and result in the bombing that kills the children in "a different possible world" (73). Significantly, the artifacts are discovered over a nine-month period (30), and when Molly examines the found penny in the Pit and wonders if the penny is another such artifact, she looks up and describes the sky "as the color of milk" (9). That it is Molly's motherhood state that causes her to discover the objects—along with the maternal references to the length of pregnancy and milk—suggests again this mothering dualism of wonder and menace. Phillips elaborates: "It's because she had children [that] Molly started to notice the weird objects that she might've just thrown away. [Motherhood] makes you more aware in a way and more sensitive to the world. At the same times, it is her discoveries that put her children at risk in a really concrete way" (qtd. in Iversen). Indeed, as Molly herself acknowledges, "It *was* her fault" that the Pit had become "a roadside attraction" (21), which later causes the bombing and the alternate reality in which her children are killed and the eventual emergence of Moll: "another version of [Molly] that is at once horrifying and at the time somewhat comforting" (Phillips qtd. in Yackell).

Initially presented and positioned as Molly's nemesis, Moll becomes, as the novel unfolds, Molly's ally and the comother to "their" children. When they first meet, Molly "repulsed by the hunger shimmering in [Moll's] eyes, calls Moll evil (130). Later, when Molly sees Moll with her children, she was "suddenly appalled at herself; she had handed her children over to a woman mangled by grief. There was no way such a mother could do all that needed to be done" (161). However, near the end of the novel, Molly is resolved "to use the words that would cast Moll out of her life forever" (164). But as she searched, "she could not find the right words [as] the unassailable argument against their arrangement ... eluded her" (164). The arrangement referred to is Molly and Moll sharing the care of the two children, as one waits in the basement for their turn with the children, and the other is upstairs with the children. As they share mothering duties, their identities begin to merge. When the phone rings with David's, Molly's husband, call, they both reach for the phone. And as they both shiver in the cold basement, Molly hands Moll her robe, since she found "ominous, that simultaneous shiver" (150). Later, Molly hides in the bushes to watch her children with Moll and realizes "with a chill that Moll had hidden in the same spot plenty of times [watching the family]" (154). Significantly, this dual mothering, as with the dualisms of mothering discussed above, is enacted and symbolized as maternal embodiment. When the two children are with the babysitter and Molly's milk comes down at work, she thought of Moll in the basement and wondered if her milk had come down too (175), and later as she watches Moll nurse Ben in the park, Molly "became aware of the weight of her own milk" (160). As Molly throws from the bridge Moll's clothing, blood stained from the death of the children, "she was acutely aware of the two wet patches of milk on her chest" (195). When Ben begins to cry, they hover "together in the seconds passing too swiftly as the sound intensif[ies], the escalating need, the milk heavy in them" (138). Moll explains to Molly that when she is with the children, she "feels like [she] never lost them. And [she] feels like [she's] losing them every second." Molly then remembers "the freshness of the amniotic fluid. Whooshing out her, the cleanest thing she had every encountered. The otherworldly liquid in which their impeccable bodies had been suspended, safe" (186). Profoundly, at this moment, the two embrace, and for Molly, it is the most intimate human sensation she had ever experienced despite having conceived, birthed, and nursed children (186). Although Molly thinks she needs to step back, she could not: "She was addicted to it ... the lack of gaps between them" (186). In that instant, "their lips matched themselves up" (186).

After David returns home unexpectedly and Molly watches her husband have sex with Moll, Molly imagines the uncontainable pleasure in her own body, but when she looks into Moll's eyes, it is grief, not pleasure, that she sees (217). Moll then disappears, and Molly goes in search of her, not knowing if it is with "the urgency of tracking down an enemy or the urgency of looking for a friend" (228). She is terrified of Moll but also worries about her. Near the end of the novel, Molly and her two children become seriously ill with the flu, and Molly wonders if she can make it out of the bed alive or whether her children will be left with no one to care for them. Significantly, it is Moll who arrives to care for them, and Molly "could muster no resistance, no rage, only an irrepressible sensation of relief" (244). And she only thinks: "So what if someone was taking advantage of her at her weakest moment?" (244). As Moll cares for the children, and tells Molly to return to bed, Molly "was loath to admit that this was the realization of an old fantasy of hers: to be in two places at once. To have two bodies. To give herself over to her own recovery while her children were in the hands of someone who loved them exactly as she did" (245). Molly's fantasy, as Phillips explains, is a common one for mothers:

"If only I could clone myself, then all my problems would be solved." I have heard many parents say that; it's a cliché. And I'm often interested in a cliché that if you actually look at it, what would it be like? What if you actually had a doppelganger who wanted to do the things you do; how would that displace you from your life? How would you feel, being displaced from your life? If you actually follow through on that. What if? (qtd. in Williams)

In The Need, Molly realizes this fantasy by allowing Moll to finally become one with her. When Molly hears Moll say, "It's always going to be a duel," she thinks, "Or maybe she said: 'It always is going to be dual'" (253). The novel ends with Moll lying on Molly: "She matched her shoulders to her shoulders. Her feet to her feet. Her thighs to her thighs. Her forehead to her forehead. Lungs to lungs, womb to womb, teeth to teeth" (254). The final image of Moll "pressing down on her, as though trying to press past her skin, into her blood, her muscles, her bones"—as well as Molly's thoughts, "It felt good, until all at once it became too much to bear" (254)—does leave the reader to wonder who the mother is in the epilogue: Molly, the protagonist or Moll, the nemesis. I suggest that this image symbolizes the disintegration of dualisms to create the mother of the epilogue: Molly "with superhuman strength, eyes tougher, in awe of her vigor, her rigor, and keeping her children safe as she bore them onward" (258). As Phillips explains:

> I do think that there is a version of the ending that is a happy one, where there might be a newfound appreciation and strength after what Molly has gone through.... The heart of the book is about the things that we take for granted every day. [The arrival of Moll] throws Molly into a moment where she no longer takes for granted her day-to-day life. My intention with having what she takes for granted come under threat and making it seem precious in a new way is that it makes her better at it. (qtd. in Yackell)

Phillips comments further: "Dislocation can provide perspective. It enables Molly to perceive the sacredness of her daily grind, something she had taken for granted" (qtd. Van Den Berg).

The novel is replete with Molly's newfound appreciation of her life as it becomes threatened by Moll and her realization that it could have been Molly with the dead children in "the different possible world" (81). The evening after she meets Moll, Molly arrives home "stunned by the serenity of her home" (87) and later reflects upon the "ostentatious peace of her home" (113). As Molly tidies the home the night after meeting Moll, she thinks: "The final hour of the day often felt insurmountable but tonight it felt sacred to hold the bin while the children cleaned up the blocks" (53). Later, while Molly is cleaning up after Viv's birthday party, she realizes: "This drudgery was part of love, part of the mission of mothering a human. Today, though, she appreciates the concreteness of the task ... the scattered evidence of the children's vitality" (125). Then, when Moll asks to nurse Ben, Molly feels "it like a solid thing, the awareness of her outrageous abundance in comparison to this woman, this refugee from a far crueler reality" (138). Indeed, it is Moll who bequeaths to Molly the awareness of, and appreciation for, the "renewed happiness of the home" (257).

I argue further that the merging of Moll and Molly signifies and enacts Molly's acceptance of the inevitable ambiguities and inherent vulnerabilities of mothering. In making this argument, I am not diminishing and denying the complexities and contradictions of mothering or suggesting that *The Need* does so. Rather, the novel shows how Molly, in accepting and embracing the vulnerabilities and ambiguities of mothering, is finally able "to move quickly despite her burdens" (258). In an interview, Phillips comments: "All my writing arises from my anxieties. Writing about them is a way of acknowledging them and learning to live with them" (qtd. in Wang). Likewise, Molly learns to live with the anxieties and apprehensions of mothering: "the push and pull of the abyss inherent in motherhood" (qtd. in Wang). Although *The Need* begins with the abject terror of mothering, it becomes, in Molly's eventual acceptance of the inevitable distresses and dreads of mothering, "an exquisitely tender meditation on motherhood's joys and comorbid torments" (Fallon).

"It May Just Send You Mad:" The Uncertainties and Insecurities of Becoming a Mother in Melanie Golding's *Little Darlings*

Whereas *The Need* employs the speculative fiction tropes of home invasion and doppelgangers, *Little Darlings* uses those of child abduction and changelings to evoke the vulnerabilities and ambiguities of mothering to render mothering terrifying. Jamie Portman describes the novel as "an ambiguous tale of motherhood," whereas Charlotte Duckworth writes that *Little Darlings* is "a haunting, addictive take on new motherhood gone wrong." *The Need* evokes the terror of mothering through the inevitable ambiguities of mothering and the inherent anxieties of raising and protecting children, but *Little Darlings* does so by dramatizing how women's sense of self is, in the words of one critic, "destabilized by new motherhood" (Kerry Claire). Indeed, as Lauren, the mother, reflects: "She'd been deconstructed by nature and then by man, then nature again, and finally by man—the two forces tossing her hand over hand, back and forth like a volleyball. Where was Lauren in this maelstrom of awfulness. Where was the person she had previously thought herself to be? (21). Melanie Golding evokes and signifies how becoming a mother changes and destabilizes women through the folklore of changelings. Doris Sutherland explains that the novel "is based on the widespread folkloric concept that fairies sometimes steal away human babies and replace them with changelings." Golding elaborates: "[The novel] was inspired by my theory that the folklore of the changeling would have once been an explanation for post-partum psychosis. Before we knew about psychiatry and such, there was still post-partum psychosis—just nobody knew what it was. So, stories explained elements of life that people didn't understand" (qtd. in Hedlund). Golding explains that she had always wanted the novel to be a realistic book: "So I set out to write it as if the folklore was a real thing that happened. But I also set out to write it as if it was a theory about post-natal psychosis. I was holding these two things in my mind almost the entire time.... It was a case of 'I'm going to tell a story in the way it needs to be told'" (qtd. in Hedlund). Indeed, in *Little Darlings*, as noted by Hedlund, "reality is rendered ambiguous" to elicit the terror in becoming a mother, including all of its vulnerabilities and ambiguities.

Whereas *The Need* opens with the terror of protecting children, *Little Darlings* does so with the terror of bringing children into the world. Lauren reflects: "All I cared about was that the pain had been taken away. With it, the fear and the certainty she would die" (3). During the birth, Lauren describes herself as "hiding as best she could, sheltering in the back of her psyche," and when the doctor places the needle in her hand, "she barely recognized it as her own" (21). After the birth, "Lauren was convinced that nothing could be as awful.... She was a pulsating piece of meat full of inconvenient nerve endings and uncauterised vessels" (21); she was "flaccid, weak, beaten. She was all shock and pain and sorrow" (21). In an interview, Golding emphasizes the significance of the traumatic birth and its aftermath:

> I was exploring the myths surrounding having a baby, specifically how it's supposed to be a joyful time, despite how often the experience is very traumatic. I felt no one could hear me when I said that the births of my children and the early days were not glorious; they tended to laugh as if I were joking. I found that

very interesting, as a cultural phenomenon. What if I took that fear and isolation and make it as bad as it could possibly be? I wanted to start a conversation surrounding mental health, but frame it in an accessible way.... If I made horror out of the reality of having a baby, it would not only be understandable, but relatable, and ultimately therapeutic. (qtd. in Lindsay)

In showing the horror of birth, Golding enacts what Susan Maushart defines as the unmasking of motherhood. The mask of motherhood, Maushart explains, is an "assemblage of fronts—mostly brave, serene, and all knowing—that we use to disguise the chaos and complexity of our lived experience" (2). In her examination of the mask of childbirth, Maushart explains the following:

Where previous generations of women approached childbirth expecting the worst—and usually getting it—today's generation suffers from an even crueler indignity. Having been led to expect the best, the disjuncture between anticipation and experience is a yawning psychic chasm from which we emerge not only battle-scarred but angry. For many women, that anger is self-directed: it is experienced as guilt, a sense of shame that we have failed to perform to standard. (114-15)

For Lauren, there is "no intrigue, no mystery, no power" (20) to the birth, as she feels only shame and disappointment afterwards: "Nothing would change what had happened during the birth, her stupid decisions, her worthless birth plan.... She hadn't done well. She'd been washed through the birth powerless on a tide of medical intervention. She didn't feel that she'd done anything but fail. The regret was heavy on her" (48). However, I suggest that in delineating Lauren's birth and its aftermath specifically as trauma (21), the novel not only unmasks the realities of childbirth but also specifically renders birth as terror. Indeed, as Golding emphasizes: "The reality of just how traumatic and life-altering having a baby can be, physically and mentally is a complete surprise" (qtd. in Lindsay).

The novel unmasks another myth of motherhood—that mothers will instantaneously and instinctively love their babies and bond with them following birth. When Lauren is holding her twin babies, she is waiting for a rush of love: "That one you feel, all at once the second they're born, like nothing you've experienced before. The rush of love that people with children always go on about. She'd been looking forward to it. It worried her that she hadn't felt it yet" (7). When later both of her twins begin to cry, and not knowing which one to tend to, Lauren knows she must quickly react: "She'd read so much about attachment disorder and rising cortisol levels in the brains of babies in pregnancy and early childhood. You couldn't leave children to cry. It had damaging effects and might do radical things to brain development, causing terrible long-term consequences. Already they seemed so angry" (15). In an interview, Golding argues that the idea "you will have this rush of love and look at the baby and think, 'I'm in love' is almost a folktale in itself. Attachment is a gradual process" (qtd. in Hedlund). Indeed, as Lauren realizes near the end of the novel: "She hadn't loved them immediately, but she loved them after a spell. It seeped into her. Slowly. Like the love was something she'd been sipping at. Intoxicating. Accumulating. Snowballing. Slowly, quietly but unstoppably until she was quite drunk with it" (189). The masks of motherhood, in Golding's words, are "those sugarcoated stories" that women tell themselves; they believe "that a bad experience can be made better if [they] don't know it's going to be bad" (qtd. in Hedlund). The postbirth experience, Golding emphasizes, is still taboo: "Nobody wants to talk about how frightening having a baby can be. The book confronts that head on" (qtd. in *The Qwillery*). In *Little Darlings*, there are no sugarcoated stories of birth or the postpartum period; instead, terror is enacted and signified by Lauren's conviction that a woman wants to steal her babies and replace them with changelings. Through this language of folklore, Golding articulates and amplifies the anxieties and apprehensions women experience as they become mothers. The changeling story, as Golding explains, is "an allegory for the current unaddressed epidemic of postnatal depression among new mothers" (qtd. in *The Qwillery*). This is the terror of mothering.

The fears, anxieties, and doubts that render mothering terrifying as women birth children and adjust to motherhood are enacted and symbolized by Lauren's confusion and uncertainty about whether the river woman is real or imagined and whether the babies returned to her are her twins or the changelings. After giving birth to her twins, Lauren awakens in her hospital room to find a horrible woman with two crying babies in a basket who demands: "Choose one or I'll take them both. I'll take yours and you can have mine. You'll never know the difference. I can make sure they look just the same. One's fair. Two is justice done" (30). Later, when Lauren is interviewed by Detective Harper, she describes meeting the river woman as "terrifying" but then says: "But the doctor said it wasn't real. It didn't happen. They said I imagined it" (43). Lauren says to Harper, "I don't think I can trust what I think right now" (45) and comments to her husband: "I don't know why I keep crying. I'm fine, I'll be fine. Nothing happened. I think I'm going mad, that's all" (47). Although the doctors explain to Lauren it was a hallucination, for her, "it seemed so real" (49). When Lauren is later at home and sees the woman hiding outside in the bushes, she knows what she saw was "solid and real" yet still wonders if she is "back around at mad again" (91). Even though Lauren may question her sanity, she continues to believe the woman is real, as she refuses to leave her house and stays cocooned with the babies in her bed, where she knew they will be safe (120). Staying in bed with her twin babies is for Lauren "precious hours [that] were hers alone, safe in the locked box of the bedroom, just [her] and two miraculous boys she'd created from within her body, who belonged to her, who were part of her and through whose veins, her own blood flowed" (122). However, at her husband's prompting, Lauren finally leaves the house after several weeks to join her mother friends for coffee. That afternoon, as Lauren falls asleep on a bench, the twins are abducted. Detective Harper later finds a woman pulling the twins' stroller in the river, a woman we later learn was having an affair with Lauren's husband. However, when the twins are returned to Lauren, she knew they weren't her children anymore: "Something else was looking at her.... That creepy, evil woman—she'd done it, somehow, exactly as she'd threatened she would. She'd taken the boys and put her own in their place" (145-46). Without hesitation, Lauren turns and runs to the river (146).

At the psychiatric hospital, Lauren tries to convince the doctor and nurses that the babies returned to her are changelings; unsurprisingly, the staff members do not believe Lauren and assure her that they will make her better. To this, Lauren thinks: "Better from what? The only thing that's wrong with me is that someone's got my children" (156). When Lauren realizes that no one will ever believe her, she lies to the doctor and says she knows that the babies are hers, but all the while "her brain kept supplying the truth: I know they *aren't.* I have never been surer of a thing" (166). Yet Lauren continues to wonder: "Am I mad ... I might be. What If I am? What if I've got it wrong and the boys are my boys and I did all of that for nothing? I feel like I know. But what if I can't trust that feeling? (166). Despite her resolve to "keep it together to get out of the hospital to put things right," Lauren speaks her thoughts out loud, describing the twins as "somebody's babies" and explaining that her babies are now in the river calling out for their mother (169). Later when she hears the twins crying, Lauren's "breasts remained indifferent" (187), which for her was the confirmation: They are not her boys. And when she looks at the babies in the stroller, she has no love for them: "It existed in her as a painful yearning, a missing part, reaching out to her real babies" (189). However, Lauren soon realizes that "she had to play the game, even before she knew what the rules were" (170). She must "pretend all was fine" (187)—a reference not only to what Lauren must do to be released from hospital but also to what all women must do as they become mothers. Moreover, Lauren thinks that perhaps she deserves her babies being taken from her for "being a bad mother" and not "loving them immediately, the way you're supposed to do, the way she expected she would" (189). This again signifies that Lauren's uncertainties and insecurities are caused not only by the folkloric changelings but by the larger social conditions of motherhood.

The novel ends with Lauren emerging from the river with the twins and believing that they have been returned to her. Later, Lauren says to her husband: "I knew it. I keep doubting it. But it's true, it worked. What I did was worth it; those boys are mine" (304). When he responds, "Of course they're yours ... they always were," Lauren thinks: "He meant, *not because of what you did, but in spite of it*" (304). But Lauren "knew the truth of what happened underneath the water, when they were switched back ... and in the end the river woman knew she'd be wrong; that the best place for [her babies] was under the water, with their loving mother" (304). The novel's conclusion, like that of *The Need*, is open to interpretation, as Golding emphasizes: "I really wanted an ambiguous ending.... It's like a puzzle. I hope I've allowed readers to decide either it's one way or the other" (qtd. in Hedlund). Indeed, the 1976 incident—when another mother reported the attempted abduction of her twins, the shadows on the recording, the witness who saw a filthy and ugly woman near where Lauren's children were abducted, and the body of the woman and her twin babies discovered in the drowned village—certainly suggest a folkloric interpretation. Yet the discovery that the third voice on the 999 recording was Lauren's, her conviction that her six-week-old babies were singing and talking, and, of course, the fact that changelings are the stuff of folklore and not reality all indicate postpartum psychosis. Indeed, as Portman emphasizes, "The reader is left with ambiguity and uncertainty—and it's creepy." I suggest that because the changeling folklore is used as an allegory for real-word anxieties and apprehensions of motherhood, this ambiguity and uncertainty are deliberate to evoke and signify the creepiness, or perhaps more accurately, the terror of mothering. When Golding is asked the one thing she really wanted to say with this book, she responds: "The love we have for our children is both limitless and terrifying; while becoming a parent is without question worth the sacrifice, it may just send you mad" (qtd. in Hedlund).

Conclusion: The Monster Outside

In this conclusion, I return to two questions posed at the opening of the chapter. How may the terror of mothering be conveyed in women's writing, and how does this shift to the terror of mothering from the terrible mother serve to trouble normative motherhood? Phillips and Golding use the genre of speculative fiction and its horror tropes of changelings and doppelgangers and thriller plots of home invasion and child abduction to conceive of and then convey the terror of mothering. What I briefly consider here are the implications and limitations of speculative fiction to evoke and examine the terror of mothering. Annie Neugebauer defines speculative fiction as "any fiction in which the 'laws' of the world" (explicit or implied) are different than ours." Speculative fiction, thus, considers what is not possible in our world— to explore what could not happen in real life. I suggest that while the anxieties, apprehensions, doubts, dreads, uncertainties, and insecurities of becoming and being a mother certainly occur in real life, they are so denied, discounted, disregarded, and disparaged in normative motherhood and by patriarchal culture that it takes the genre of speculative fiction to render them visible. The inherent ambiguities of mothering perhaps can only be conveyed through the speculative device of the doppelganger and the latent insecurities of becoming a mother through that of changeling folklore. Perhaps it is only through speculative fiction that permission is granted and is space created for what cannot be conveyed in realistic depictions of motherhood—namely, that mothering itself is terrifying. However, in its fantastical renditions, the larger social implications of the genre's commentary on mothering may be muted or missed. In both novels, the critique of normative motherhood is imparted through an unreliable narrator whose very sanity is in question. Thus, the terror of mothering that the narrator delineates could be easily dismissed as delusional or discounted because of the mother's madness. Nonetheless, and to return to the second question, I do believe that the two novels, precisely in the disruptions offered through speculative fiction, serve to challenge normative motherhood by rendering not mothers but mothering as terrifying. In their attention to the inherent vulnerabilities of mothers and the latent dichotomies of mothering, both novels confirm and affirm that it is the ambiguities of mothering rather than maternal ambivalence that render the maternal monstrous. Indeed, the monster is not the mother but mothering. It is not within but outside.

Works Cited

Almond, Barbara. *The Monster Within: The Hidden Side of Motherhood.* University of California Press, 2010.

Alter, Alexandra. "What to Expect When You're Expecting Evil." *New York Times,* 6 July 2019, www.nytimes.com/2019/07/06/books/horror-fiction-motherhood-helen-phillips.html. Accessed 9 Mar. 2021.

Barenbaum, Rachel. "The Apparent Enemy Is Not the Actual Enemy: An Interview with Helen Phillips." *Los Angeles Review of Books,* 7 Aug. 2019, lareviewofbooks.org/article/the-apparent-enemy-is-not-the-actual-enemy-an-interview-with-helen-phillips/. Accessed 8 Mar. 2021.

Brennan, Kailey. "Helen Phillips: On Writing to Explore Anxieties, Remaining Neutral through Failure and the Expanding Experience of Motherhood." *Write or Die Tribe,* 6 Aug. 2019, www.writeordietribe.com/author-interviews/interview-with-helen-phillips. Accessed 8 Mar. 2021.

Briefel, Aviva. "Motherhood and Other Monsters." *Public Books,* 27 Mar. 2020, www.publicbooks.org/motherhood-and-other-mon sters/. Accessed 8 Mar. 2021.

Clare, Karry. "Little Darlings, by Melanie Golding." *Pickle Me This,* 16 May 2019, picklemethis.com/2019/05/16/little-darlings-by-melanie-golding. Accessed 24 Mar. 2021.

Crumb, Maddie. "On Success, Failure, and Working within Con-straints." *The Creative Independent,* 10 July 2019, thecreative independent.com/people/writer-helen-phillips-on-success-failure and-working-within-constraints/. Accessed 9 Mar. 2021.

Duckworth, Charlotte. "Mums Who Write: Melanie Golding." *Charlotte Duckworth,* 19 May 2019, www.charlotteduckworth.com/ blog-2/2019/5/18/mums-who-write-melanie-golding. Accessed 24 Mar. 2021.

Fallon, Claire. "Motherhood Is a Horror Story in 'The Need'." *Huffington Post,* 7 Nov. 2019, www.huffingtonpost.ca/entry/the-need-helen-phillips-horror motherhood_n_5d262d8ae4b0cfb 595ffcf53?ril8n=true. Accessed 11 Mar. 2021.

Golding, Melanie. *Little Darlings.* Crooked Lane Books, 2019. Gordan, Doug. "Novelist Helen Phillips Explores Complexities of Motherhood in New Thriller 'The Need.'" *Wisconsin Public Radio,* 24. Aug 2019, www.wpr.org/novelist-helen-phillips-explores-complexities-motherhood-new-thriller-need. Accessed 11 Mar. 2021.

Greenblatt, Leah. "Motherhood Meets the Sci-fi Surreal in Helen Phillips' Brilliant *The Need. The Guardian,* 9 July, 2019, https://ew. com/book-reviews/2019/07/09/helen-phillips-the-need- review/. Accessed 11 Mar. 2021.

Hedlund, Dani. "An Interview with Melanie Golding." *F(r)iction,* frictionlit.org/an-interview-with-melanie-golding/. Accessed 3 Mar. 2021.

Iversen, Kristen. "'The Need' Perfectly Captures Motherhood's Duality, Its Terror and Ecstasy." *Nylon,* 10 July 2019, www.nylon. com/helen-phillips-the-need-interview. Accessed 9 Mar. 2021.

Kelly, Hillary. "What's Scarier Than Motherhood?" *The Vulture,* 8 July 2019, www.vulture.com/2019/07/helen-phillips-the-need-profile. html. Accessed 9 Mar. 2021

Lindsay, Leslie. "Fear, Isolation, and the Shame of Not Being 'Good Enough,' Plus What She Did 'Right,' in This Deeply Moving and Authentic Debut by Melanie Golding Steeped in Fairy Tales & New Motherhood." *Leslie A. Lindsay*, 15 May 2019, leslielindsay. com/2019/05/15/fear-isolation-and-the-shame-of-not-being-good-enough-plus-what-she-did-right-in-this-deeply-moving-and-authentic-debut-by-melanie-golding-steeped-in-fairy-tales-new-motherhood-litt/. Accessed 14 Mar. 2021.

Lindsay, Leslie. "Helen Phillips on THE NEED." *Leslie A. Lindsay: Always With a Book*, 9 Oct. 2019, leslielindsay.com/2019/10/09/helen-phillips-on-the-need-how-she-couldnt-have-written-this-speculative-fiction-if-she-wasnt-a-mother-reconciling-love-and-loss-a-fabulous-reading-list-and-so-much-more/. Accessed 8 Mar. 2021.

MasterClass. "What Is Speculative Fiction? Defining and Understanding the Different Genres of Speculative Fiction." 8 Nov. 2020, www.masterclass.com/articles/what-is-speculative-fiction-defining-and-understanding-the-different-genres-of-speculative-fiction#what-is-speculative-fiction. Accessed 30 Mar. 2021.

Maushart, Susan. *The Mask of Motherhood: How Becoming a Mother Changes Everything and Why We Pretend It Doesn't*. Penguin Books, 2000.

Neugebauer, Annie. "What is Speculative Fiction?" *Annie Neugebauer*, 24 Mar. 2014, annieneugebauer.com/2014/03/24/what-is-speculative-fiction/. Accessed 14 Nov. 2020.

Parker, Rozsika. *MotherLove/Mother Hate*. Basic Books, 1995.

Phillips, Helen. *The Need*. Simon & Schuster, 2019.

Portman, Jaime. "Little Darlings, an Ambiguous Tale of Motherhood, Strikes Spooky Note." *O.Canada.com*, 31 May 2019, o.canada.com/entertainment/books/little-darlings-an-ambiguous-tale-of-motherhood-strikes-spooky-note. Accessed 14 Mar. 2021.

Rich, Adrienne. *Of Woman Born: Motherhood as Experience and Institution*. 2nd ed., W. W. Norton, 1986.

Ruddick Sarah. *Maternal Thinking: Toward a Politics of Peace*. Beacon Press, 1989.

Sutherland, Doris V. "Changeling Times: Melanie Golding's Little

Darlings." WWAC, 26 Nov. 2019, womenwriteaboutcomics.com/2019/11/changeling-times-melanie-goldings-little-darlings/. Accessed 14 Mar. 2021.

The Qwillery. "Interview with Melanie Golding, Author of Little Darlings." *The Qwillery,* 30 Apr. 2019, www.theqwillery.com/2019/04/interview-with-melanie-golding-author.html?m=1. Accessed 24 Mar. 2021.

Van Den Berg, Laura. "Dislocated Realities: A Conversation between Helen Phillips and Laura Van Den Berg." *The Paris Review,* 21 Aug. 2019, www.theparisreview.org/blog/2019/08/21/dislocated-realities-a-conversation-between-helen-phillips-and-laura-van-den-berg/. Accessed Mar. 11, 2021.

Wang, Mary. "Helen Phillips: 'Living with the Awareness of the Abyss Is Probably a Good Thing.'" *Guernica,* 19 July 2019, https://www.guernicamag.com/miscellaneous-files-helen-phillips/.Accessed 8 Mar. 2021.

Williams, Kyle. "Helen Phillips." *Full Stop,* 20 Feb. 2020, www.fullstop.net/2020/02/20/interviews/kyle-williams/helen-phillips/. Accessed 8 Mar. 2021.

Yackell, Frances. "Both Ways at Once: Talking with Helen Phillips." *The Rumpus,* 9 Oct. 2019, therumpus.net/2019/10/the-rumpus-interview-with-helen-phillips/. Accessed 9 Mar. 2021.

A Trace of What It Is Not: The Hauntings of the Monstrous Mother

Andrea O'Reilly

I n their introduction to *Bad Mothers: Regulations, Representations, and Resistance*, Michelle Hughes Miller, Tamar Hagar, and Rebecca Jaremko Bromwich argue that "the Bad Mother trope arises from the cultural inculcation of the Good Mother and its successful institutionalization" (6). Moreover, they go on to explain that "the Good Mother shapes the Bad Mother through its mechanism of accountability to the expectations that it holds" (6). The tropes of the good and bad mother are thus divergent yet symbiotic: The meaning of one depends on that of the other. As the good and bad mother tropes are oppositional yet interdependent, I argue that the trope of the monstrous mother troubles and undoes the dichotomous interplay between the two. The bad mother is often seen as synonymous with or analogous to the monstrous mother, but the trope of the monstrous mother, I suggest is a distinct discursive construct that troubles the polarity of the good and bad mother through the rhetorical strategies of fusion and contextualization. Writing on the women's noir, Lee Horsley argues that "these narratives disrupt polarized judgements, so that 'good' and 'bad' mothering are no longer distinct, but instead are aspects of a psychologically split character who is humanized and rendered sympathetic" (9-10). I suggest that the monstrous mother trope functions in a way similar to the maternal in the women's noir. In one instance, the trope fuses the good-bad maternal binary by positioning the mother as a psychologically split character, and in another, it exceeds the binary by providing context to the mother's life to humanize her character. In this fusion and contextualization, the monstrous trope confuses, collapses, and conflates the good-bad bifurcation that structures normative motherhood and on which it depends to regulate and surveil mothers. In her elusiveness—transcending and blurring maternal polarities—the monstrous mother deeply disturbs and distresses normative motherhood.

The chapters in this collection present and position the monstrous mother as a distinct discursive construct, recalling Jacques Derrida's concept of the trace: All signs contain a trace of what it does not mean, especially if the other half of it is a binary pair. The trace dislocates, displaces, and refers beyond itself. The trope of the monstrous mother becomes this trace precisely in the fusion and contextualization of its monstrosity. In her chapter on monster mothers in *Dracula* and *Stranger Things*, Melissa Dinsman explains that "the term 'monstrous' is generally used to explain things that are beyond our comprehension and therefore not classifiable or categorizable." Maria Beville elaborates: "We use the word [monstrous] to explain things that we cannot understand ... this applies to behaviour when it is seen to have transgressed the limits of what we ourselves imagine doing" (as qtd. in Dinsman). Categorization, Beville argues, makes the unknown no longer monstrous; However, the monstrous mother trope, I argue, resists and refuses classification and categorization because in its excess and incomprehensibility, it fuses and/or contextualizes the good and the bad to unify and/or transcend the maternal polarity to become a trace of what it is not. In this, the monstrous mother is not simply a bad mother but is, more importantly, a transgressive one—a mother who defies and violates through fusion and contextualization, the good-bad mother dichotomy on which normative motherhood depends to regulate and surveil mothers.

Fusion: Simultaneously a Devil and an Average Mother

In six of the chapters in this collection, the monstrous mother is rendered transgressive in her refusal to be categorized; she is neither completely good nor bad as scripted under normative motherhood. Rather, monstrous mothers are fickle and capricious entities who haunt the spaces between categorizations or shift to and from them. In their chapter on cyborg mothering and posthumanism in *Orphan Black*, Susan Harper and Jessica Smith explore how the three central mothers in the series confuse, collapse, and conflate the normative binary of good and bad motherhood. Helena is depicted as wild, primitive, and feral living in abandoned places and she herself wonders "if she is human, divine, or evil." However, of all the mothers in the series, she is the most protective of her twin babies and will kill to protect them. While the character Coady goads Helena by saying her babies would be better off being raised by Dyad because "what kind of mother could [she] possibly be?" (11-12), Helena embraces motherhood to become a devoted and nurturant mother in the home she has created for her children in Alison's converted garage. In contrast, as Harper and Gullion argue, "If Helena represents the archetypal monstrous mother, Alison Hendrix embodies the role of the good mother." However, as Harper and Gullion observe, all is not as it seems. Alison—the quint-essential good mother with her minivan, church potluck dinners, and community theatre in middle-class suburbia—is also addicted to pills and alcohol, becomes a drug dealer, sleeps with her friend's husband as revenge, watches as this friend is choked to death by the garbage disposal, and helps her husband dispose of Leekie's body in their basement floor. Moreover, this good mother Alison is infertile (her two children are adopted), whereas the bad mothers—Sarah, who is a young single mother, a criminal, has had an abortion, and has abandoned her daughter, and Helena, who is feral and has killed many without remorse—are fertile. In its rendition of the bad mothers as fertile and the good mother as infertile, the show inverts the signifiers of normative motherhood. This inversion along with the ambiguity and instability of good and bad mother identities serve to upend and rupture the good-bad polarity of normative motherhood.

Rebecca Jaremko Bromwich's analysis of Karla Homolka's similarly shows how tenuous and mutable the categorizations of good and bad mothers are. Homolka remains Canada's most notorious female serial killer who, along with Paul Bernardo, sexually tortured and killed three young women, one of whom was her sister. Bromwich's review of mainstream media texts and Facebook posts confirm that the dominant discursive configuration of Homolka is that of monstrosity and that she has become a symbol of what is beyond redemption. However, since her release from prison, Homolka has become a mother of three children and has come to embody normative motherhood as a white, middle-class, stay-at-home mom. As Bromwich writes: "The present existence of Karla Homolka as a suburban, middle-class mother—in all visible respects now compliant with institutional expectations of mother-hood—troubles common understandings of subjectivity, agency, and identity." More specifically, Homolka's mainstream motherhood challenges societal norms about maternal virtue to reveal that good mothers are more complex than assumed. That Karla Homolka is simultaneously monstrous and an average mother upsets (in both meanings of the word) our cultural assumptions about good mother-hood and shows it to be shifting, tenuous, and variable.

My chapter on Sue Klebold's *A Mother's Reckoning* and Monique Lépine's *Aftermath* similarly disturbs and debunks the rigid dichotomy of normative motherhood through a critique of the myth of maternal omniscience and the judgment of maternal culpability. The two memoirs deliver a potent critique and corrective to two salient beliefs of normative motherhood: first, good mothers raise good children and bad mothers raise bad children; and second, good mothers, as involved parents, should and must know their children. In the chapter, I argue that if the dictates of normative motherhood were true, the Columbine tragedy could not have happened, since Sue was a loving and involved mother. And although Monique was not the attentive and engaged mother demanded by normative motherhood, as Sue was, she still loved her children, and did the best she could given the conditions and circumstances of her life. In her memoir, Monique comes to understand that she is not responsible for her son's mass killing. Both memoirs interrogate the myth of maternal omniscience as well as the judgment of maternal culpability to show that what is truly incomprehensible is not the tragedies of Columbine and the Montreal Massacre but the blame and responsibility placed on the mothers for them. The memoirs show that mothers may be good but still have bad things happen to them and their children. In these interrogations, the memoirs expose the omniscience required and culpability expected in normative motherhood to be both fallacious and fictitious. And in so doing, the texts blur and confuse the rigid demarcations of good and bad mothering on which normative motherhood depends.

The shifting and elusive boundaries of good and bad motherhood are likewise explored in Dinsman's chapter, as she examines three types of so-called bad mothers—the negligent mother, the sexual nonmother, and the working mother—in Bram Stoker's gothic horror novel *Dracula* (1897) and the Netflix series *Stranger Things*. In their transgressions of cultural norms, the mothers are depicted as monstrous. However, as the mothers are monstrous, the monsters are also rendered maternal: Dracula symbolically breastfeeds Mina, and in *Stranger Things*, the mother and monster are merged into one with Eleven's birthing of the Demogorgon. Moreover, the mothers in *Stranger Things,* like those in *Orphan Black*, cannot be confined to the normative categorizations that seek to define them. Joyce, the bad, single, working-class mother in *Stranger Things*, similar to the feral Helena of *Orphan Black*, is portrayed as "the "fighter mother," whereas Karen, like Alison of *Orphan Black*, is presented as "the 1980s mother that women were supposed to be." Karen is also a neglectful mother, as she never knows where her children are, which results in their endangerment. In merging the maternal with the monstrous and inverting maternal stereotypes—good mothers are often bad, and bad mothers are frequently good—the monstrous mother trope bridges the bifurcation of normative motherhood. Similarly, Abigail L. Palko's chapter explores how *Maleficent* and its sequel *Maleficent II: Mistress of Evil* both repudiate and depend upon notions of monstrous mothering. The chapter unpacks the ways that the live-action films first trouble this trope by reimagining the villainess in *Maleficent*, but then reinscribe the trope in the sequel by leaning on matrophobia to pervert Maleficent's character and introduce another stereotypical monstrous mother.

In her reading of *Patchwork Girl*, a cybertext fiction that reworks Mary Shelly's *Frankenstein*, Anitra Goriss-Hunter explores how the fluid medium of the electronic text enables readers to question and revise normative images and concepts of motherhood. In *Patchwork Girl*, the female monster of *Frankenstein* is recreated by the author: She stitches together the female body parts that Frankenstein had torn asunder. The scars and seams of Patchwork, as both hypertext and shape-shifting character, "create a hybrid monstrous maternity of gender indeterminacy and fragmented identity." Maternity in *Patchwork Girl* is thus dynamic, fragmented, subversive, and queer—not mired in the binary notions of the good mother and bad mother. As Goriss-Hunter writes, "Shelley and the monster she creates move beyond and within texts; Shelley shifts from being the author of *Frankenstein* to a character in *Patchwork Girl*, to birthing and loving a monster, and to becoming monstrous herself." Goriss-Hunter further describes the hypertext as "cunning" and Patchwork as "slippery," and in its cunningness and slipperiness, this text, like the ones discussed above, unsettles and unmoors the good-bad maternal polarity that defines and determines normative motherhood.

Contextualization: A Victim Twice

As the texts examined in the previous section disrupt the bad-good bifurcation of normative motherhood through the rhetorical strategy of fusion, the texts here disturb it through the rhetorical strategy of contextualization. With nuance and attentiveness, the texts narrate the intricacies of the mothers' lives to elicit understanding and arguably empathy. The monstrous mother is humanized to render a complexity that cannot be confined or contained to idealized or disparaged maternal stereotypes. In her chapter on the TV series *Homeland*, Aidan Moir exposes the problematic of the good and bad dichotomy of normative motherhood in her reading of Carrie Mathison as an aberrant mother. As Walters and Harrison write: "Neither monster nor angel, the aberrant mother is not quite a twenty-first-century feminist heroine but she does upend more traditional depictions of maternal identity. Unabashedly sexual, idiosyncratic to a fault, and seriously delirious in her caretaking skills" (qtd. in Moir). The aberrant mother trope Moir argues may be read as "a progressive representation because for her, motherhood is a secondary identity—one that is behind other professional and personal roles and obligations" (4). When Carrie becomes a mother, she leaves her newborn in the care of her family to continue her work as a Kabul station chief, and upon her return to the United States, she assumes her maternal identity with reluctance and unease. After her daughter, Franny, slips in the bathtub and Carrie submerges her further into the water with the possible intent of committing infanticide, she realizes she is a danger to her daughter and returns to her overseas work to protect her.

Critics have described Carrie as a psychotic and narcissistic villain. However, what these condemnations fail to acknowledge is Carrie's mental illness: She is bipolar and likely has PTSD from her CIA work and possibly PPD as a new mother. Moir argues that the fact that Carrie cannot balance her career and mothering while experiencing mental illness and prioritizing her patriotic responsibility over her daughter does not instantly transform her into a monstrous or aberrant mother. Instead, as Moir concludes, *Homeland* in telling Carrie's story provides a highly destabilizing representation of motherhood. The show's humanizing portrait of Carrie and its destabilizing representation of motherhood nuance and hence problematize the good-bad maternal binary that grounds and structures normative motherhood.

The aberrant mother is likewise a theme in the novels examined by Jennifer Martin in her exploration of maternal abandonment in the literature of women writers from the American South. In each novel Martin explores—Gail Godwin's *Father Melancholy's Daughter* (199), Doris Bett's *Souls Raised from the Dead* (1994) and Dorothy Allison's *Bastard Out of Carolina* (1992)—the mothers ultimately abandon their children because they are unable to reconcile maternal ideals with their personal desires. The social mores of the South, Martin argues, prevent the women from practicing empowered mothering that allows for the needs of the mother along with those of the children. However, the novels, Martin argues, trouble the notion of these mothers as monstrous mothers by revealing an interior to their lives that shows them to be "victims of a society that makes unrealistic demands on mothers and denies any form of individual expression." Indeed, as Martin concludes: "perhaps mothering abandonment is not monstrous but is instead a reaction of women to the conditions of their lives" (20). Similar to Martin's reading, Jessica Turcat in her analysis of the mothers in the poetry of Ai, who starve, beat, and maim their children, argues these mothers have been a victim twice—by both the experience and institution of motherhood—and they use violence to ward off their own victimhood. As Adrienne Rich has written: "Instead of recognizing the institution of violence of patriarchal motherhood, society labels those who finally erupt in violence as psychopathological" (qtd.in Turcat). The novels and poems demand, as Susan Griffin has commented, that "we pay attention to the context within which women mother and the structures that constrain their mothering choices" (qtd. in Miller, Hager, and Bromwich 1). In providing this context and in eliciting understanding and perhaps sympathy for these bad mothers, the texts problematize the rigid demarcations and harsh judgments of the bad mother.

The demand for contextualization is likewise what drives Josephine L Savarese's reading of the story of Laura, an Indigenous mother who was blamed for her daughter's disappearance and had her other children apprehended by the state. What is needed, Savarese argues, is "a feminist perspective that contextualizes women's lives by accounting for the poverty, violence, addiction, and racism that mothers experience." In her close reading of interviews with Laura, we learn that Laura and her mother both attended residential schools, that her family lived on a reserve as a result of the violent settlement of the prairie regions, and that Laura left her home at thirteen and became homeless in the city of Regina. However, the colonial framing of this narrative presents Laura and her family as wild and unruly and characterizes them as irredeemable (9). Given this pathologizing narrative stance, Savarese argues, "it becomes easier to overlook the systemic vulnerability that predisposed Laura and her family to violence." In 2005, Laura willingly consented to a three-month prison term as a step towards regaining custody of her six children. In 2008, a court decision offered a more sympathetic evaluation that described her "as a caring, even while imperfect, mother who bonded with her children." However, the order for the children's return to Laura was later overturned by a court of appeal. Savarese describes her intent in writing the chapter "as a feminist decolonial love" that attempts to "revision Laura beyond a criminalized, monstrous, failed and failing caregiver." Emphasizing Laura's humanity as a mother who has been harmed by colonialism and the criminal justice system reveals that it may be societal judgments, not the mothers themselves, that are monstrous.

In her chapter about the monstrous maternal in Anna Burns' *No Bones*, Shamara Ransirini argues that the monstrous maternal trope works to trouble the anxieties surrounding nationalist women in Northern Ireland and to protest the uneasiness generated by Republican women's feminine embodiment in nationalist iconography" (1). Although the novel does not provide insight into Bronagh's character as happens with the other texts, it does, as Ransirini notes, raise a series of pertinent questions. What does it mean for a woman, a mother to adopt angry and violent politics, and how can feminine anger in politics be reimagined? This questioning complicates simple categorizations or explanations. Moreover, as Ransirini explains, during the Troubles the roles of the perpetrators, victims, and witnesses were blurred as were the distinctions between political and inter-personal violence. Moreover, in highlighting and protesting the fears of female corporeality in violent politics, the trope of the monstrous maternal, as Ransirini argues, queers the gaze on the nonnormative female body. Moreover, the trope exposes the gaps and omissions in Irish national and masculinist imaginary to materialize the embodied narratives of women. The questioning, queering, and unveiling enacted in the novel, I suggest, are rhetorical strategies of contextualization that serve, as with the other texts examined, to nuance and hence problematize the categorizations of the good-bad maternal schism of normative motherhood.

The final chapter, also written by me, explores maternal ambiguities and vulnerabilities in Helen Phillips's *The Need* and Melanie Golding's *Little Darlings*. It asks what happens when we shift our focus from the mother to the experience of mothering in theorizing the bad and monstrous maternal and what is revealed when what evokes terror and is made terrifying is not the mother but mothering itself. The chapter argues that in using the genre of speculative fiction, Phillips and Golding expose the latent vulnerabilities and ambiguities of mothering—as well as its uncertainties, insecurities, apprehensions, and anxieties—to reveal what normative motherhood denies: It is mothering that is terrifying, not mothers themselves. Under normative motherhood, mothers are demonized and serve as repositories for cultural fears. However, in both *The Need* and *Little Darlings*, what is rendered frightening is not mothers themselves but what is expected and required of mothers in the institution of motherhood.

The Monstrous Mother

Patriarchal culture, as Abigail L. Palko notes in the introduction to this volume, censures and polices women through the idealization of the good mother and the demonization of the bad mother. She argues further that mothers are an easy and favourite scapegoat and readily become a proxy for our cultural fears and uncertainties. In this coda, I have argued that the trope of the monstrous mother—through the rhetorical strategies of fusion and contextualization—confuses, collapses, and conflates the good-bad bifurcation of normative motherhood and that on which it depends to systemize, surveil, and scapegoat mothers. This reading is certainly not the only way to situate and assess the monstrous mother trope as examined in the twelve chapters of this collection, but I suggest that the of positioning the monstrous maternal as a trace of what it is not deeply disturbs and distresses normative motherhood. In this, the monstrous mother is not only troubling but also haunting—poignant, evocative, and difficult to ignore or forget.

Works Cited

Derrida, Jacques. *Of Grammatology.* Johns Hopkins University Press, 2016.

Horsley, Lee. "Meres Fatales: Maternal Guilt in the Noir Crime Novel." *Modern Fiction Studies*, vol. 45, no. 2, June 1999, pp. 1-40.

Miller, Michelle Hughes, Tamar Hager, and Rebecca Jaremko Bromwich, editors. *Bad Mothers: Regulations, Representations, and Resistance.* Demeter Press, 2017.

Notes on Contributors

Rebecca Jaremko Bromwich is a lawyer, legal scholar, activist, and mother. She works as an equity, diversity, and inclusion manager for the offices of the multinational law firm Gowling WLG. Prior to taking on that role, she was director of the Graduate Diploma in Conflict Resolution Program at the Carleton University's Department of Law and Legal Studies. She also served as a crown attorney and worked as a lawyer in private practice for a large, national firm. Rebecca is the author and co-editor of several academic books as well as a novel.

Melissa Dinsman is an assistant professor of English at York College-CUNY and author of *Modernism at the Microphone: Radio, Propaganda, and Literary Aesthetics during World War II* (2015). Her current research focuses on WWII women writers, the politics of the domestic, and information networks. Some of Dinsman's most recent work can be found in *Modernism/modernity, International Yeats Studies*, and *Public Books.* She currently serves as co-president of the Space Between Society.

Anitra Goriss-Hunter is a lecturer at Federation University Australia. Her research and teaching focuses on gender and education, inclusion, and preservice teacher (PST) education. Anitra received the Australian Women's and Gender Studies Association award for most outstanding PhD thesis. Her current projects include investigating women's careers in higher education; increasing female participation in STEM education; and developing inclusive pedagogies for PSTs. Anitra received the Federation University Vice-Chancellor's Award for Outstanding Contribution to Student Learning in 2020.

Jessica Smartt Gullion, PhD, is the associate dean of Research for the College of Arts and Sciences and Associate Professor of Sociology at Texas Woman's University. She studies qualitative methodology, environmental sociology, and motherhood. Her most recent books include *Researching With: A Decolonizing Approach to Community-Based Action Research*, the award-winning *Diffractive Ethnography: Social Sciences and the Ontological Turn*, and the forthcoming second edition of *Writing Ethnography*.

Susan Harper, PhD is an educator, activist, advocate, and scholar based in Irving, Texas. She holds an MA and PhD in cultural anthropology from Southern Methodist University and an MA in multicultural women's and gender studies from Texas Woman's University. She serves as coordinator for Student Activities and Multicultural Programs at UNT Dallas. Her research interests include queer motherhood, contemporary paganism, feminist pedagogy, and qualitative inquiry and ethnography as a tool for justice.

Jennifer Martin, PhD, found the experience of motherhood both baffling and exhilarating, which drew her to motherhood and food studies as a lens to understand her own world and to explore the ways other women experience the highly personal and unique experience of motherhood. She is the coauthor of *Devouring Cultures* and author of several chapters and articles involving motherhood, women, and food. Jennifer is now an entrepreneur and cofounder of Gray & Martin Consulting.

Aidan Moir received her PhD in communication and culture from York University. Her research analyzes the influence of branding on the circulation of iconic identities in contemporary media culture. She has previously published on the symbolic power of celebrity maternal lifestyle brands and the complications that arise when iconic female celebrities are required by promotional culture to reconcile their public personas with motherhood.

Andrea O'Reilly, PhD, is full professor in the School of Gender, Sexuality and Women's Studies at York University, founder and former director of The Motherhood Initiative (1998–2019), founder/editor-in-chief of the *Journal of the Motherhood Initiative* and publisher of Demeter Press. She is coeditor/editor of twenty-five books, including *Feminist Perspectives on Young Mothers and Mothering* (2019); *Feminist Parenting: Perspectives from Africa and Beyond* (2020); *Mothers, Mothering, and COVID-19: Dispatches from a Pandemic* (2021); and *Maternal Theory: Essential Readings. 2nd Edition* (2021). She is editor of the *Encyclopedia on Motherhood* (2010) and coeditor of the *Routledge Companion to Motherhood*

(2019). She is author of *Toni Morrison and Motherhood: A Politics of the Heart* (2004); *Rocking the Cradle: Thoughts on Motherhood, Feminism, and the Possibility of Empowered Mothering* (2006); and *Matricentric Feminism: Theory, Activism, and Practice. 2nd edition* (2021). She is currently completing a monograph on mothers and mothering in post-2010 women's writing. Dr. O'Reilly has received more than 1.5 million dollars in grant funding for her research including the current projects "Older Young Mothers in Canada" and "Mothers and COVID-19 in Canada and Australia." She is twice the recipient of York University's Professor of the Year Award for teaching excellence and is the 2019 recipient of the Status of Women and Equity Award of Distinction from OCUFA (Ontario Confederation of University Faculty Associations).

Abigail L. Palko, PhD, is the director of the Maxine Platzer Lynn Women's Center at the University of Virginia, where she teaches a course on the politics of motherhood for the Department of Women, Gender & Sexuality. Her scholarship focuses on cultural and literary representations of mothering practices, with a particular interest in the ways that rhetoric about motherhood shapes and influences women's mothering practices. Her book, *Imagining Motherhood in Contemporary Irish and Caribbean Literature* (Palgrave, 2016), analyzes the ways that Irish and Caribbean women writers negotiate new understandings of the figure of the good mother in their writing. She is the coeditor of *Feminist Responses to the Neoliberalization of the University: From Surviving to Thriving* (Lexington Press, 2020) as well as *Mothers, Mothering and Globalization* and *Breastfeeding and Culture: Discourses and Representation* (both from Demeter Press; 2017 and 2018). In addition to numerous scholarly articles and book chapters, she also writes a monthly column for the UVA Women's Center's blog, the *Palko POV.* She serves on the Steering Committee for IAMAS (the International Association of Maternal Activism and Scholarship).

Shamara Ransirini completed her PhD in the University of Queensland, Australia. Her thesis, *Dangerous Women: Literary Representations of Women Involved in Violent Political Conflicts,* drew on intersectional and new materialist feminist theory to explore the literary embodiment of women militants across several cultural contexts. Her essays have appeared in *Hecate* and *Outskirts.* Shamara currently works at the University of Queensland.

Josephine L. Savarese is a scholar based in Fredericton, New Brunswick, and has a passion for decentring colonial narratives and fostering decolonial love; she serves on the Senate Committee on Reconciliation at St. Thomas University. She recently exhibited her painted piñata (cocreated with an organic farmer and youth) in "From Harm to Harmony," a community arts project documenting climate change and possibilities for collective action hosted by the Conservation Council of New Brunswick. Josephine is coediting a manuscript with Demeter Press on mothers who kill and infanticide.

Jessica Turcat's latest work has appeared in *San Diego Poetry Annual*, *Indiana Review*, and *Rewilding Anthology: Poems for the Environment*. While obtaining her doctorate in poetry, she had the opportunity to study under the poet Ai. She currently teaches for the Gender, Women's, and Sexuality Studies Program at Oklahoma State University.

About the Cover Artist

Tobiah Mundt is a self taught fiber artist who was born and raised in Houston, Texas. She studied Architecture at Howard University in Washington, DC and eventually left the field of Architecture for sculpture. She uses needle felting, wet felting and rug tufting techniques to create colorful forms and figurative pieces that illustrate and invoke emotion.

She is the Co-Owner and Creative Director of The Hive, an arts and crafts bar in Charlottesville, Virginia where she teaches fiber arts, blurring the line between art and craft. Tobiah has exhibited her work in Texas, Washington DC, Maryland, and Virginia.

www.tobiahmundt.com